Indian Writing in English

Speculations and Observations

Indian Writing in English
Speculations and Observations

Arvind M. Nawale

AUTHORSPRESS
Publishers of Scholarly Books

Worldwide Circulation through Authorspress Global Network

First Published 2011
by
Authorspress

Editorial
Q-2A Hauz Khas Enclave,
New Delhi-110 016
e-mail: authorspress@yahoo.com

Marketing
E-35/103, Jawahar Park
Laxmi Nagar, Delhi-110 092
e-mail: authorspress@yahoo.com

Indian Writing in English: Speculations and Observations

ISBN 978-81-7273-585-2

Printed in India at Tarun Offset, Delhi.

Dedicated to my elder brother Dr. Sanjay Nawale,
Associate Professor, Shivaji College, Barshi,
Director, SW, Solapur University
And
A renowned critic, translator and writer of dozen books in Hindi
for inspiring and paving me a way for such literary ventures....

—Dr. Arvind M. Nawale

Preface

Ever since the first English novel *Rajmohan's Wife* by Bankim Chandra Chatterjee, Indian English writers, creative and critical, have immensely explored their self-selected genres. Decade after decade, Indian writing in English is contributing to its fullest. This anthology of 21 scholarly observations and speculations on various themes and techniques presents a sensible approach towards understanding the vast literary corpus of Indian English writing.

The first twelve papers make an honest attempt to explore the enigmas and excitements that contemporary Indian English novel has to offer. Dr. Arvind Nawale's paper "Primitivism in Arun Joshi's *The City and the River*" probes into the primordial, elemental and ethical choices that a man has to make. Dr. Ketaki Datta's paper "R.K Narayan's *The English Teacher*: A Journey from Natural to Supernatural or Beyond?" makes a brilliant approach to acquaint the reader with an emotional, intellectual, and spiritual journey through her argumentative discussion. Dr. Bhaskar Roy has made an honest approach to comparing two veteran novelists: Mulk Raj Anand and Raja Rao. Dr.Vimmie Manoj the studies status of women in the novels of Ruth Prawer Jhabvala in her paper. In the paper, "Women's Rights: A Study of Rohinton Mistry's *A Fine Balance*", Dr. B. Indira presents a feminist concept. A joint venture by Dr. Arjun Jadhav and Dr. Sujata Bamane is a depiction of middle class modern Indian woman's woes through their introspective study of Shashi Deshpande's novel *The Dark Holds No Terrors*. In the similar tone, the next paper by Dr. Vishwanath Bite explores a brilliant search for self-identity through the novels by written Shashi Deshpande. Sahabuddin's paper is based on the fine portrayal of the journey the women in Kamala Markandaya's novel travel through. Two consecutive papers on the Booker Prize winner books *The God of Small Things* by Arundhati Roy and *The White Tiger* by Arvind Adiga written respectively by Dr. Neerja Sachdev and Dr. A. Ramesh Babu make a remarkable presentation on postmodernism through their profound studies.

The next two papers, Dr. N.K Deb's "Cultural Dynamics and Contemporary Indian English Novel" and Dr. Anju Bala Agrawal's "A Study of Globalisation and Changing Social Behaviour in Indian English Literature" present the socio-cultural scenario that exists in Indian English Literature.

Short story is also one of the popular forms of Indo-English writers. Creative writers like Dr. Aju Mukhopadhyay and scholars like Dr. M.G Hegde and Dr. Beena have separately but in tune with each other presented a historical background to short-story writing, and have made a reflective and thoughtful study in the selected genre. Dr. Beena Rathi brings before us the social realism in the immortal stories by Premchand. A Sahitya Academy award winner, poet Dr. Dinesh Kanwar Singh explores the chaos of values and ethics in Modern Indian English Poetry in his scholarly paper. Dr. Jayadeep Sarangi's masterly paper, "The Metaphors of Conquest: Trends in Contemporary Indian Woman Poets in English", is a definite guideline to getting acquainted with Indo-English poetry.

The last four papers by Dr. Nagori, Dr. Mitra, Dr. Wadikar and Dr. Jagadale delve deep into the intricacies of the Modern Indian-English Dramas. Dr. Smita R. Nagori (Lakhotia) examines Karnad's *Naga-Mandala* with its blurbline while Dr. Zinia Mitra evaluates Karnad's monologues. Dr. Shailaja Wadikar makes a remarkable presentation of lust and power politics in Tendulkar's *Encounter in Umbugland* and *Ghashiram Kotwal* while Dr. Umesh Jagadale makes a brilliant and technical analysis of communication in drama with examples of a few Indian English plays.

This anthology purports to be a significant study of Indian writing in English. On one hand, it has covered knowledgeable writers like Mulk Raj Anand, Raja Rao, R. K. Narayan, Kamala Markandaya, Shashi Deshpande, Kamala Das, Girish Karnad, Tendulkar, Premchand and so on. This anthology also helps in examining the creative impulse of Booker Prize Winners like Arundhati Roy and Aravind Adiga. With such a high variety of issues, this book would surely catch the eye of knowledge seekers. The deep insights of exceptionally scholarly contributors in the Indo-English Writing would surely benefit the students, teachers and researchers in general, as well as their selected areas of interests. I am honoured and privileged in editing papers of exceptionally scholarly contributors and present this book to the vast local and global readership.

The present anthology has strictly followed blind peer review procedure while selecting the papers. I am thankful to respected P.C. Katoch (IAS), a critic, poet, novelist and essayist, Palampur, Himachal Pradesh. My friends Dr. Sunil Sharma, a critic, poet, essayist and fiction writer and Vice-Principal of Model College, Mumbai and Dr. N. P. Pawar, Dean, Faculty of Arts, Solapur University and Associate Professor in English, Mangalweda for reviewing and selecting papers, making suggestions and sharing with me in critical arguments.

I must record my deep sense of indebtedness to Sudarshan Kcherry, Managing Director, and the whole team of Authorspress, New Delhi for pursuing me to edit the present volume. I must not forget to express my gratitude to my respected father Shri Manikrao Nawale and mother Sow. Mandakini Nawale, my brothers, Dr. Sanjay Nawale, and Mr. Sunil Nawale, my sister Jyoti Khurpe, brother-in-law Prof. Manohar Khurpe, my father-in-law Mr. K. G. Tudame, my wife Manisha, daughter Apurva and son Amit for their inspiration and constant support.

Capt. Dr. Arvind M. Nawale

About Contributors

Dr. Arvind M. Nawale is Head, Department of English in Shivaji Mahavidyalaya, Udgir, Dist. Latur (M.S.). He has edited more than half a dozens of books and is also on the editorial board of three international journals.

Dr. Ketaki Datta is Associate Professor, Department of English in Acharya Brojendra Nath Seal College (Govt.), Coochbehar (W.B.). She is also a novelist, critic and a translator.

Dr. Bhaskar Roy Barman, DLitt (USA) is an internationally published poet, short story writer, novelist, critic, translator, editor and book reviewer. His awards and honours include "Man of the Year 1997" from the American Biographical Institute, USA (ABI), "20th Century Award for Achievement" from the International Biographical Centre, Cambridge, England (IBC).

Dr. Vimmie Manoj, Ratlam is an expert on gender studies, postcolonial studies, and the translated works of Indian regional writers. She was Asst. Professor, Department of English in S V Govt. College of Commerce, Ratlam (M.P.)

Dr. Babbellapati Indira is Associate Professor, Department of English in A.U. College of Engg, Andhra University (A.P.). She is also widely published poetess and a critic **C.V. Padmaja** is Asst Professor, Department of English, GITAM University, Visakhapatnam (A.P.).

Dr. Arjun Jadhav is Associate Professor & **Dr. Sujata Bamane** is Asst Professor, Department of English, Fergusson College, Pune (M.S.).

Dr. Vishwanath Bite is Asst. Professor, Department of English in MBSK Kanya Mahavidyalaya, Kadegaon (M.S.). He has edited few books and is also Editor-In-Chief of *The Criterion*, an international journal in English.

Sahab Uddin is Asst. Professor, Department of English in HAA College, Dabaka (Assam) and a Research Scholar, North-Eastern Hill University (NEHU) Shillong, (Meghalaya)

Dr. Neerja Sachdev is Associate Professor, Department of English, S.S.K. Girls' Degree College, Allahabad (U.P.).

Dr. A. Ramesh Babu is Asst. Professor, Department of English, Kamala Institute of Technology and Science, Huzurabad (A.P.).

Dr. N. K. Neb is Associate Professor, Department of English, D.A.V. College, Jalandhar (Punjab). He has co-edited four books on Indian-English fiction and is Editor-In-Chief of a national journal.

Dr. Anju Bala Agrawal is Associate Professor, Department of English, R.C.A.Girls P.G.College, Mathura (U.P.). She has edited few books on Indian-English Literature.

Aju Mukhopadhyay, a poet, author and critic, is a bilingual writer of fiction and essays from Pondicherry. He has authored 28 books and received several poetry awards. Many of his works have been translated in other languages and anthologised. He has travelled widely in Asia, Europe and America for his study.

Dr. M. G. Hegde is Head, Department of English, Dr. A. V. Baliga College of Arts and Science, Kumta, N. Kanara District, (Karnataka). He has edited the tenth volume of *Complete Works of Gourish Kaikini* and a book of critical essays for Karnataka Sahitya Akademi.

Dr. Beena V. Rathi is Associate Professor, Department of English, Smt. Radhabai Sarda College, Anjangaon Surji, Dist.Amravati (M.S.).

Dr. Kanwar Dinesh Singh, a Sahitya Academy Award winner English poet of India, is an internationally published poet, critic, translator, editor and book reviewer.

He has authored and edited a number of books and is also Editor-In-Chief of *Hyphen*: an international journal in English. He is also Asst. Professor, Department of English, Government Postgraduate College, Solan (H.P.)

Dr. Jaydeep Sarangi is Associate Professor, Department of English, Jogesh Chandra Chaudhuri College (Calcutta University), Kolkata (W.B). He is a perceptive critic and bi-lingual Indian English poet. He has authored more than seventy articles and twenty books in Indian Writing in English.

Dr. Smita R. Nagori (Lakhotiya) is Head, Department of English, Maharashtra Udaygiri College, Udgir, Dist. Latur (M.S.). She has published many papers and book reviews.

Dr. Zinia Mitra is Head, Department of English Nakshalbari College, Darjeeling (W.B.). She is a critic, reviewer and translator. Her travelogues and articles have won columns in *The Statesman*. Her reviews, articles and translations have been published in different books and journals including the Sahitya Akademi.

Dr. Shailaja B. Wadikar is Asst. Professor, Department of English, School of Languages and Literature, S.R.T.M. University, Nanded (M.S.). She has authored a few books in Indian Writing in English.

Dr. Umesh S. Jagadale is Asst. Professor, Department of English, Sangamner College, Sangamner (M.S.). He is a budding dramatist, theme some full length and One Act Plays to his credit.

Contents

Preface ***vii***

About Contributors ***xi***

1. Primitivism in Arun Joshi's *The City and the River* 1
—Arvind M. Nawale

2. R.K. Narayan's *The English Teacher*:A Journey from Natural to Supernatural or Beyond? 7
—Ketaki Datta

3. Indian English Fiction: Mulk Raj Anand and Raja Rao 21
—Bhaskar Roy Barman

4. Portrayal of Women's Status through Symbols and Images in the Novels of Ruth Prawer Jhabvala 37
—Vimmie Manoj

5. Women's Rights: A Study of Rohinton Mistry's *A Fine Balance* 57
—Babbellapati Indira and C.V. Padmaja

6. Middle Class Modern Indian Woman's Woes in Shashi Deshpande's *The Dark Holds No Terrors* 69
—Arjun Jadhav & Sujata Bamane

7. The Theme of Woman's Search for Self-identity in Shashi Deshpande's Selected Works 81
—Vishwanath Bite

8. Journey from Anonymity to Recognition: A Study of Kamala Markandaya's Women 91
—Sahab Uddin

9. Tradition to Post-Modernism: *The God of Small Things* 99
—Neerja Sachdev

10. The Image of Modern India in Aravind Adiga's *The White Tiger* 104
—A. Ramesh Babu

11. Cultural Dynamics and the Contemporary Indian English Novel 114
—N. K. Neb

12. A Study of Globalisation and Changing Social Behaviour in Indian English Literature 127
—Anju Bala Agrawal

13. Indian English Short Stories: A Comparative Study 137
—Aju Mukhopadhyay

14. Anthologies of Indian English Short Story—A Survey 155
—M.G. Hegde

15. Social Realism in Premchand's S`hort Stories 169
—Beena V. Rathi

16. The Inheritance of Chaos: Crisis of Values and Ethics in Modern Indian English Poetry 175
—Kanwar Dinesh Singh

17. The Metaphors of Conquest: Trends in Contemporary Indian Woman Poets in English 191
—Jaydeep Sarangi

18. Compromise as a Survival Kit in Girish Karnad's *Naga-Mandala* 205
—Smita R. Nagori (Lakhotiya)

19. The Fragrance of Flowers:
A Reading into Girish Karnad's Monologue 212
—Zinia Mitra

20. *Encounter in Umbugland and Ghashiram Kotwal*:
Tendulkar's Comment on Power Politics 222
—Shailaja B. Wadikar

21. Communication in Drama:
Exploration towards a New Analytical Model 235
—Umesh S. Jagadale

Index **244**

1

Primitivism in Arun Joshi's *The City and the River*

—Arvind M. Nawale

'Primitivism' is a condition or quality of being primitive. It is the pursuit of ways of life running counter to the development of technology. According to M.H. Abrams (1985:129):

> A primitive is someone who prefers what is "natural" (in the sense of what exists prior to and independently of man's reasoning and contrivance) to what is "artificial" (in the sense of what man achieves by thought, laws and conventions, and the complex arguments of a civilized society).

He further adds:

> Most men and many writers of literature are primitivists in some moods, longing to escape from the complications, fever, and anxieties of modern civilization into the elemental simplicities of a lost natural life, whether that is imagined as an individual's childhood, or as the classical or medieval past, or as some primitive, carefree, faraway place on earth (Ibid.:130).

Basically, primitivism is an artistic movement which is originated as a reaction to the Enlightenment. Rousseau was the first to draw attention to the concept of the 'noble savage'. He considered every man as innately good and pacific in his 'natural state', but when he came into contact with society he was bound to become impure, materialistic in attitude, corrupted codes and conventions and incapable of understanding the real meaning of life. Primitivists believe that modern society is moving away from its traditional routes, losing touch with its true primitive condition.

Primitivism is a revelation of modern man's alienation from the deepest self and from nature. "At the root of all primitivist works of art there is a strong urge for reintegration, and a sincere and passionate struggle to recover the lost vitality and wholeness of being" (Ghose 1985: 52). It finds its most distinctive expression in D.H. Lawrence's *The Woman Who Rode Away* and *The Plumed Serpent*. Emily Bronte, Byron, Wordsworth, Joseph Conrad and Nietzsche were highly influenced by primitivism. Arun Joshi's few characters also long for primitive values.

The City and the River (1994), the fifth and last novel of Arun Joshi, deals with an entirely different theme from his earlier novels. In it, "the post-modernist tendency to consider the rural, the natural [primitive] way of living against the unbanished civilization is depicted in full depth by the novelist" (Bhatt and Alexander 2001:85).

Slightly differing from the preceding works *The City and the River* is a step ahead from individuality to universality. In all of his earlier four novels Joshi focuses on the inner turmoil of the individual protagonists, while in this novel he works on a vaster canvas depicting the predicament of the whole generation or rather the whole race. In it we find the coexistence of the extremes at every level. Hermits, *yajnas,* sacrifice, primitive people coexist with electronic surveillance, ultra-modern lasers, helicopters, videos, spying and inquisition. And the novel moves on two levels simultaneously. At one level it reveals the ruthless governing of the city by the Grand Master and his fawning Council of Advisors. On the other level are boatmen like primitive people who struggle indictment of the corruption and malpractice of political leaders, businessmen, the police and armed chiefs.

The Grand Master, along with the hundred years old Astrologer, the *de facto* ruler of the city, applies new formulas with the hope of winning back the people's allegiance to him.

According to him, the boatmen cause so many troubles to him. They boatmen never let the town planner widen the narrow tortuous streets in which they live. They may spend half of their time on the river-bank in singing, talking, meditating and playing on the one-string in primitive ways and would rather live in penury than to work for anybody else except themselves. They do not even care to greet the Grand Master. He observes:

> Boatmen are not as simple as they seem.... They consider themselves to be the children of the river, and to the river, and river alone do they hold allegiance. They believe, unfortunately, with their hearts, and for their beliefs they are willing to die. And don't let their poverty mislead you into believing that they can be bought (14).

The Grand Master is disgusted with the insolent behaviour of the boatmen. He considers them as those who have turned the city into "an unruly place, a plaything of *asuras*" (15). He feels shame for their appalling condition and their going about half-naked like primitives. But the boatmen like to live like primitives. They do not believe in personal possessions. They want to lead a simple life. As their Headman, who is a woman, tells the Grand Master, "hard work or no... boatmen will get two meals a day" (16) and they expect no more.

The Grand Master is worried about their growing population which is, according to him, a hurdle in his way to better tomorrow. He tells the Astrologer, "Let their number be frozen by law... the force of arms if necessary" (Ibid.), and he asks him to announce a law, "Let there be only one child to a mother or two to a home" (Ibid.). The Astrologer proposes to the people, "The Way of the Three Beautitudes" (17) to ensure their allegiance to the Grand Master as children to their father. But the head Boatman makes it clear to the Astrologer: "The Boatmen... are children of great river, and only of the great river... How can we become children of the Grand Master or of anyone else?.... If it is a matter of allegiance, our allegiance is only to the river and cannot be shared" (19). She further says in protest: "You think an ant is born on this earth without God's will? If it is His will that there should be only one child to a mother than surely it shall come to pass. There is no need for the Grand Master or you to pass a law" (19-20). Even the Astrologer tells the Grand Master that "The river for them... is a symbol of the divine mother. Of God Himself" (22) and advises him not to be "too harsh with the boatmen. Without them the city cannot run" (Ibid.).

The opening of a new era known as "The Era of Ultimate Greatness" (23) is announced by the Astrologer to discipline the people. But the boatmen spurn his Three Truths, call him a pompous fool and even burn his effigies along the river banks. The Era of Ultimate Greatness "is a parable of evil drunk with power attempting to encroach upon the traditional primitive culture of the boatmen who worship the River and are now forced to take an oath of allegiance to the Grand Master and to salute him in place of River" (Mathur 1995:150). Boatmen are not ready to salute the Grand Master

At the Festival of the River, a *yajna* is performed by the Astrologer, and the Grand Master's son is coroneted as his successor. The Grand Master's plans, however, meet with stiff resistance from the Boatpeople, Bhumiputra or Master Bhoma, a teacher of mathematics who belongs to the Mud quarters. Hence a large number of arrests take place. Bhumiputra is held. The Headman, who refuses to swear allegiance to the Grand Master, and the Professor who takes up the cause of Bhumiputra, are condemned to the Gold Mines. Systematic attempts are made to destroy the Boat people's way of life. The Grand Master, who hates music, even destroys the simple musical instrument of the Boatmen. The Headman's eyes are pierced with long needles. The Professor dies trying to draw the attention of the authorities to the atrocities. The attempts of the boatmen, however, are fragile against the laser tanks of the Grand Master.

Now as the dream of the Grand Master is fulfilled, he becomes the unchallenged king of the Seven Hills. The Astrologer becomes the new Grand Master. The Grand Master's confrontation with man is absolutely over. No man stands in his way, which means the victory of his inhuman apathy. That, however, is not the end, nor is it the purpose of the novelist. "When sin surmounts the earth, nature, too, takes its revenge.

Nature takes its revenge on all—victims as well as victimizers" (Bande 1997:112). After the crude profanation of the sanctity of the human race, Nature takes different aspects. "Dark clouds loomed large. The Great River swelled menacingly to transform itself into a 'primordial sea' "(357). Rain lashes the city without let up and the water rises up threateningly to the Seven Hills. The King is swallowed up by the river.

The novel emphasizes the presence of the fundamental primitive force of Nature. In the words of Meithei (1997:57):

> The river in this way is indeed the main protagonist which stands out as a formidable spiritual force as old as Time it self. It represents the primitive force of Nature that remains indomitable like the Almighty God, as against the corrupting values of man-made civilization.

The river swells its level taking over everything, from the Seven Hills to the tunnel of the pyramids. Everywhere it is the mighty presence of the sea of waters that engulfs man and the solidity of things that are swallowed in its womb till all is levelled —whether man or matter. "Here the conflict between civilizing forces and the primitive untamed forces assume the proportion of the cosmic conflict between comparatively weaker man, artificial and vain, and the self generating ceaseless force of Nature or the Supreme God as in classical tragedies" (Ibid.:55).

Joshi is successful in the creation of the picture of humanity, surrounded by natural elements and primitive forces over which man has no control.

Works Cited

Abram, M. H. 1985. *A Glossary of Literary Terms*. Delhi: Macmillan India Ltd.

Bhatt, Indira and Alexander, Suja. 2001. *Arun Joshi's Fiction: A Critique.* New Delhi: Creative Books.

Ghosh, Soumendranath 1985. "Toward a Definition of Modern Literary Primitivism". *Journal of English Department*, Burdwan University. II, I: 50-56.

Joshi, Arun. 1994. *The City and the River* New Delhi: Orient Paperbacks. (All the page references in parentheses are to this edition only)

Mathur, O. P. 1995. "The Contemporary and the Cosmic in Arun Joshi's *The City and the River*." In Yaravintelimath. *et al*: 147-153.

Meithei, M. Mani. 1997. "Man, God and the Nature of Reality in Arun Joshi's *The City and The River*. In Pathak: 47-59.

Pathak, R.S. 1997. *Indian Fiction of Nineties* Delhi: Creative Books.
Sharma, Bruhma Dutta. 1992. "*The City and the River* as a Political Novel." In Dhawan. 241-256.

Yaravintelimath, C.R. *et al*. 1995. *New Perspectives in Indian Literature in English*. New Delhi: Sterling Publishers Pvt. Ltd.

2

R.K. Narayan's *The English Teacher*: A Journey from Natural to Supernatural or Beyond?

—Ketaki Datta

> A life after death is not a matter of speculation or conjecture of hope and fear; it is a practical certainty which the individual has little dreams of doubting as he doubts the reality of his conscious existence.
>
> —*J.G.Frazer*

The English Teacher (1945) is the only work of Rashipuram Krishnaswamy Narayan, where he cashes in on the incidents which actually happened in his own life. In *My Days,* where he explains in explicit terms, "She caught typhoid in early May and collapsed in the first week of June 1939. Looking back it seems as if she had had a premonition of her end, and had wanted to stay back with her parents and sister. I have described this part of my experience of her sickness and death in *The English Teacher* so fully that I do not, and perhaps cannot, go over it again. More than any other book, *The English Teacher*, is autobiographical in content, very little part of it being fiction."(150-151)

It is really interesting to note that *The English Teacher* makes his dream possible—he gets reunited with his dead wife, which is considered sheer inanity or flight of fantasy, by the critics like M.K. Naik. Most of them consider the conclusion as nonsensical. But is it not wish-fulfilment or sublimation of desire, in one way or another? If something can be achieved through dreams or otherwise, in which a troubled soul finds enough succour, considerable courage, shall it not be taken to be worthwhile? That was what exactly happened in the case of R. K. Narayan alias Krishnan, the protagonist of *The English Teacher.*

A quick look at the inventory of the incidents in the writer's life will surely help us relate the same happening in Krishnan's life too. A journey from the Natural to the Supernatural, as we find in the novel is not contrived, but natural, obvious, inevitable. Through this novel, the writer puts a soothing balm on the never-to-be-healed laceration, the sudden, untimely demise of his wife Rajam. That is why, when this novel was published in America, it was titled as *Grateful to Life and Death.* Again to quote verbatim from *My Days,* Narayan is eloquent about the verisimilitude of this novel with the incidents of his own life, "The 'English Teacher' of the novel, Krishna, is a fictional character in the fictional city of Malgudi; but he goes through the same experience as I had gone through, and he calls his wife Susila, and the child is Leela instead of Hema. The toll that typhoid took and all the desolation that followed, with a child to look after, and the psychic adjustments, are based on my own experience. The book falls in two parts—one is domestic life and the other half is 'spiritual'. Many readers have gone through the first half with interest and the second half with bewilderment and even resentment, perhaps feeling that they have been baited with the domestic picture into tragedy, death, and nebulous, impossible speculations. The dedication of the book to the memory of my wife should to some extent give the reader a clue that the book may not be all fiction; still, most readers resist, naturally, as one always does, the transition from life to death and beyond."(*My Days*,150-151)

Susila had an eerie experience while she went to see a new house to move into. Rajam, while coming back from her parental house, had another similar experience. The house-owner came with some demand, just when she was leaving for Mysore. As her father failed to accede to it, he shouted, 'Vacate my house immediately!' and a black scorpion fell from the roof-tile; however, Rajam narrowly escaped being bitten.

As Leela was not allowed to enter her mother's room during illness, the same had been clamped on Hema, Narayan's daughter. Just like Leela, after her mother's passing away, three-year-old Hema too peeped into her mother's room and found it empty, and Narayan alias Krishna, reasoned by saying, "They have taken her to the hospital."(*My Days* 152-153)

It is really interesting to note that even the séance sessions Krishna had by the lotus pond in a gentleman's place had their base in reality! In order to heal up the wound of irreparable loss after Rajam's demise, he went to his sister's house in Madras. There, he used to walk miles after miles almost every evening. Especially on the sea-beach. He almost turned into a zombie, losing all interest in living a busy life, people, surroundings, everything and all! At such point of time, one of his cousins, whom he had lost sight of long before, accosted him while he was returning home from the beach one evening, and expressed his condolence. He took him to one of his acquaintances, Raghunatha Rao, at Mylapore, who along with his wife, breathed life into his drab, dry existence by helping him come in regular contact with dead Rajam, through séance sessions. Narayan expressed his gratitude to this chance-meeting with his long-forgotten cousin near the sea-beach that day, "This street-corner encounter, though it looked so casual, led on to contacts and experiences which profoundly affected my future, and saved me from disintegration." (*My Days* 156-157)

The portrayal of the natural lush surroundings in *The English Teacher,* conducive to the séance sessions, is the brainchild of Narayan, just to fulfil the fictional need. At the behest of Raghunatha Rao's wife, when the other worldly spirits start scribbling on the blank page:

> Your band of helpers are here, and welcome your visitor today. We are aware that he has suffered a recent bereavement, lost a person he loved. We can see that his heart is still very heavy and anguished. If we could help him, and others like him, to understand the nature of life and death, and relieve the pain at heart we will have achieved our purpose.....The lady is here, but will not communicate with her husband directly yet. By and by,

> perhaps, when she is calmer. She is somewhat agitated today, since this is her first effort to communicate with her husband. (*My Days* 159-160)

We find a similar narration in *The English Teacher*, "Here we are, a band of spirits who've been working to bridge the gulf between life and after-life....Here is Susila, wife of Krishna, but as yet she is unable to communicate by herself. And by and by she will be an adept in it."(*The English Teacher* 112)

Till now, we are on a 'natural' plane, gradually elevating to the level of 'supernatural'. But we have to be clear to ourselves, at first,—is there any other plane, in between or beyond? Yes, there is one—beyond. That is, philosophical understanding of 'life and death'. That perhaps, bridges the hiatus between the natural and the supernatural. This supernaturalism needs no Coleridgean 'willing suspension of disbelief', this supernaturalism is akin to higher philosophical thinking where the gap between the natural and the supernatural gets bridged automatically. Rather, there is a need for understanding the "self", even, through inner and outer dialogues. In this regard, we can refer to a fine essay "Heteroglossia and Polyphony in *The English Teacher*" by Sravani Biswas, where she points to this fact only:

> *The English Teacher* follows a first person narrative mode where the inner dialogue of Krishna goes back and forth in a dialectical bend in order to concretize the self. It is the unfinished sense of the self in Krishna that cannot accept the finite and well-defined garb of the English teacher......
>
> It is his revolt against the centripetal force that works in terms of systems and formulas. For him, the people around him, like Gajapathy, Mr. Brown, or Rangappa, and the larger society itself constitute this force. In their eyes Krishna is the 'other' who may be complete and defined....
>
> But will a shift from teaching in a college to the role of a teacher in a nursery school resolve his debate? In fact, in the novel Krishna plays several roles but there is a constant slipping away or shifting of roles and the conscious 'self' of Krishna continues to remain as certain as ever. (Chandra145-146)

From the natural to the supernatural plane, the journey was really obvious. As in the case of R.K. Narayan, the séance sessions at Raghunatha Rao's were enthusing, refreshing; it was the same with Krishna of *The English Teacher*. Doubtlessly, Narayan and Krishna were having the same kind of pleasure out of these sessions. Narayan felt relieved when the spirits assured him:

> the lady wants to assure you that she exists but in a different state, she wants you to lighten your mind too, and not to let gloom weigh you down. She says, now you are told I am here; by and by when you have attuned yourself, you will feel without proof or argument that I am at your side and that will transform your outlook. She advises you not to let anxiety develop about the child. She is well, and she will grow up well. I watch her. I now see her in a room, wearing a blue skirt, and playing with another child; they have three dolls between them. The lady says goodbye until next week. (*My Days* 160-161)

Almost equal solicitousness is noted in the case of the dead Susila, while she keeps communicating with her husband:

> You fret too much about the child. Have no kind of mercy about her. When you are away at college, you hardly do your work with a free mind, all the time saying to yourself, 'What is Leela doing? What is she doing?' Remember that she is happy all the afternoon, playing with that friend of hers in the next house, and listening to the stories of the old lady....Do you know that she sometimes insists upon being taken to the little children's school which is nearby? (*The English Teacher* 119)

Are not the conversations very much similar? In *My Days,* R.K. Narayan in clear terms avers, "I began to sense Rajam's presence at that table. What she is supposed to have said or Rao's pencil wrote was secondary. The actual presence felt at this sitting in the stillness and dimness of that little room had a profound effect on me. When I went home that evening, I felt lighter at heart." (*My Days* 160-161)

Till this point, the supernatural has gone hardly beyond the natural. Though it is somewhat awkward to have psychic contact of a living one with a dead one, a scientific sanction has already been given by a saintly scientist long ago. Swami Abhedananda, an ardent disciple of Sri Ramakrishna, in his *Life Beyond Death*, endorses Narayan's viewpoint and he says that a dead soul can easily commune with the living one if the latter so desires. In the chapter *Rebirth of the Soul,* Swami Abhedananda proffers his view in this regard:

> Pythagoras, Plato and their followers believed in the theory of transmigration and metempsychosis of the soul. Pythagoras says, 'After death, the rational mind, having been freed from the chains of the body, assumes an ethereal vehicle, and passes into the region of the dead, where it remains, till it is sent back to this world, to inhabit some other body, human or animal.' Plato also believed in this theory of transmigration. He describes in an allegorical way how and where the souls go through the process of transmigration in Phoedrus. (Abhedananda 94-95)

In the same book, Swami Abhedananda gives reasons for the individuality of the soul even after the negation of the body:

> But it is very obvious that the body is constantly changing. Then where is that permanency in our bodies? This material form or the gross physical organism will be destroyed. Then where will lie our permanency? Not in the body, but in the soul. It is the sense of 'I', which will continue to exist after this body is gone.
>
> Having understood this solution of the problem concerning the existence of the soul, we question: if the soul continues to exist, what will become of it afterwards, and what ill its destiny?...We get the answer from the Vedanta, which is most universal and most un-sectarian. It possesses the sense-powers, life-force, mind and intellect as well as the impressions of its physical and mental activities, and this soul manufactures the body through the mediums of parents.
>
> Now a question may arise: if the soul continues to exist after death, does it lose its individuality? We get the answer from the Vedanta that it retains its own individuality. It can remember where it was, who were its parents, etc.

> Modern spiritualism and the result of the psychological researches have given us ample proof of the individual soul after death... (Abhedananda 108-110)

If we argue about the space that the other-worldly creatures, including the dead wife of R.K. Narayan, occupy, we are sure to delve into the issues of space/place, syntopos/diatopos controversies. Prof. Nirmal Selvamony in his erudite essay "Place and Ecocriticism: A Reading of R.K.Narayan's *The English Teacher*", while expatiating about spacio-temporal context goes on to say:

> When space is spoken of in terms of objects, space is thought of as 'place', as space occupied by objects. Such space or place could be denoted by means of the term. 'diatopos' [after Saussure's 'diachrony']. But when the object does not occupy any place other than consciousness, consciousness as place can be spoken of as 'syntopos' [after Saussure's 'synchrony']. If diatopos is measurable/ markable space, syntopos is unmeasurable /unmarkable space...In the case of the human person we need to situate him /her in both these spaces. If the body of the person occupies diatopos, his/her persona does syntopos. Matter is basically diatopic and tends to get syntopic when becomes consciousness. However, it is possible to distinguish matter from consciousness and hence, diatopos from syntopos....At no time is life/consciousness without a body. Syntopic existence, on the other hand, presupposes being in more than one place at the same time. (Selvamony & Dasan 190-191)

Thus, the psychic séances which Narayan was attending quite regularly during his stay at his sister's place in Madras, were by no means figments of heat-oppressed imagination. But, there is some logic in its support. For the sake of argument, even though we call them ways of the journey 'from the natural to the supernatural', it leaves much to be desired. It is perhaps a quest for something beyond, which transcends mere supernaturalism. It is, perhaps, an understanding of the philosophical meaning of existence.

In *My Days*, Narayan speaks of all the nitty-gritty that his dead wife, Rajam, felt concerned about, taking right from the daily happenings at home to her treasured worldly belongings to the questions that frequently kept assailing Narayan. But, amazingly enough, with each séance, he began to feel transformed into a new individual who had a philosophy of his own. His wife began to help him, too, in this regard. He speaks his mind in *My Days*:

> All that factual side seemed to me immaterial. Even if Mr. Rao had had his own sources of enquiry and was dashing off the information at the sitting, even if Rao caught telepathically whatever went on in my or anyone else's mind, it did not matter to me. Even if the whole thing was a grand fraud, it would not matter. What was important was the sensing of the presence in that room, which transformed my outlook. (161)

His wife begins to teach him how to communicate with her "without any intermediary." And, herein lies the attempt to bridge life and death. She chastens him for living on the superficial plane of consciousness which gives rise to concern for petty materialistic issues. She asks him to hone his perception to that limit that he would remain unperturbed by any external problems, grievous events, and so forth. She, in one séance session, says:

> Two nights ago, when you were about to fall asleep, your mind once again wandered off to the sick-bed scenes and the day you mourned my passing over...No harm in your remembering those times, but at the root there is still a rawness and that interferes with your perception. Until you can think of me without pain, you will not succeed in your attempts. Train your mind properly and you will know that I am at your side....After coming over, I have learnt so much more about the human mind, whose working, whose working I can directly perceive....In your plane, your handicap is the density of the matter in which you are encased. Here we exist in a more refined state, in a different medium.....I wish I could explain all that I see, think and feel....When you are prepared for it, I'll be able to tell you much....(*My Days* 162-163)

Perhaps, the renowned Bengali novelist, Tarashankar Bandyopadhyay's Pushpa, (of the novel *Devjan*) could have engaged in similar séance sessions if she remained in a lower syntopic level. But as her lover (who got married later, when their love did not materialize) died and joined the same syntopic plane, she began to make him understand the significance of the beyond-death existence. In *The English Teacher,* the writer speaks in considerable detail of Susila's philosophical elevation, almost in the same vein:

> 'Time in your sense does not exist for us,' she replied. 'Our life is one of thought and experience. Thought is something which has solidity and power, and as in all existence ours is also a life of aspiration, striving and joy. A considerable portion of our state is taken up in meditation, and our greatest ecstasy is in feeling the Divine Light flooding us....We've ample leisure. We are not constrained to spend it in a particular manner....Music is ever with us here, and it transports us to higher planes....Things here are far more intense than on earth; that means our efforts are far more efficient than yours. If by good fortune we are able to establish a contact with our dear ones who are receptive to our influence, then you say that that person is inspired.....
>
> Between thought and fulfillment there is no interval. Thought is fulfillment, motion and everything....In your state a thought to be realized must always be followed by effort directed towards conquering obstructions and inertia—that is, the nature of the material world. But in our condition no such obstruction exists. When I think of you or you of me I am at your side.' (*The English Teacher* 131-133)

And Susila meant it. Again, she wanted Krishna to feel in the same vein, transcending all barriers. Therein lies the *summum bonum* of metaphysical union of two souls. It is not a matter of mere feeling, but deep understanding. This is the manifestation of true love, where no separation is considered to be separation at all. Was it for no reason that the great metaphysical poet, John Donne, said:

> ....
> Dull sublunary lovers love
> [Whose soul is sense] cannot admit

Absence, because it doth remove
Those things which elemented it.

But we by a love, so much refin'd,
That our selves know not what it is,
Inter-assured of the mind,
Care lesse, eyes, lips and hands to misse.

Our two soules therefore, which are one,
Though I must goe, endure not yet
A breach, but an expansion,
Like gold to ayery thinnesse beate.
....

A Valediction: forbidding mourning

Susila, the dead wife of the English teacher, Krishna, succeeded in developing a philosophical wisdom in her husband. The teacher who lost all interest in living, found a new meaning of existence, where his wife, the source of his inspiration, is constantly beside him. Though, at first, he concentrates upon the ten jasmine buds plucked at night as a remembrance of his wife, however, he does not need that later.

Krishna seemed to transcend all encumbrances of 'distance and loneliness.' He was blessed with a higher knowledge, where mere thinking could lead to fruition. That is really impossible to achieve in this being but with the persistent aid of Susila, he attained it. He says, at the end of Chapter Five:

> On my way home, through the dark night, across Nallappa's Grove my feet felt lighter, because I knew she was accompanying me. Her presence was unmistakably there. I could sense it. The darkness of the night was not felt by me. The distance and loneliness were nothing to me. She was with me. I quietly enjoyed the fact without stirring the slightest thought. Far off I saw the dark night lit with a fire of cremation. But it did not disturb me! 'I know more than this...'I remarked. (*The English Teacher* 132-133)

This knowing is no supernatural knowledge, but a higher philosophical perception.

But, how was it possible? Can we refer to Narayan's coming in close contact with Paul Brunton, the saintly philosopher, who came to understand India through its secret philosophical power and mysticism? In *My Days*, he admits:

> Following the directions given, I practiced psychic contacts regularly for some years, almost every night. I found it possible to abstract myself from my physical body [a process taught by Paul Brunton] and experience a strange sense of deliverance. And then gradually the interest diminished when I began to feel satisfied that I had attained an understanding of life and death. (*My Days* 164)

In the subsequent chapters of *The English Teacher*, many reflections of actual happenings, though futile, find place. For example, his aversion towards astrology, his notion of the role of an ideal headmaster, and so forth. His father-in-law was a headmaster and he says about him that "he was a book-lover and interested in literary matters, and we found many common subjects for talk."(*My days* 118-119).

He fell head over heels in love with the daughter of this headmaster. One day, while talking about matters of varied common interest, he interrupted him by putting forth the overture of marrying his daughter, quite abruptly. His immediate reaction was really strange! "He was taken aback, but did not show it. In answer to my proposal, he just turned to the god in the shrine and shut his eyes in a prayer." (*My Days* 118)

"A few days after that, he started tallying our horoscopes, her daughter's with mine. And, judging himself and consulting with others, he found that the two horoscopes were found incompatible." In Narayan's horoscope, the Seventh House, which indicated matrimonial aspects, was occupied by Mars which was considered inauspicious. Though setting all odds at naught he got married to Rajam, the girl of his dreams, but she died within five years of their marriage. Since then, he abhorred astrology. So, by way of wishful thinking, he proved the calculations of an astrologer totally wrong in case of the fictitious headmaster, who had staunch faith in astrology. This man used to believe that he would die on a particular day, as predicted by a hermit-astrologer whose each and every soothsaying came true. But, the last one was proved wrong! Ah, if the same had had happened in Susila's alias Rajam's case!

Relinquishing the job of an English Teacher in Albert Mission College, on the one hand, is a protest against the colonial imposition of the language and literature, *per se,* and on the other hand, as for deeper meditation and spiritual enlightenment *Karmatyag* (renunciation of work) is essential, he gave up the cushy job in order to settle for a less-paid one (job in kindergarten school) though a worthy alternative in his eyes. Along with each passing day, Krishna began to believe that Susila was always with him. He, rather, entered into meditative rituals to feel the constant presence of her beside him, with him. But, Susila came to object to it once:

> I must tell you now that your sittings for development must be even more relaxed than they are at present. Why don't you allow your mind to move round about me? Now you just picture me in your mind and do not allow your thoughts to move an inch this side or that. This rigid exercise does not help our contact. By your intense and severe thought you make almost a stone image of me in your brain...you should be able to receive my thoughts. It can be done only if you do not make a stone image of me. I want you to behave just as you would if I were conversing with you... (*The English Teacher* 160-161)

But, Krishna was trying to come to terms with the inevitable loneliness and separation which he began to feel was the ultimate truth in a man's life, especially after transferring the responsibility of his daughter, Leela, to his father:

> There is no escape from loneliness and separation. ...Wife, child, brothers, parents, friends....We come together only to go apart again. It is one continuous movement. They move away from us as we move away from them. The law of life can't be avoided. (*The English Teacher* 177)

The English Teacher gave up all inhibitions that came in his way of communicating with his wife. In order to lead a "harmonious existence", he gave up all eternal engagements, even his "college job."

After giving up the college job, when he was walking down the secluded jasmine-embalmed street, at night, he felt the presence of Susila. Entering his room, when he whispered the name of Susila thrice, he felt her presence and for the first time he talked to her in person. He made room for her on the bed. He lauded her elegant look, her complexion, her sparkling eyes, her saree with a blue shimmering splendour and the fragrance of jasmine that surrounded her!

She even accepted the jasmine garland he handed to her. She tied it to her coiffure. And both of them greeted the dawn that peeped through the window, being ushered in readily by the cock, which crowed as usual.

As Krishna got engrossed in her, even the dead soul appeared alive to him. R.K. Narayan makes the moment seem real by writing:

> The boundaries of our personalities suddenly dissolved. It was a moment of rare, immutable joy—a moment for which one feels grateful to Life and Death.(*The English Teacher* 184)

The highest possible realm of philosophical thinking is what Krishna achieves. And Narayan corroborates the same feeling in *My Days*:

> Out of all this experience a view of personality or self or soul developed which has remained with me ever since. 'Now we know in part, then fully, face to face..' said St. Paul; our faculties are limited by 'now' and 'here'. The full view of a personality would extend from the infant curled up in the womb and before it, and beyond it, and ahead of it, into infinity. Our normal view is limited to a physical perception in a condition restricted in time, like the flashing of a torchlight on a spot, the rest of the area being in darkness. If one could have a total view of oneself and others, one would see all in their full stature, through all the stages of evolution and growth.....(*My Days* 164-165)

Is it not a corroboration of the fact that Susila and Krishna's selves stood united on the mental plane?

What, then, is this perception? Mere supernatural? No, doubtlessly, it is something beyond, something related to higher philosophical thought! *The English Teacher* is a journey from the natural to the supernatural and to a higher philosophical understanding where the barrier between Life and Death vanishes.

Works Cited

Abhedananda, Swami. *Life Beyond Death* (Calcutta, India, Ramakrishna Vedanta Math), 1944.

Chandra, N.D.R. ed. *Contemporary Literary Criticism: Theory and Practice*, Vol I (New Delhi, India, Authorspress, 2005)

Grierson, H.J.C. ed. *Metaphysical Lyrics and Poems of the Seventeenth Century, Donne to Butler* (New York, OUP), 1986.

Narayan, R.K. *The English Teacher* (Mysore, India, Indian Thought Publications), 1955.

_____ *My Days* (New York, USA, The Viking Press Inc) 1974.

Selvamony & Dasan, ed: *Essays in Ecocriticism* (New Delhi, India, Sarup & Sons), 2007.

3

Indian English Fiction: Mulk Raj Anand and Raja Rao

—Bhaskar Roy Barman

India has sixteen recognized languages and major among them are Hindi, Bengali, Urdu, Tamil and Malayalam. Compared to the major literatures existing in these major languages, Indian English fiction is a newcomer to the literary scene, its beginnings linked to the publication of R.K. Narayan's first novel, *Swami and Friends* (1935), Mulk Raj Anand's *Untouchable* (1935) and Raja Rao's *Kanthapura* (1958). The 1930s was marked in the history of India's struggle as a time that witnessed how India's struggle for wresting freedom from the hands of the British rules gathered momentum under the able leadership of Mahatma Gandhi. The three Indian literary triumvirs made proper use of the novel borrowed from the West a—literary form—they bequeathed this form to the writers who followed and were inspired by, them—as a vehicle of social and political inquiry. It also served as the means by which the non-native reader could be carried across into the world of the text.

I shall deal with those works of Mulk Raj Anand and Raja Rao, which are considered their masterpieces and have arranged, for the sake of the article, two novelists in the following order: Mulk Raj Anand and Raja Rao. The reason why Anand has preempted Raja Rao is because Anand's Untouchable appeared much earlier than Rao's Kanthapura.

Mulk Raj Anand has found himself catapulted into a whirlpool of controversy by the appearance of his novel, *Untouchable*, and received much wider acclaim than Raja Rao and even R.K. Narayan. The reason behind this is E.M. Forster's preface to his novel, *Untouchable* and it has served, suffice it to say, to heighten Anand's prestige as a novelist. This novel and the novel, *Coolie* that followed it conspired to bring him the recognition he rightly deserved, which ensured him the status of a novelist capable of portraying and delineating a particular situation which is realistic and true to life. E.M. Forster's frank confession to his failure to do himself in his *Passage to India* what Anand has done in his *Untouchable* sort of mesmerized a coterie of critics that cropped up into heaping a plethora of praise on Anand as a novelist.

The moment he made his appearance as a novelist, the winds of change had already started blowing across the sub-continent. The end of the First World War, a watershed in European history, proved to be a significant period in Indian life and gained its significance in the Gandhian whirlpool, sweeping over the length and breadth, upsetting on its way all established political strategies and ushering in refreshingly new ideas and methods which sent a-tremble Indian life in several spheres.

The tempo of political agitation was kept up after the war by Tilak, who emerged, shaking off the temporary spell of retirement after his release from prison in 1914, to rejoin the Congress. Two years later, in 1916, he himself founded the Home Rule League and paved the way for Mrs Anne Besant to establish a similar league called 'All-India Home Rule League' the following year. Gandhi had meantime returned from South Africa, refreshed with his Satyagraha triumph there. He returned in 1915. After having undergone a one year's probation, guided by his guru, Gokhale, Gandhi tested successfully his new weapon of non-violence in the Champaran campaign against the exploitation of the tenants of the indigo planters in 1917, the Kaira Satyabraha against the unjust land-assessment demands during the famine of 1918 and the Ahmedabad land dispute in the same year. The 1919 agitation against the Rowlat bills led to the Jallianwala Bagh slaughter which remains a permanent black spot on the British escutcheon, and drew a scar across Indo-British relations much deeper than any which had been inflicted since the Mutiny. By this time Gandhi's leadership had already taken on an All-India character, and it was symbolic of the fact that an age had ended, and another age began on the death of Tilak on 1 August 1920 in Bombay. The countrywide non-cooperation movement spearheaded by Gandhi created an unprecedented awakening and converted Indian nationalism from a middle-class movement to a mass emotion.

Ten years later, in 1930, Gandhi led the civil disobedience movement and it substantially differed from the non-cooperation movement, but the goal remained the same. The first was aimed at bringing the Government to a standstill by withdrawing from the administration, whereas the second was aimed at paralyzing the Government by mass-performing specific illegal acts. Among these the one that captured the imagination of the people most was the illegal making of salt. Gandhi's twenty-four-day march with twenty-nine chosen followers from Sabarmati Ashram to Dandi to break the salt law in 1930 electrified the entire civilized world. Another ten years later in 1940 the third and last Satyagraha campaign to be followed two years later in 1942 by the historic 'Quit India' movement prompted violent activity while Gandhi and his lieutenant languished in jail. After the end of World War II the political and economic exigencies compelled Britain to concede independence to India on 15 August 1947.

Indian English literature owes itself to the influences of these epoch-making developments in Indian life. Highly significant is the sudden flowering of the novel during the thirties when the Gandhian movement reached its zenith, and by this decade the nationalist upsurge had sent a-tremble the entire Indian society on an unprecedented scale; it made the society acutely conscious of the pressures of the present in all national spheres. Fiction constituted the web and texture of society emerging out of this consciousness and finding a fertile soil in a society in ferment. During the Gandhian age Indian English fiction discovered such compelling themes as the freedom struggle, East-West relationship, the communal problem and the plight of the untouchables, the landless poor, the downtrodden, the economically exploited and the oppressed.

Mulk Raj Anand's fiction is shaped and moulded by "the double burden on my shoulder, the Alps of the European tradition and the Himalayas of my Indian past." (*Apology for Heroism*, Bombay 1946, p. 67). He is, on one hand, critical of the deadwood of the hoary Indian tradition characterized by obscurantism, and aware on the other of its finer and enduring aspects. But Anand has derived his fervent socialist faith from the European tradition, and this inculcated upon him a vision of modern egalitarian society. His novels faithfully chronicle his eclectic humanism and humanitarian compassion for the underdog. To fan his socialist view, Anand has shackled himself to political evangelism, and has taken it upon himself to advocate the downtrodden and the underprivileged.

It is worthwhile to focus our attention on the controversy pertaining to his post-independence achievement as a novelist. After independence Anand's art seems unable to develop new dimensions. It so turned out that instead of fighting against the bourgeois government, he accepted the patronage of the Congress and the Congress Government, and thus made a dramatic shift from the well-established political novelist to a critic of culture. This controversy is premised by a critical expectation that Anand, on his return from England, should demonstrate a significant progress in his vision and work. But it should be remembered at the same time that Anand returned to India from a highly complex intellectual atmosphere of Europe which was befuddled, on one hand, by an aesthetic debate on modernism, anticipating an onslaught of anti-modernism and post-modernism and, on the other, by the moral and philosophical unresolvabilities which resulted from the barbarity of the two world wars. It was certainly difficult for him to accommodate himself to the changed situation in post-independence India. But he never departed from his war against colonialism, imperialism and other similar socio-political structures of human oppression and subjugation.

As I have said a bit earlier, the Indian English novel flowered during the thirties when the Gandhian movement reached its zenith. During the thirties appeared Anand's four novels: *Untouchable* (1935), *Coolie* (1936), *Two Leaves and a*

Bud (1937) and *The Village* (1939). His fifth novel, *Across the Black Waters* appeared in 1940.

Though there are other novels written afterwards such as *The Big Heart* (1045) and *The Private Life of an Indian Prince* (1953), I shall limit myself to dealing with the novels written during the thirties and in 1940. Since Anand is at his best in *Untouchable* and *Coolie*, I shall discuss them in some detail and touch upon the rest.

In his special preface to the second Indian edition of *Two Leaves and a Bud* (1951), Anand has hinted at his early fire and drive that helped shape his first novel. In writing about the pariahs and the bottom dogs he has ventured into the territory hitherto unexplored. In reading the novel, *Two Leaves and a Bud* one can easily see that humanitarian compassion distorts the action and the character disastrously. The locale is a teaplantation in Assam to which Gampu, a poor Punjabi peasant, is lured away by holding out fabulous promises only to find himself compelled to work in unhygienic conditions and starved. A British officer who tries to rape his daughter shoots him dead.

Despite all the violence and bitterness, the novel has a very jewel of a title, inspired by the coolies' song:

> I will make a good sheaf
> Plucking, plucking, plucking
> Two leaves and a bud.

Angular and sharp is the characterization, as in the indictment of an inhuman system that blurs the lines of humanity in the picture. But the intellectual framework of the novel thrives over the human content and reminds us of Forster's novel, *Passage to India* in which hovers the atmosphere of suspicion and strife and racial intolerance and antagonism; there is the small talk in the club, the reign of prejudice and unreason. In portraying Reggie and other very unpleasant characters, Anand's writing is infiltrated with disgust and hate.

A Punjabi peasant is the protagonist in Anand's trilogy, *The Village*, *Across the Black Waters* and *The Sword and the Sickle* which appeared in 1942. In the trilogy Anand traces the career of Lalu Singh over a period of some years from shortly before the First World War to the disturbed post-war year in India. Thus his boyhood, youth and early manhood are the themes of the trilogy. *The Village* gives a realistic picture of life in a typical Punjabi village, seen through the eyes of young Lalu Singh. He rebels against all the village mores and escapes them by running away. In *Across the Black Waters* he joins the army and fights in Flanders in the First World War. The third novel, *The Sword and the Sickle* shows Lalu Singh returning home from a German prison, hobnobbing with communists and ending up in prison.

Now we should steer our attention round to Anand's two masterpieces, *Untouchable* and *Coolie*, which have catapulted him into prominence.

Of all the novels Anand wrote before and after the independence *Untouchable* is the most compact and artistically satisfying, while *Coolie* is the most extensive in space and time, actuating multiplicity in variegated action. In *Untouchable* the unities are admirably presented in the manner of a classical play, inasmuch as it covers the events of a single day in the life of a low-caste boy round whom revolves the action of the novel. Many critics have compared *Untouchable* to Daniel Defoe's *Robinson Crusoe*, because they are both canonized discourses. In *Robinson Crusoe* the mythic allegory of Crusoe carries multiple meanings, social, political, economical and moral to the point where the narrative has become provocative commentaries and Crusoe has become a culture-hero, an embodiment of a synthetic structure of history and ideology. The parallel with *Untouchable* extends only to restructuring a new myth that integrates in its fabric culture, history, value and ideology. Bakha of whom Anand speaks as the hero-anti-hero symbolizes the evil of untouchability. Bakha is destined to remain a victim of social and religious determinism, a system that has bondaged him since his birth which itself strips him of the courage to rebel against the combined forces of religion and culture. But a scion of the twentieth century, Bakha has become susceptible to the impact of the new influences. Securing a pair of breeches from a Tommy and a pair of old boots from a sepoy, he wears them and dreams of being in 'fashion'. But the dawning of the day shatters his dream and reminds him of his work of latrine-cleaning. Anand dexterously describes Bakha's morning round of duties, bringing out the efficacy with which the boy does this essential service and the callousness with which the beneficiaries receive it. Bakha had to clean three rows of latrines single-handedly and several times in order to bring cleanliness in the place of filth and possible diseases, and turns his daily toil into a dexterous art. His sister, Rohini is, too, dexterous in her own way of cleaning.

In the afternoon Bakha attends the marriage of his friend Ram Charan's sister whom he could not marry. Ram Charan, the washerman's son, Chota, the leather-worker's son and Bakha forget for the nonce the minutae of sub-low-caste differences, and share the sugar plums and plan to play in the evening. At Havildar Charat Singh's, again, caste is forgotten and the Havildar treats Bakha affectionately and gives him a hockey stick. Fighting against the 31st Punjabis, Bakha sends a goal which starts a free fight. In the fight a little child is injured. Bakha ires the child's mother by touching and polluting the child. When he returns home, his father scolds him severely for having idled all the afternoon away and turns him out, thus filling Bakha's cup of frustration and misery.

Untouchable deals with the life of a sweet sweeper worse off than a slave. Untouchable himself, he pollutes others when he happens to touch them. Polluted they purify themselves. Thus he becomes a disquieting as well as a disgusting object to the orthodox. Whenever he walks along the public roads he is required to adduce and warn them he is coming.

Anand lavishes all his sympathy upon Bakha in delineating his character. As a child he gained a deep experience about the life of a sweeper through playing and mixing with the children of sweepers. In the novel he has displayed a right mixture of insight and detachment. It is wellknown that he has come to fiction through philosophy which has imparted him the depth that has helped make lively and realistic the character of Bakha. Bakha is presented as the prototypical untouchable, because he has turned out to be a unique individual and, in some measure, an exceptional untouchable. The many things that happen to him still happen somewhere or other even today. Only the telescoping of many events in the course of a single day purports to be Anand's.

The life in the town and a cantonment with all its colours and smells, the chants and the noises, the filth and the cruelty, the kindness and the humanity, the shifting scenes in the temple, the marketplace and the playground, with the quiet of the hillside and the stir of the public meeting, is described with so uncanny an accuracy that *Untouchable* strikes us as a picture of a place, of a society, of a custom and of certain persons not to be forgotten. The picture has acquired the force of an indictment of the evils of the decadent and perverted orthodoxy. By addressing himself to the task of giving expression to certain evils, Anand has to some extent acquired the effectiveness of Dickens.

Now let us turn to Anand's second masterpiece, *Coolie*. The action of the novel spreads over some years and moves from village to town, from town to city, thence to Bombay and from thence to Simla. *Coolie* is what is called a character novel, for it extends primarily in space. We finds ourselves, too, moving with the hill boy, Munoo, and following his fortunes, or rather his misfortunes. Munoo's character is drawn in the image of a childhood playmate of Anand's.

Munoo is forced to leave the village in Kongra valley to work and see the world around him. His first contact with reality shatters his dream of bettering his life. Arriving in the house of a minor bank clerk, he incurs the wrath of a shrewish and vindictive housewife. Before fleeing from the frenzied rage of his employers he wreaks vengeance by relieving himself near their doorsteps, thus lowering their social prestige. Then he gets employed at a primitive pickle and jam factory. The proprietor who has befriended him is reduced to bankruptcy owing to the thievery of his partner. Munoo is once again thrown onto the street to resort to coolie-ing. He faces a desperate competition from other coolies, seeking for a chance to become a beast of burden. A circus elephant-trainer rescues him from this struggle and helps him to reach Bombay, where he attaches himself to a vagrant family to become one of the workers in a cotton mill. He sweats out his living in appalling working conditions in leaky straw huts and, when these are washed away by monsoon, in dilapidated and insanitary tenement houses. He makes friends, has his first glimpse of life in a red-light district and witnesses a Hindu-Muslim feud instigated by the bosses to break the impending strike. Finally he is knocked down by the car of an Anglo-Indian woman. The Anglo-Indian woman takes him over to Simla to make him her servant. Here he dies of tuberculosis, the disease caused and aggravated by his having to pull a rickshaw for his mistress. He dies, watching the peaceful hills and valleys he has abandoned for the plains.

The pace of writing, as in *Untouchable*, is swift and the scenes follow in quick succession. The novel is verily a cross-section of the horrible and the holy, the inhuman and the humane, the sordid and the beautiful. The general effect is panoramic, as good and evil are thrown together, as in a real life. But we are not allowed time to ponder on the general effect, for we find ourselves constantly shifted and engulfed by a new situation at every turn and confronted with new cruelties and absurdities. Village, taluka headquarters, district headquarters, presidency capital, national capital—this is but a spatial progression, because human situation hardly alters wherever we find ourselves placed. Munoo represents all the downtrodden who are exploited all the time, one way and the another, by the socially privileged. As is Bakha of *Untouchable*, Munoo is a passive character always acted upon. What is common between Bakha and Munoo is their active warm-heartedness, their sense of gratitude for the least show of kindness, and particularly their desire to emulate the sahibs. But Munoo is the more attractive of the two, and his attractiveness owes itself to his curiosity and zest for life. But he is not able to attain to the status of a tragic hero. With his death nothing but his zest for life is lost. But we can't help grieving over his death caused at human machination.

In several ways *Coolie* makes a big departure from *Untouchable* by taking us into a much more complicated and circuitous world. Even though kicked and abused for offending the law of caste, the untouchable is not deprived of his place in society, and is necessary in the society. The coolie, on the other hand, though free to move about and choose his own work, is in fact functioning under a system even more rigid. He has nowhere to go; he is often underpaid and overworked, is cheated by his employers and lives in constant dread of losing his job. With Munoo, it is not his place in the old caste system that is being questioned—he belongs by birth to the second higher order—but it is his place in the new caste system created on the basis of cash nexus that is being questioned. The plight of Bakha emanates from a system that has prevailed in India for centuries, and the English have had nothing to do with it. But the plight of Munoo and his kind does emanate directly from the British rule and from the industrial revolution initiated by their rile without consideration for social reform. At the root of evil in the case of both Bakha and Munoo is poverty diffused all over India and infecting all our society.

In *Coolie* Anand explores the relationship of master and servant such as exists between Munoo and Nathoo Ram. Anand censures such kind of relationship, because it is inhuman, unhealthy and nearly submissive. He stresses the importance of the relationship that exists between equals, particularly the relationship that exists between the poor. *Coolie* transports us into a world in which exists comradeship among the poorest people. With nothing to hope for, their common humanity is all they possess. The relationship between Munoo and other factory employees is tinged with humaneness. We are at the same time treated to another picture depicted on a different scale, a picture of a different world characterized by unrestrained hysteria benuded of self-respect. The picture of the world is best illustrated when Prabha, the proprietor of the primitive pickle and jam factory, goes bankrupt and is beleaguered by his creditors. They shout obscenities and fight among themselves for what little might still be got from auctioning the property.

Raja Rao was aware of the forces engineered by the Gandhian movement and, at the same time, of the deep draughts of past tradition. Hail as he did from the Mysore state,

Raja Rao could not disentangle himself free from the influence of the Hindu culture or rather found himself tethered to his immutable moorings invisibly stringed by the traditional Hindu culture in which he had been brought up. Besides *Kanthapura*, he wrote three other novels, namely, *The Serpent and the Rope* (1960), *The Cat and Shakespeare* (1963) and *Comrade Kirillov* (1976), and a short story collection, *The Crow of the Barricades* (1947). I shall discuss in brief his novels only and leave his short story collection out.

Raja Rao is not, as are Mulk Raj Anand and R.K. Narayan, a prolific writer. His first novel, *Kanthapura*, considered his masterpiece, is an exuberant retelling, at once celebratory and elegiac at the same time, of the impact of Gandhi and the freedom movement on a small South-Indian village caught in the maelstrom of freedom struggle during the nineteen thirties. The tremors of the Gandhian impact on this South-Indian village are recorded in this novel in a chatty language peculiar to an elderly village woman, a loquacious story telling grandmother presented in the novel as a repository of Kanthapura's history. We find woven into her rich account of actual events, legends and myths the overwhelming changes brought about through the influence of Moorthy, an educated young villager and a staunch follower of Gandhi. In this small South-Indian village situated high on the ghats (mountain ranges) up the Malabar coast ploughing the fields at the first rains has been the traditional event, but the harvest reaped in 1930 is the whirlpool of Gandhianism. The initial reaction of Kanthapura to the entry of the Gandhian whirlpool is apathy. The young Moorthy, known as he does that the masterkey to the Indian mind is religion, puts new wine in the old bottle of the traditional Harikatha, a legendary narrative of God, and indoctrinates the Kanthapurans to Gandhian thoughts. Yet Gandhianism encounters stiff resistance in the form of orthodoxy. In fact, the theme of the novel may be summed up as Gandhi versus the small South-Indian village. But "the style of narration makes the book," says K.R. Srinivasa Iyengar in his book *Indian Writing in English* (published 1962 by Sterling Publishers Pvt. Ltd, New Delhi, India) on page 391, "more a Gandhi Purana than a piece of mere fiction. Gandhi is wielding his sceptre from afar in the person of Moorthy. The characters divide into two antagonistic camps: the rulers (and their supporters) on one hand and the Satyagrahis (and their sympathizers) on the other." There are other divisions and sub-divisions, but we are not concerned with them here. The main motif of the novel is the conflict between the Satyagrahis and the bureaucracy over the breaking of the salt law by Gandhi and his chosen band of followers. The breaking of the salt law has enforced passive resistance to 'alien' authority. Salt is manufactured in open distance of the Government, forest laws are broken and toddy shops picketed. Though what happens in Kanthapura is by no means a unique exception, the telling of the story embellishes the whole affair with a historical and puranic tinge. The following message is worth quoting in this connection:

> The narrative is hardly very straightforward: there are involutions and digressions, there are meaningful glances, there are rhythmic chains of proper names (Rachanna and Chandranna and Mandanna; Sampanna and Vaidyanna; Satamma and Rangamma and Puttamma and Seettamma), there are hypnotic repetitions and refrains, and there are also sheer poetic iridescence. A village, a picturesque region, an epoch of social and political change, a whole complex of character and motive, reason and superstition. Idealism and cold calculation, all sprang up before our eyes, demanding recognition and acceptance: it is almost a tour de force. (*Indian Writing in English*, p.392)

Although Raja Rao has had a grandmother tell the story with the result that the feminine touches and mannerism to some extent jolt the flow of narration, there is nevertheless consummate art, and the novelist himself justifies it in his foreword to the novel. He writes "We cannot write like the English. We should not. We can write as Indians. We have grown to look at the large world as part of us. Our method of expression therefore has be a dialect which will some day prove to be as distinctive and colourful as the Irish or the American. Time alone will justify it." The narrative techniques offers the requisite justification. The narrator, as we have already come to know, is an old woman, the grandmother teller of folk tales, who tells the story in the garrulous, digressive and breathless style of the Indian purana, emulsifying narration, description, reflection and religious discourse. Like Mulk Raj Anand, Raja Rao has interspersed his English with many Indian words, phrases, idioms, expletives, particularly those borrowed from his native Kannada, translated into English.

I shall pick on another novel to discuss in this article and make flitting mention of other novels, for we should consider space.

The Serpent and the Rope has a strong autobiographical flavour. Apropos of the novel in their review published in the *Sunday Times* Diana and Meir Gillon:

> confessed that the book defied "the discipline of reviewers' word limits" and pointed out that it was "certainly an epic and could ...have been a great novel. Even as it is, it remains a magnificent guide to India, and, for those who are prepared to work for their pleasures, a book to read and re-read." The reviewers in the Times, on the other hand, said succinctly: "It is rather as if the wisdom of Sanskrit had been into story- book form...The writing is utterly beautiful. No other word will do."
>
> (*Indian English Writing*, p. 397)

Here in this novel, the storyteller is Ramaswamy, himself the central character in the novel. He leads the readers deep into the novel and his personal reflections. In course of the narration of his diverse experiences, he projects contradictory qualities which often collide against each other. We find him sometimes subtle, sometimes sensitive, sometimes sensual and sometimes spiritual. Proud of being the eldest son of a professor of Mathematics at Hyderabad, he traces his lineage via Madhwacharya (Vidyaranya) far back to the *Upanishadic sage*, Yajnavalkya. Of himself he says, "I wandered my life away, and became a holy vagabond," and describes himself as a European brahmin, as a 'French Vedantin', as the neo-Tristan and the pseudo-Satyavan. He had read the *Upanishads* at the age of four, is conversant with Sanskrit and knows English, having gone via school to college in India. His mother tongue is Kannada and he fluently quotes Puranadaradasa. In 1945, at the age of 21, he goes out to France, equipped with a Government scholarship to pursue a course of research in

European history, and meets at the University of Caen Madelein, a teacher of history, destined to be his wife, even though she is older than him by five years. They marry three years later and a child is born and christened 'Krishna' and dies within a year of his birth. Ramaswamy, popularly known as Rama, returns to India early in 1951, on hearing of the illness of his father. Here, at this point starts the novel, whereas his going out to France and marrying Madeleine is said to serve as a prelude to the novel, the 'events' to take place during the next three years constitute the action of the novel. He has inherited, from his mother, his sensitiveness and poetry, his spirituality and his delicacy of build, and, from his father, the fanaticism of a mathematician. His father dies soon after he returns from France and on his death he feels as if orphaned.

Rama's four years' stay out in Europe infuses him with a realization of what India, beautified by Himavant and Ganga in the North and Kaveri and Kumari in the South as it stands, really means to him. Two different cultures, thanks to his stay out in Europe, commingle in his sensitivity and contributes to his mind becoming a seething whirlpool of cultural currents and cross-currents. An Indian brahmin, he has married a French girl, a catholic, and this marriage is construed as an attempt at fusion of two conflicting religions and cultures. Instead of being fused, as I have said a bit earlier, it has created a seething whirlpool in his mind.

There are both physical and psychological sides to the action of the story. The physical action is characterized by superficial global sweep. Rama's travels take him round to Benaras, Mussorie, Delhi, Bombay (now Mumbai); from thence over to Aix-en-provence, Montpalais, Pau, Cambridge, London; back again to Hyderabad, Bangalore, Harihararpur (the village in the novel), Kodaikanal, Madurai, Bombay; and finally, to Aix-en-Provence, Oxford, London, Paris. He visits India first in 1951 after he has gone out to Paris, on hearing of the illness of his father (his father succumbs to it), a second time the next year to be at the wedding of his sister, Saroja. He plans to visit India a third time in 1954, towards the end of the novel, to work out his salvation. Within this time-and-space framework are interwoven different and interesting characters drawn from different social milieux.

Madeleine, a Catholic French girl married to Rama, towers over other characters drawn from India, France, England, Russia and Spain. Her drifting away from Rama whom she loves over to Buddhism is but the manifestation of her conflicting personalities. She experiences, by marrying a Hindu brahmin, she being a French Catholic, the glory in the blending of two religions, and the agony out of non-fusion of the two religions and goes beyond them to embrace Buddhism. She also has the tit-bit of motherhood and its transitoriness owing to the death of her son which sort of unshackles her off the bond of love to pave the way for her embracing Buddhism. Even though she undergoes such transformation, she retains humaneness.

Savitri, another triumph of characterization, is no less an interesting character and commands the attention of the reader. She is attracted, though affianced to a poor jagirdar in the civil service, to Rama, and Rama, too, to her. Thus, mutual is their attraction, each exercising a catalytic effect upon the other and each growing upon the other's consciousness. But it is the spiritual affinity that draws them together and they are, so to say, spiritually united. She goes back to India to get physically united with the person she does not love, that is, Jagirdar, and Rama returns to Madeleine at Aix-en-Provence.

There is a third woman who comes upon his life. She is Lakshmi, another man's wife with whom he had but a brief liaison at Bombay towards the fag end of his second visit to India. Since this liaison is not supported or sanctified by spiritual love, Rama quickly disentangles himself from his bondage to physical love, and flies over to Aix and to Madeleine.

The psychological action is far more active and far more important than the physical action, and takes place in the theatre of Rama's heart, mind and soul. The readers find themselves transported into the world where men and women assemble from different nations and where different phenomena juxtapose themselves and, above all, the movements of the world itself are reflected in the mirror of his sensitivity. The reader is given a rare opportunity to peep deep into the soul of Rama, in fact, the soul of Raja Rao. Rama is the reality, the rope and everyone else is illusion, the serpent.

Madeiline, Savitri and Lakshmi are but fragments of illusion. We are all enslaved to illusion, to the phenomenal world which is the serpent to us. Like Rama, we all try to wriggle out of the bondage of the illusory world. To Madeleine says Rama:

> The world is either unreal or real –the serpent and the rope. There is no in-between-the-two – an all that's in-between is poetry, a sainthood...And looking at the rope from the serpent is to see paradise, saints, avatars, gods, heroes, universes. For wherever you go, you see only with the serpent's eyes. Whether you call it duality or modified duality, you invent a belvedere to heaven, you look at the rope from the posture of the serpent, you feel you are the serpent—you are—the rope is But in true fact, with whatever eyes you see there is no serpent, there never was a serpent. You gave your own eyes to the falling evening and cried, "Ayyo!" "Oh" It's the serpent!" You run and roll and lament, and have compassion for fear of pain, others' and your own. You see the serpent and in fear you feel you are it, the serpent, the saint/ One—the Guru—brings you the lantern; the road is seen, the long and white road, going with the statutory stars. "It's only the rope". He shows it to you. And you touch your eyes and there never was a serpent.
>
> (Quoted in *Indian Writing in English*, p. 403)

The truth revealed in the above *ipse dixit* maybe the rope, but the Guru is yet to come, a lantern in hand to differentiate the rope from the serpent. The immediate experience in the absence of the lantern we find ourselves perennially searching for the Guru to bring the lantern, is the experience of the serpent with its speckled bands and seductive scales.

Works Cited

Anand, Mulk Raj. *Apology for Heroism: A Brief Autobiography of Ideas*. 1946. New Delhi: Arnold-Heinemann, 1975.

_____. *Coolie*. 1936. London: Penguin, 1945.

_____. *Untouchable*. 1935. London: Penguin, 1986.

Iyengar, K.R. Srinivasa. 1973. *Indian Writing in English*. Bombay: Asia Publishing House.

4

Portrayal of Women's Status through Symbols and Images in the Novels of Ruth Prawer Jhabvala

—Vimmie Manoj

> I want to drink poisons, To lose myself in mists, in dreams![1]

Symbols are a complicated association of ideas represented by a mixture of metaphors to communicate inimitable feelings. Images are not a mere mental picture but those, which vitalize expressions and infuse it with copious suggestions; they are the carriers of symbols. When an image reappears in work of literature as a *leitmotif* of the thematic design it becomes a symbol.

Ruth Prawer Jhabvala, the 1975 Booker Prize Winner, in her novels, uses symbols and images to highlight the cultural disparity and gender hierarchy to redefine the status of women. She focuses on the women's struggle to be in harmony with society, elevated by social and cultural variances in the novels: *To Whom She Will* (1955), *The Nature of Passion* (1958), *Esmond In India* (1958), *The Householder* (1960), *Get Ready For Battle* (1962), *A Backward Place* (1965), *A New Dominion* (1972), *Heat and Dust* (1975), *In Search of Love and Beauty* (1983), *The Three Continents* (1987), *Poet and Dancer* (1993) and *Shards of Memory* (1995).[2] Shortlisting the structural techniques used by her one finds that she repeatedly uses many symbols and images imparting a rhythm to her works.

Jhabvala has used Indian symbols like *purdah* and kites to present an authentic picture of India. She does not use the Indian symbols and images as structural compulsion, but these symbols portray India's authentic sensibility and present the genuine depiction of women in India. Through the use of symbols she has approached the feminine psychology not as a 'riddle' but has developed femininity as an easy and simple process. She uses other symbols and images that are universally relevant, for example, the symbol of sky, colour and car-ride, and images universally acclaimed, for example, the images of relationships, animals, mountains, rains and houses. She uses these devices to depict women's status against the backdrop of the clash between the oriental and the occidental, traditional and modern.

I

Jhabvala thematically uses the device of symbolism in *The Nature of Passion* to portray the women characters as symbols. The character of Nimmi, the rebel, is in sharp contrast with that of Usha, the submissively obedient woman. Usha accepts her status as that of a slave to the male members in the family while Nimmi's refusal to accept their command irritates them. She goes to the club and even gets a "haircut" (6), which is symbolical of her attempt to cut off the bonds of slavery. Ultimately, her revolt subdues as she succumbs to emotional and social pressures. The characters of Lalaji's wife, Shanta and Usha symbolize the women as submissive slaves, while Phuphiji stands for the strict authority of age-old traditions. Phuphiji is pictured as a dry and thin lady with an ugly face, ruthless like the customs and traditions whose meaning has no standing in the modern world. Kanta (the attractive) symbolizes the urban woman who, in an attempt to outlook the modern standards, is ready to sacrifice her joint-family ties but hypocritically lingers on its monetary gains. Jhabvala pictures through these women characters their devalued status, irrespective of their age, education and financial standing.

Jhabvala extends the pattern of using characters as symbols in *Esmond in India* where the European Betty and the

Indian Lakshmi, Madhuri and Kanta exhibit the women who accept their devalued status. Shakuntala initially does seem to rebel when she opposes her mother's command and adopts the modern ways to recognize her liberation. Ironically she ends up being a slave to the physical desires of Esmond. These women characters are placed low in the gender hierarchy and Jhabvala uses them to signify the generally low status of Indian and Western women.

Jhabvala adopts the pattern of symbolizing through her character the plight of women as a widow; for example, in *The Householder,* the character of Prem's mother symbolizes the pathos of the lonely widow. Her self-pities expose the purposeless life after the death of her husband. Similarly the death of the beggar widow in *Heat and Dust*, the novel that won her the Booker Prize in 1975, accounts for the rigidity adopted by the society towards the widowed women. In the same novel, the event of *sati* unravels the Indian society's incapability to accommodate widows.

The symbolic characters of Phuphiji in *The Nature of Passion* and Bhuaji in *A Backward Place* as child widows expose the hollowness of the male-dominated society, which seems to decide the status of women. Jhabvala boldly symbolizes the widow's struggle of survival in the male-dominated society through the character of Asha in *A New Dominion*. Her survival is not on monetary grounds but on the physical planes. The rich widow, taken over by boredom and restlessness, has sexual links with Gopi. Her live-in relation with Gopi becomes a symbol of her revolt against the inferior standards set for women.

Jhabvala's women characters as symbols include prostitutes like Tara in *Get Ready for Battle* and Tara Bai in *A New Dominion.* Although Tara Bai is a film actress, the society assumes her as a "glorified prostitute" (6). The symbol of their free mingling with the opposite sex presents the dual nature of society. Tara moves to prostitution due to poverty but even Brij Mohan who seems to be ideological throws her out after using her. On the other hand, Tara Bai's free movement with the men is stressed and her talent is ignored. Jhabvala has symbolically stressed the nature of men to relate women as sexual objects.

Besides the submissive women characters Jhabvala presents some women characters as warriors against male domination. The characters of Indu, Gulab and Sarla Devi stand as symbols of the new era that places women as equal to men. In *The Householder* Indu symbolizes the practical modern woman who knows when to act. In contrast to Prem's mother, Indu's silence in moments of tensions adheres to the fact that "Indian tradition lays down time-honoured rules for a wife's conduct"[3] Indu's intentions to be a model housewife gives way when she serves Prem with "a defiant little slam"(79). Her going off to sleep before Prem's arrival or scolding the servant before her mother-in-law and Prem, displays her subtle revolt. Her revolt against Prem's authority aids to enhance her status. Prem and Indu's frequent disputes end in asserting their claims to respect each other as householder and housewife. Through them Jhabvala symbolizes the reality that wants husband and wife to act as friends and lovers, and thus enhance their status, both as individuals and as a couple.

Jhabvala interprets Gulab in *Esmond in India* as a lady with sensuous, instinctive awareness of reality that acts habitually by instinct. Gulab refuses to be ruled over by Esmond, and terminates her marriage with him. She becomes a symbol of the free-thinking Indian woman. Similarly Sarla Devi on the path of self-exploration breaks all her ties with her family in *Get Ready for Battle*. Jhabvala's inclination towards Hindu symbolism is highlighted in *Get Ready for Battle* through Sarla Devi who becomes the symbol of *karma*. Sarla Devi on the path of self-realization touches those around her, engages in their problems and becomes free. She acts like a catalyst and is ever ready to fight the battle. Although her status as a mother, a wife or a sister does not enhance she remains unaffected.

Jhabvala's main interest in the clash of humans is the struggle of women to be in harmony with the patriarchal society. Cultural disparity and gender hierarchy season the fundamental differences that are heightened by external circumstances. Jhabvala, as a connoisseur of divided souls, conceives characters whose inner longings are at odds with their outer protective coloration. Shakuntala and Nimmi who desire and achieve more tidy, "modernized" existences, later feel as if someone had stolen their life forces: Westerners like Etta, Clarissa, Junior Olivia, Lee and Harriet who eagerly hand themselves over to India's chaotic bliss in the end find it too rigorous to endure.

Characters like Sarla Devi and Gulab symbolize the birth of a "new woman" who is conscious of her identity though she is not very eager for social recognition and status. Gulab's potential to grow and develop in the hidebound society, in spite of all adverse situations, succeeds to struggle, attain and shape her own individual identity. On the other hand, Sarla Devi, agonized with social constraints and moral inhibitions, preserves her identity and she moves to another path after failing in one task. Her striving for betterment thus proceeds without any inhibitions of victory or loss, thus symbolizing the title 'Get Ready for Battle'. Gulab symbolizes the more active woman, although throughout the novel she is portrayed as a submissive, lazy woman who can think only of eating and sleeping, yet throughout the novel her inactiveness pictures her revolt and in acceptance of Esmond's tyranny.

Through the story of Gulab and Sarla Devi, Jhabvala has ventured to tear apart the veil of romantic haze from the not-all-lovely face of wedlock. Like her other Indian contemporaries, Jhabvala is also concerned with the issue of colonial imagery in Western Oriental literature. She adopts fictive strategies that liberate her characters from the denigrating and confining images of the "other." As R.S. Pathak points out, Jhabvala portrays various types of seekers after the realization of the self. Faced with a series of crises her characters are in a perpetual quest for identity.[4]

Jhabvala emblematically presents the dichotomy existing between men and women, and suggests the struggle that an individual must endure to live in harmony with each other. The external racial, social, religious and gender differences repeatedly highlight the fundamental personal difference. The recurrent symbol of the 'sky' in accordance with other famous symbols like that of Melville's great white whale in *Moby Dick* and Coleridge's albatross in *The Rime of the Ancient Mariner*, marks the rhythm in her works and provides a sense of deeper dimension. The frustration and failing of Esmond in his relation with women in *Esmond in India* is highlighted when his attitudinal rigidity to adopt and accept the woman's viewpoint leading to his futile existence is symbolized through the Indian sky " [...] which dwarfed all human life into significance"(264). The women here are imaged like the sky; just as Gulab dwarfs his existence so does the Indian sky. His relation with Gulab ends because she refuses to be dominated. He enjoys domination over Betty and Shakuntala, and demotes their status. Esmond's sexual encounters with Western women symbolize his manly dominance. His sexual moves towards Shakuntala after his separation from his Indian wife symbolize the fact "intercourse yes, intimacy never." Here the European Esmond uses his sexual dominance over women to impose their demoted status. Jhabvala thus uses symbols to communicate Esmond's unique feelings.

The symbolism of the clash between the spiritual and materialistic is represented through Sarla Devi and Gulzari Lal. Sarla Devi is termed as the sage, an embodiment of goodness, whilst her husband, Gulzari Lal, reflects the Western representative of wealth and evil in *Get Ready for Battle.* The battle is of self, between the materialistic passion and the spiritual desire. Similarly in *Poet and Dancer*, Angel, as the name suggests, stands for innocence and devotion in contrast to Lara, the epitome of experience, domination and evil. Jhabvala symbolizes through their story the battle between the two forces, mythical like the battle between Godly goodness and satanic evils. The story ends with the downfall of both since they refuse to part. Angel and Lara symbolize the women in their extreme states who become responsible for their deteriorated status.

Jhabvala presents the symbolic awareness of sexuality of the women characteristically. In *The Nature of Passion*, Nimmi gets carried away because of her desire for self-realization and almost challenges to dwell in sexual links with Pheroze. Similarly in *Esmond in India* Shakuntala's desire to explore her individuality and womanhood compels her into a hasty relationship with Esmond and offers herself to him, wanting him to arouse her dormant sexual sentiments. Sumi desires to explore her sensuality in *Get Ready for Battle.* Sumi, the maiden who is in love with Vishnu, desires sexual pleasures from him. The character of Mrs. Saunders in *Heat and Dust* symbolizes the sexually active Western woman whose pornographic visualization of her Indian servants makes her mentally sick whilst in the other extreme is Ritu, whose sexual deprivation makes her mentally sick. Olivia and Olivia Junior undergo the same situational sexual praxis but both tackle their problem differently. Olivia submits to the Nawab's sexual moves and Olivia Junior makes the move towards Inderlal to display her communion with the Indian land. Whilst the Nawab impregnates Olivia, who becomes symbolical of the Indian revenge against the British Rulers, Olivia Junior's pregnancy symbolizes the Westerner's acceptance of India and its ways. Lee in *A New Dominion* considers her sexual intercourse with Gopi and Swami as holiness in order to attain self-fulfilment of the mind, though the men in context sexually abuse her. In *Three Continents* the sexual encounter of Harriet with Crishi results as she correlates it with her spiritual journey. Her passive desires put her before Crishi like a lamb before the wolf. Jhabvala points out that in political, cultural and spiritual struggle it is women who are exploited, thus the status of women remains unchanged in all circumstances. She expresses her convictions with reference to the status of women using symbols as a medium. The women characters like Shakuntala, Nimmi and Sumi symbolize the newer generation women, who get carried away by the stream of physical demands. In case of Shakuntala, Nimmi and Sumi total destruction is prevented with their marital involvement; however, any improvement in their status is doubtful. Whilst Jhabvala has portrayed the Indian maidens in quest of emotionality and sexuality, she portrays the Western maidens in quest of spirituality. In *A New Dominion* the Western maidens like Lee, Margaret and Evie, in their spiritual journey get sexually exploited and Harriet in

The Three Continents undergoes the same experience. The self-styled guru Leo, who exploits Marietta on physical and spiritual levels, charms her in *In Search of Love and Beauty*. Etta and Clarissa in *A Backward Place* exploit those around them; they are neither on any emotional, sexual nor spiritual quest. Instead their quest is materialistic. Jhabvala symbolizes these maidens, who irrespective of their quest become the fodder to male exploitation. They thus symbolize the fact that young women, irrespective of their culture and goals, remain yoked to men. Jhabvala shows physical intercourse between Western women exploited by Indian men, or Indian women exploited by Western men. Nowhere has she portrayed the physical union between Indian man and woman or Western man and woman, except the married Indian couples. This becomes a symbolic reason for the cultural cataclysm in context to the devalued status of women.

Another symbol frequently used by Jhabvala in her works is the incident of the car ride. This symbol becomes synonymous with the sexual advancement made by young women. In *The Nature of Passion* Nimmi's car ride with Pheroze leads to her sexual experience. Similarly, Sumi's car ride with Vishnu in *Get Ready for Battle*, where she openly invites Vishnu "Just once again! Only once!"(152), symbolizes her eagerness to experience the passion of the flesh. However Vishnu does not feel the same sexual attraction towards Sumi, and turns down her advances as he puts his foot "on the brake"(153). The car ride of Olivia with the Nawab in *Heat and Dust* symbolizes Olivia's hidden sexual wanting and her mute acceptance to the clever moves of the Nawab. Her frequent car rides to the Palace symbolize her desires. Harriet's car rides in *Three Continents* links with her sexual awareness. Jhabvala has thus used the car ride as a general symbol of sexual desire.

Symbolism forms an integral component of her fiction, as it enriches the narrative by pulling its message down to the level of our unconscious and anchors it there. The universal use of the "sky" links the Indian sensibility of Jhabvala's fiction with the rhythm of the world. The scene outside Etta's flat in *A Backward Place* signifies the magnificence of the Indian "sky," [...] Most prominent of all was the sky, which covered and dwarfed everything [...] had black kites wheeling slowly round and round against it."(7). Here the sky symbolizes the difference between the two genders. It reflects the negating power of the male-dominated society and its superimposition over women. The Indian symbol of kites against the sky expresses Etta as part of society. The kites appear to have lost their colour, and appear black just as Etta has lost her identity and is aimlessly moving "round," a shape that has no end. She has lost her identity and her superior status of being a white woman. She is an object like the "kite" with the string in the hands of men who move her aimlessly. The symbol of the kite is a remark on her lowered status. The symbolic use of kite explores the not so-clear status of Etta and thus creates curiosity in the reader about her destiny.

Jhabvala has picturesquely used the sky to paint the Crishi's dominance over Harriet in *Three Continents*. Harriet is forcefully convinced by Crishi to write Michael's suicide note, her confused state of mind and sighted surety of her doom is symbolized by the sky, "The colour had gone from the sky and it was that sort of dim, translucent light there is at dawn as well as dusk, for it seems that light dying is the same as light being born"(382). The sky is the symbol of the state of human life and points to the emptiness that chains the human life. The cycle of life and death directs towards the existence of the Divine soul. The symbol of the colourless sky relates to the uninteresting life-pattern of women. The time of dawn and dusk relates to the hope of a new beginning, where women will be not dominated but considered as an equal. The status of the Western Harriet is that of a bonded slave to the Eastern Crishi. Harriet symbolizes the Western woman who, in quest of spirituality, gets overpowered by dominating male forces and finally settles with a demoted status like the "dim and pale" moon.

Jhabvala symbolizes that the position of women is sometimes lowered because of her own social setting. The absence of man in the lives of woman reflects the state of desolateness where neither sun nor rains can give refuge in

Poet and Dancer indicating the hopeless and waywardness of the lives of the two cousins, "[...] all the lights had been extinguished in the buildings as well as the sky; the promise of dawn had not been fulfilled, and it was a gray, neutral day, neither sun nor rain"(194). Here the 'gray neutral day' symbolizes the fruitless lives of the two cousins. The relationship between the two cousins symbolizes the negation of life forces when women try to overlook the existence of men in society. Their relationship finds no productive result, thus the status of the two young women remains "neutral."

Jhabvala's pictorial depiction of women, drawn against social, cultural and historical context has several dimensions delivered through varying artistic moods. A symbol she uses to differentiate between the genders is in terms of fair and dark. For example, Esmond, the fair European, is married to the dark-skinned Gulab. Olivia, though married to the fair Douglas Rivers, gets attracted to the dark Nawab and Junior Olivia gets involved with Inderlal. All of these relations fail mainly because the two in relation are not on the same plane, culture as well as status-wise.

In *Heat and Dust,* Jhabvala evokes the pathetic position of women through the symbolic use of names. The name of the city Satipur, as derived from the word *sati,* symbolizes the degradation of women like the "collapsing houses"(166), and the Nawab's princely state "Khatm" meaning the end, swallows their desires like a venomous snake. The cities dissolve the identity of the women it inhabit.

Jhabvala brings into her fiction the symbol of women's digression, the *purdah.* In *Heat and Dust* she uses the symbol to comment on women's distancing from reality as "[...] something dead and mouldering"(13) and relates it with the antiquated practice. The free Western women Olivia and Beth joke about the Begum's inferior status; on the contrary their independent status is mythical. Sandy, the educated wife of the Nawab, rebels against the *purdah* and refuses to be masked. But the entrenched *purdah* values suppress her aspiration for freedom. Olivia too does not succeed in evading the *purdah,* and her abortion too is conducted in *purdah.* The "burqa" is denial of individual identity. The *purdah* becomes a symbol of backwardness and resistance to change. In the same novel Ritu is kept in *purdah*, her mental illness symbolises the tribulations generated by *purdah* attitudes. Jhabvala highlights the dilemma of the exploited women like Ritu and Olivia who suffer *purdah* on their senses and desires. Olivia is confined within the *purdah* of the British colonial policy that isolates her and discriminates 'her individual needs'. What is worth taking note of is that Jhabvala has very precisely defined the strength of the *purdah* when she describes the veiled women as 'hawkers' or the strength of the *purdah* when rendered to hide diabolic plots as that of the attempt of murder of the chorus girl, and Olivia's abortion asserts the dual nature of the custom. In the modern perspectives, Jhabvala examines Indian social practices and cultural norms exposing the reality of liberalized codes set for women just as Nimmi, Sumi and Shakuntala are denied freedom from *purdah*. Jhabvala indicts through the symbol of *purdah* the constrained codes that suppress the liberated expressions of women, and exposes the status of women in the tradition-bound Indian society.

Jhabvala symbolizes the free-thinking that replaces the traditional dejection, as Vera in *Shards of Memory* rejects Henry because she is aware of the failure and suffering associated with spiritual involvement. She does not long for any spiritual journey and disapprovingly says, "[...] it was better to marry someone whose eyes were in keeping with the rest of him"(272). She rejects the probable relation with Henry and saves herself from the agonies and sufferings resulting due to it. Jhabvala presents Vera as a symbol of a new woman who will not hesitate to reject love if she senses any devaluation in her status.

II

Jhabvala's fictional genius is basically imagistic. A common image pattern underlying her fiction can be seen: house images, branching into furniture images, animal and bird images, sky images and flower images, atmosphere images like heat, dust and mist images. Isolated images such as body images, swirl images and characters as images prevail in the fiction of Jhabvala.

In the novel *The Householder* Jhabvala uses the sky image to impart special effects throughout the story. The awareness of life by the couple's existentialistic approach reflects when they make love in the open, "The sky, vaulting huge and black above them, nailed with silver points of stars and a slice of moon, seemed closer than the earth" (163). The images of the sky is pictured as a vault like the social pressure that unites Prem and Indu as husband and wife without their consent. The image of the stars and the moon appear to be in symphony with the earth just as the lovers are content in each other's arms. This image reflects the compassion dwelling between the two that leads to their equal status as man and wife irrespective of their situational limitations.

In *Shards of Memory,* Jhabvala uses the sky image to picture the reality that exists between the relation of Vera and Henry. As Vera pushes Henry's wheelchair "he felt that he was not in the least impeding her but that they were scudding along like leaves blown over the earth, clouds over the sky [...] he continued to feel as free as in a field or meadow"(160). The weightlessness felt by Henry illustrates his physical and emotional dependency on Vera. His thinking of not impeding Vera is too sceptical because physically he is handicapped, his male ego withholds the thought that he is a hurdle in Vera's way because it a woman's duty to look after her man (which he desires to be). The image thus creates points to the free-thinking of the male that accounts for caretaking as a compulsion of woman.

Jhabvala predominantly uses the land image to picture the efforts made by the young Nimmi in *The Nature of Passion* where she goes for a ride with Pheroze and experiences the sensuality of being kissed. Here the images of "[...] out on the barren plains, a pack of jackals cried like inhuman children"(104) associated with the episode signifies the failure of her struggle to enhance her status. Later the image of "Green parrots flew in and out of the sun and a gush of bright orange blossoms flowed down the length of the crumbling old wall,"(190) reflect the success of Nimmi's hunt for a life partner. The image of birds flying symbolizes the free soul of women. The lightness in the atmosphere shares her joy, "The sunlight was bright but gentle, winter sunshine full of the birds". The image does not end here and it proceeds, "In the distance, out on the barren plains, the broken flight of steps of a vanished place led to nowhere and a man with a stick and a loincloth walked behind two yoked and shabby bullocks" (190). The description reflects the life of women led by men where women were "not thought of nor looked at, but nearby" (191). Jhabvala uses the image of the yoked animals to signify the devalued status of women in the patriarchal society; "the man with a stick" speaks of the atrocities done on women by men. The land is barren symbolizing the non-futility of women's existence in the world. The "broken steps" symbolize the hurdles placed on women's path whilst the road that "led to nowhere" envisions the reality of the destination that the social pressures levied on women lead to. Jhabvala focuses on the land image in *The Householder* where Prem's pride of owning his impregnated wife, Indu, is represented through the image of "lush grass, the bushes heavy with rain, the swollen lake" (181). The land image reveals Prem and Indu's content wedding life like the "lush grass" and Indu's pregnancy is portrayed through the "swollen lake". The image of flying birds against the backdrop of the sky echoes the loneliness of Sarla Devi on the path of spiritual accomplishment in *Get Ready for Battle;* it produces a coherent rhythm:

> [...] remote but seemingly attainable- she saw a sky huge and soft with evening. There was a last, lingering, fading, orange streak on the horizon and flung out against it a flight of silhouetted birds with outstretched wings (223).

The status of Sarla Devi as a woman on the path of spirituality is lonesome; the "orange streak" symbolizes the spiritual quest as orange colour stands for spiritualism. The world symbolized by the "huge sky" is softened as dusk encroaches symbolizing that dusk is followed by dawn, a new beginning. The image of "birds with outstretched wings" symbolizes Sarla Devi's flight and struggle for independence from the materialistic ordeals of the world. Jhabvala symbolically creates images of the spiritual quest, of *karma* and *moksha*. Similarly in *A Backward Place*, the image of Mrs. Kaul as a "bird in a gilded cage" reflects her status as a creature in captivity. In *Heat and Dust*, the symbolic representation of the sky and the atmosphere creates a suitable background for the story. The atmosphere is heavy and unbearable for the British Olivia junior, the heat and dust engulfs her senses, the 'Dust storms' signal of some approaching misfortunes, "Leaves that were once green are now ashen, and they toss around us in a dervish dance [...]. Every position is uncomfortable; and one's mind too is in turmoil" (79). Junior Olivia's encroaching misfortune is alarmed with the image of the once green leaves that are un-embarked and covered with dust. They toss around symbolizing the endless movement; the "dervish dance" signifies the wild rituals to be performed on her. The summer dryness withers life.

Junior Olivia seems confused, firstly because she is not sure of her status as a woman and, secondly, because her being a British woman in the Indian land alienates her from the rest. Similarly the hot dry weather alters her thoughts. She seeks refuge in the claims of the Nawab to escape from the clutches of the "the vast distances, the vast sky, the dust and the sun and occasional broken fort or mosque or cluster of tombs"(85). The image of the "vast sky" reveals her insignificant status. The "broken fort" symbolizes the lost glory associated with women and the "cluster of tombs" symbolizes the evident downfall of women. Her relationship with the Nawab is an escape from the dry reality, the futile meeting of the East and the West, but Olivia does not have the strength to accept the futility; instead her vision of the sky is, "The sun was beating down of course-the gold dome of the Nawab's mosque gave out blinding beams-..."(103). The image forges her view. She tries to find her existence, but is not aware of the fact that in the procedure of doing so she is being used by the Nawab. The image of the "gold-dome" weaves mystery about her survival. She bluntly refuses to foresee the future, "In the distance, beyond the pearl-grey palace walls, lay the town in miserable stretch of broken roofs, and beyond that the barren land: but why look for that far?" (103). Jhabvala projects the young British woman's refusal to foresee the downfall as the present soothes her wandering soul, a temporary escape from her anonymous identity.

Junior Olivia goes up to the mountains to escape from the social and cultural strain, where she finds that, "The rain had made everything shinning green and wet. [...] and in the distance more clouds, but of a very dark blue, were piled on each other like weightless mountains" (165). The "rain" had made the dry barren land fertile and the "blue" sky symbolizes the tranquillity in contrast to the blazing sun viewed by Olivia. The image of clouds "piled" symbolizes the arrival of a compassionate era that would surpass the standing of men and women as separate identities.

Olivia gets drowned in the confusion of her existence, but Junior Olivia tries to walk on the path, rising above the realms of worldly differences. The narrator's journey to the mountains symbolizes the journey on the spiritual path, a recluse to the absurdities of survival arising due to cultural, social and gender differences, "I rarely look down. Sometimes, when the rains stop, the mist in the valley swirls about and afterwards the air is so drenched with moisture that the birds seem to swim about it and the trees wave like sea weed" (180). Jhabvala presents the image of the valley filled with "mist" as a symbol of the non-concrete and the "air" symbolic of the soul is shown drenched and in motion. The "swirls" represent the gyre's centrifugal motion used by Yeats in *The Second Coming* (1921). The rains, as Jhabvala symbolizes, are her acquaintance with the basic conception of the soul tied to the cycle of birth and rebirth. As in the teachings of the *Upanishads*, an individual's quest lies in identifying the self with the supreme source. The "birds" appear to "swim"; this antithetical image symbolizes the mystical union in which the ego frees itself, and thus the ego of men and women will be diminished. The core of the individual as man and woman is joined to the essence of the universe. The image of the tree waving like "sea weed" states the heightened sense of being conscious and enchanted. The narrator's statement "[...] more difficult to get down again, even if I should want to" (181) represents the irreversible journey to search the self.

Jhabvala rightly points that the universe does not differentiate between gender and culture. The status of man and woman can be the highest if they walk on the road of self-realization. Thus at the end of the novel the heat and dust is replaced by rains and greenery symbolizing the positive stride of life.

Jhabvala has structurally used symbolism to highlight the similarities and dis-similarities between Olivia and her successor. She points out through the two women characters, the doomed destiny met by Western women who flock to India. Although both are doomed by their fate they both select their path of destruction and both deal with their survival crisis differently.

Jhabvala frequently uses the image of house and furniture to depict the the inner self of the individual. The image of house and furniture used by Jhabvala in *Esmond in India*, to describe Uma's house signifies the spiritually free Indian lifestyle. Gulab memorizes Uma's house with "vast rooms and little furniture" (20), contrary to Esmond's flat depicting the rigidity in the atmosphere "hemmed in by furniture" with "no room to move at ease [...]"(20). Here the image of the two houses contradict each other, whilst Uma's Indian house gives Gulab the freedom, Esmond's Western flat obstructs her mobility symbolizing her state of prison. The lavish Western lifestyle does not soothe the Indian Gulab who, unable to analyze the utility of so much furniture, concludes, "[...] It only prevented one from being comfortable"(20). The Westerns are "as alien and uncomfortable as their own flat" (47).

The characters in the novel are well collaborated with their lifestyles, just as Gulab hates the made-up environment. "She knew her room was not very clean; she knew she herself was not very clean; but that was the way she lived"(46), symbolizes the natural animal instinct in her, which cannot be tampered with nor modified into a so-called civilized one.

Gulab resembles the character of father in D.H. Lawrence's *Sons and Lovers* (1945). Esmond too fails in changing Gulab and regrets staying in his own flat "[...] though he had completely followed his own tastes in the furnishing and decorating"(50) yet Gulab's "heavy smell and her languor," weighed him down, as if "swallowing him up"(50). Gulab thus has been delineated as a symbolic creature who, in spite of being ignored by Esmond, succeeds in "superimposing her presence" making him "aware of it." Her presence cannot be denied, she represents the power in women. Her identity dwarfs Esmond's existence, thus reflecting the status of the wife as a valued member in the Indian family.

The door image is situational when the servant defiles her chastity. She realizes Esmond's incapacity to protect her chastity and she packs her belongings and, "She left the door open [...] "(261). The "open door" images the freedom of Gulab from the possession of Esmond. Leaving the door unlocked symbolizes Gulab's refusal to be caged, signifying the free status of women. In the same novel Jhabvala depicts Uma as an authority who guides the life of those around and her open-minded thinking is symbolized by the image of her house with "[...] open verandahs overlooking the courtyard"(34). Uma's requirements are minimum and she seems to be living in sacrament. Jhabvala explores two violently opposed modes of being: one, the intimate experience of feeling, and the other, the more orderly social virtues of " in India". The neatness against the coarseness of the flats symbolizes the state of mind, one in deep stability and the other in conflict.

The image of the Nawab's Palace in *Heat and Dust* that pictures his royal past is pre-figurative. The image of the Palace with the carved sofas, brocade upholstery and furniture symbolize his passion for a majestic life but the absence of piano, a western instrument symbolizes the denial of entry to Olivia in his Palace. The "Palace walls" shadow the houses in the town of Khatm beside the "slummy lanes." Olivia on her way for abortion reaches the midwives house "descending some slippery steps" and the "tumble-down"(166), condition of the house image her destined doom. Olivia's boredom is imaged through "her black and white prints."(18). Her habitual tendency to remain isolated from the others is imaged through "her Japanese screen"(18). She becomes a decorative tableau like the chair and embroidery frame, thus her status is reduced to that of an object.

In the novel *A Backward Place* as the East stands for a mystifying pattern of life, a symbolic of 'emotion', with mastery she parallels the mood and projects through the image of flowers. The scenic space is in sharp contrast with the interior of Etta's flat where: "Everything was so elegant, so conditioned, in such good taste: just like Etta herself [...] There were two flowers each in two tiny delicate vases"(6). The flower images stand for the two European women, Etta and Clarissa. The tiny vase depicts the flat. The two women fail to emerge or adopt Indian norms and face destruction. Similarly in *Heat and Dust* the image of flowers frequently appear imparting an imaginary inclination to Olivia's nature: "Olivia could not live without flowers" (36). She leads her life in hallucination and refuses to accept the reality. The delusion leads to the European women's destruction and demolished status.

The writer's device utilizes the colour image to show the futile attempts of Etta in *A Backward Place*, to make a small Europe in India. It is expressed when the flat is described as neat and systematic in contrast to the oriental with the "sophisticated black and white prints hung on the walls"(6). The contrast of black and white highlights Etta's unsure traits. The absence of colour other than black and white in the European context is related to sophistication, a satire on the European attitude, just as Judy was taught by her European parents "to draw the curtains" (12). In contrast is the English suburban life, with its neat security and well-defined aims tight and cold. Judy becomes briefly aware of her material poverty and makes desultory attempts to reorganize her makeshift furniture, but as she plans to replace her tatty sofa, she is lulled by its "comfort into dreamy acceptance" (12), signifying the love and compassion of the East. Her mother is shown devoting her life to dusting bric-a-bracs and protecting her from the outside world, until her poignant agoraphobia leads her to the logical extreme of suicide. Jhabvala uses the colour images to show the contrast between Gulab's and Betty's houses in *Esmond in India* and marks their diverse thinking. The bright colours and " rich dark green" depict Betty's untangled nature (42), whereas Gulab's unclean style of living relates to her non-bothering nature.

In Jhabvala's works image enlarges the meaning and makes it capable of newer interpretations. The image of Prem's mother in *The Householder* with her belongings consisting of a steel trunk with a big padlock and a number of cloth bundles tied with a string signify her elaborate flawed nature and non-detachment from the family woes. Her longing for regard disgraces her status. Further; with her interference in Prem's house chores and in the moments of Prem and Indu's privacy, denigrates her status. Her departure pictured with overladen baggage and her occupancy in the train spreading her luggage to other luggage racks symbolize her penchant of interfering into space not meant for her. She fails to lead a life of isolation, and her unwanted indulgence into the matters of others puts her into pathetic situations.

In Jhabvala's *To Whom She Will* the body image links Hari's infidelity towards Amrita with his visions of Sushila as: "[...] strong and brown and stark naked, bending in the shadowed light of the moon and her hair springing out like a black flame"(147). The above image explains the devalued status of women as a mere physical existence. The body is strong but brown devoid of any covering, not erect but bending, symbolizing the slave position.

Jhabvala has modified certain images associated with the Indians. For example, the image linked with the Indian woman as a submissive nonentity is broken by the portrayal of characters like Sarla Devi in *Get Ready for Battle*, Uma in *Get Ready for Battle,* Maji in *Heat and Dust* and Gulab in *Esmond in India*.

Conclusively, Jhabvala is intent on presenting the gender collision of men versus women through a highly symbolic view of their status. Jhabvala relates, as Paula Moya points that, "Experiences happen to us, and it is our theoretically mediated interpretation of an event that makes it an experience."[5] Jhabvala expresses through symbols and images what cannot be said directly; she adumbrates the various attitudes and activities that affect the life of women. She welds these diverse paths through delicate use of symbolic motifs so that they form a satisfying pattern of life and art. She takes a dip into the treasure-chest of symbols and images, and uses them to illustrate a commonality in the women's predicament, and constructs an implied set of values. For Jhabvala the combination of illusion and realism in varying degrees seems to provide some solution, in art, to the problem of creating an authentic, self-liberating identity of women holding the view mentioned in *A Passage to India* on perception and reality:

> We exist not in ourselves but in terms of each other's minds.[6]

References

1. Gustave Flaubert *Le Temptation De Saint Antone,* trans. Lafcadio Hearn (Pyhän Antoniuksen kiusaus suom. Jorma Kapari,1874).
2. All textual references to Ruth Prawer Jhabvala's novels have been given in paranthesis. The following editions have been used:
   To Whom She Will (London; George Allen & Unwin. 1955. American edition retitled *Amrita*. New York: W.W.Norton, 1956).
   The Nature of Passion (London: George Allen & Unwin, 1958).
   Esmond In India (London: George Allen & Unwin. 1958; rpt. London; John Murray 1978).
   The Householder (London: John Murray, 1960.
   Get Ready For Battle (London: John Murray, 1962).
   A Backward Place (.London: John Murray, 1965).
   A New Dominion (London: John Murray, 1972. American edition retitled *Travellers*. New York: Harper & Row, 1973).
   Heat and Dust (London: John Murray, 1975.
   In Search of Love and Beauty (London: John Murray, 1983)
   Three Continents (London: John Murray, 1975).
   Poet & Dancer (London: John Murray, 1993).
   Shards of Memory (London: John Murray, 1995).
3. R. Agrawal, " An interview with Ruth Prawer Jahbvala", *Quest:* 91 (1974) 36.
4. R.S. Pathak, Quest *for Identity in Indian English Writing* (New Delhi; Bahri Pub.,1992) 19.
5. Paula Moya, "Postmodernism, "Realism, and the Politics of Identity: Cherríe Moraga and Chicana Feminism." In *Feminist Genealogies, Colonial Legacies, Democratic Futures.* Ed. M. Jacqui Alexander and Chandra Talpade Mohanty. (London; Routledge, 1997) 136.
6. E.M. Forster, *Passage to India* (London; Arnold Publications, 1924) XXV.

5

Women's Rights: A Study of Rohinton Mistry's *A Fine Balance*

—Babbellapati Indira and C.V. Padmaja

Rohinton Mistry's second novel *A Fine Balance* with the narrative spanning the pre/postcolonial India highlights the period of Emergency imposed by the then Prime Minister, Indira Gandhi. Emergency in its wake saw, for the first time in post-independent India, the suspension of the basic fundamental rights guaranteed by the Constitution of India to its citizens. Strong opposition and healthy dissent are indispensable to an effective functioning of any democracy. And crushing the voice of the opposition jeopardizes its very foundation. Since 1947, when India had been declared independent, democratic institutions were suspended for the first time during the Emergency, and any voice of dissent or a semblance of opposition was ruthlessly stilled; what followed was one of the most inglorious chapters in the history of contemporary India. Rohinton Mistry's *A Fine Balance* is an honest record of this dark shameful episode. Mistry states:

> It seemed to me that 1975, the year of the emergency would be the next important year, if one was preparing a list of important dates in Indian history and so it was 1975[1].

A Fine Balance, yet another landmark in Indian English fiction, is a stark and moving portrayal of life during Emergency. It shows how absolute power can corrupt a leader absolutely, all in the name of restoring peace and order in the country. Emergency rule unleashed organized horror under the autocratic leadership of Indira Gandhi. Though it is meant to target her political opponents, it is the common man who was the worst affected in the process of a leadership that was at its tyrannical worst.

Corruption, injustice, discrimination, caste-exploitation, bloodshed, linguistic strife and communal disharmony ruled the roost during the period. The novel focuses on the Indian polity's struggle for power, with the nation torn by internal dissent with power-hungry politicians controlling the strings of administration. Mistry depicts this post-independent India where caste, class, ignorance, poverty discrimination and, above all, the common man were exploited by self-serving leaders whose only objective was to enhance their own power and wealth with utter insensitivity to those around them.

Corruption, an age-old phenomenon, has been eating into the social fabric of India, and the ordinary man remains caught between an unsympathetic and hostile system and his own individual aspirations. Portraying the struggle for survival and empowerment on one hand and poverty and exploitation on the other, Mistry depicts the most volatile and violent spectrum of the contemporary history which shook the socio-political-economic fabric of the country during the Emergency era, 1975-77.

On a wide canvass of epic proportion, in the novel *A Fine Balance*, the portrayal of women in their marginalized roles commands the readers' attention. In fact, the conflict in the novel revolves around Dina Dalal, twice marginalized as a woman and a Parsi. Through a study of her character, we get to know the place of women in Parsi culture, and in her struggle we see a woman's fight for her rightful place in the world at large. In living a life of her choice, she has to wage a lone battle for her personal as well economic independence. Hers is a small, subdued voice but heard strong to free herself of the shackles of male supremacy. Her life shows women in general and Parsi that women in particular have a long way to go to proclaim themselves 'independent.' Dina struggles to defend her fragile independence from an autocratic brother as well to protect herself from a rapacious landlord. Hers is a life symbolic of a woman's rebellion within patriarchy and religious taboos.

India is a founder member-state of the United Nations and is party to its Charter of Human Rights. The Indian Constitution on its part enshrines the principles of human values in the form of guaranteed rights. Despite the constitutional guarantee for equality and special protection, in every walk of life and at every stage of life, women suffer discrimination, exploitation or violence. The doctrine of equality, which is the foundation of social justice, enshrined in Article 14 of the Constitution is a galaxy of concepts of equality before law and equal protection of law. The primary imperative of Article 14 is equal opportunity to all. Article 15[1] prohibits discrimination on the grounds of religion, race, sex, place of birth or any of them.

The Right to Life and Personal liberty is the most fundamental of all the fundamental rights guaranteed by the Constitution. This takes within its sweep every opportunity necessary to develop one's personality and potentiality to the highest level possible in the existing stage of our civilization. Mere right to exist will have little value, if it is bereft of any chances to develop or to bring out what is in every man and woman. Being the basis of all the rights, the right to life is effectively provided under Article 21 of the Constitution. It has become "a sanctuary for human values" and therefore has been rightly termed as "the fundamental of fundamental rights."

The Right to Personal Liberty postulates the creation of a climate wherein there is no suppression of the human spirit, wherein there is no denial of opportunity for the full growth of human personality, wherein the head is held high and there is no servility of the human mind or enslavement of human body. In a society where definitions, policies and rules are male-oriented, the need is to understand woman and her rightful place in the society.

The International Convention on the elimination of all forms of Discrimination against women (ICDAW) (1979/1981) is one of the core human rights measures for the advancement and empowerment of women in private and public life, particularly in the areas of education (Article 10 of ICDAW) employment, (Article 11 of ICDAW) health (Article12 of ICDAW) marriage and the family (Article 16 of ICDAW). But the life of Dina proves that violence against women is a manifestation of historically unequal power relations between men and women.

Widowed at the age of 24, Dina Dalal is a lonely figure in the novel, estranged from her parental family and condemned to a monotonous existence. Her life has been a cyclic pattern which begins at her brother's house and after a brief spell of independence and happiness, ends with her accepting the emotional subjugation of patriarchy, Nusswan, her brother symbolizes.

Dina feels a strong affinity to her philanthropic father whose "fervor to ease suffering" (15) eventually leads to his own death in the course of a medical camp in the interiors of the country. Instead of trying to seize the deadly sickles or at the very least to blunt them (15) Dr. Shroff dies of a cobra bite. After his death, Nusswan presides over the household. For Dina, it is hard to stomach Nusswan, obsessive of power and control, as a replacement to a warm and loving father. Her personal freedom gets restricted and Nusswan forces her to neglect school and burdens her with the entire household work. His personality is too weak to tolerate a teenager's harmless deviation from an adult norm: "Dina's defiance, her stubbornness, was driving him crazy," (20) but he discloses the shortcomings of his own personality by establishing an authoritarian family regime based on surveillance. "The little devils needed monitoring" (21) and corporal punishment (23). His attempts to conform to the role of his father proves not only disruptive to the family but severely affects Dina's peace of mind. If he turns into a despot to compensate for his own shortcomings, it is Dina who is always at the receiving end of his whims. As a result her life becomes a nightmare in an autocratic system characterized by restriction and tyranny.

Dına gets obsessed with the idea of personal freedom because of the misery suffered under her brother's guardianship typical of the Parsi tradition. It is clear in the prologue of *A Fine Balance*, that Dina holds independence in high esteem. Talking about her tailoring business, which eventually sanctions her economic freedom she says:

> No need to now to visit her brother and beg for next month's rent. She took a deep breath once again, her fragile independence was preserved (11).

For Dina, having to rely on Nusswan's money means losing her freedom; giving into her brother's rule equals giving up her independence. Therefore, her small tailoring business is not at least of all an attempt to escape the sphere of her brother's influence[2]. Dina relies on male career patterns of entrepreneurship in order to leave behind a male sphere that prevents her from coming into her own as a modern woman.

In an act of rebellion against Nusswan's manipulative power, the young Dina falls in love with Rustum Dalal, a compounder, and marries him against the wishes of her class-conscious brother. Unfortunately, her happy married life with Rustum comes to an abrupt end when Rustum is killed in a cycle accident on the day of their wedding anniversary. Despite her brother's genuine offer of help, she decides to live by herself. Nusswan cannot not understand her "strange idea of independence" working like a slave to earn a pittance even as a widow (369).

She earns her livelihood by sewing and maintains her independence as a dress maker. When failing eyesight threatens to end her tailoring career and the independence it provides, she refashions herself as an entrepreneurial middle person; she undertakes to stitch readymade garments for Au Revior Exports owned by Mrs Gupta, a client of her classmate and friend, Zenobia. She hires two slum-dwelling tailors, the low-caste Ishvar and his nephew Om for commercial piece-work making her back room as their workplace. She soon takes a student, Maneck Kohlah, the son of an old school friend of hers, from the same community as a paying guest.

Her life as a widow is harsh and filled with an endless struggle to survive in a set-up where single woman has to struggle twice as hard to lead a life with dignity. Initially, with class-conscious Dina playing it strict and exploitative of the tailors, relations among the four are tense and guarded; the tailors on their part too are suspicious of her while Maneck, the paying guest, is divided in his allegiances. Gradually, with Om and Ishvar, her struggle for independence becomes a struggle for control. She decides to maintain her distance in order not to lose control.

> I have nothing against them, but they are tailors,-my employees. A distance has to be maintained (293).

She locks them up whenever she has to leave the house thereby relying on strict boundary maintenance. Her decision is motivated by the fear of losing both control and independence at the same time. She is anxious not to lose her intermediary position in the process of manufacturing and selling dresses.

> The tailors will put me out of business if I don't lock them in (285).

She assumes that control guarantees economic success which means independence from Nusswan. In order not to suffer from her brother's rule again, she draws on the model of her brother's rule in her dealings with Om, Ishvar and Maneck. Maneck slowly makes friends with Om and takes their side and disapproves of Dina's treatment of the tailors, especially when she displays her class consciousness. The Parsi Dina at first regards the Hindu tailors Om and Ishvar as dirty (cf.302), indisciplined and irresponsible (cf.272), lazy (cf.288), liars (cf.276), as alcoholics (cf. 272) and promiscuous (cf.305). Control over the tailors is not only for economic independence but it is something deeply ingrained into her personality of the difference between class and ethnicities as determined by her culture that developed in her a fear for others. She reminds Maneck:

> there is a difference, and you cannot pretend there aren't – their communities, their background (293).

She advocates segregation between the representatives of the two communities on the grounds of ethnicity. Her indifference towards the tailors is also revealed when she is not ready to accommodate them under her roof, when their shack is bulldozed to the ground as part of the slum evacuation programme during the Emergency. Her knowledge of the "crookedness" in the city never allows her to risk offering shelter.

> A trunk, a bag or even a satchel—is the first step into a flat. Personal items stored on the premises—that's the most common way of staking a claim. And the court system takes years to settle the case, years during which the crooks are allowed to stay in the flat (305).

Though within her own community she suffers as a woman, Dina is not free from her personal prejudices against class, caste and community. Maneck is put off by Dina auntie's refusal to accommodate even the tailor's trunk.

> He was not ready to forgive her while the tailors remained un accommodated in the night (305).

When Dina comes to know through Maneck the long-drawn suffering of Ishvar and Om as victims of caste oppression thinks:

> compared to theirs, my life is nothing but comfort and happiness—People keep saying god is great, God is just, but I'm not sure (340).

Moved by their plight Dina offers the tailors her veranda to live in and their overwhelming gratitude makes her feel guilty. She sheds several of her other defences and pretentions, and starts sharing her kitchen with them. Soon the four have their meals together.

> Sailing under one flag: There were always four people, or at least two, busting about the kitchen in the evening. My bleakest hour, thought Dina, has now become the happiest. (401)

Her decision to take them is a sign of her "affection breaking barriers." [3] In the microcosm of Dina's flat all prior hierarchies and ethnic prejudices now cease to be of relevance. The foursome face and survive many upheavals that take place because of the imposition of internal Emergency. But they do not see their struggle for survival as linked to the existing political scenario. For Dina, the much spoken of Emergency is "government problems—games played by people in power. It does not affect ordinary people like us," (75). For the common man it is nothing but "one more government tamasha" (5).

Very soon they are proved wrong. Even their simple dreams are thwarted by the blows dealt by the Emergency. The bright future of Om and Ishvar is clouded due to the government's massive countrywide family planning programme to check the population explosion in the country. Dina is compelled by her landlord to vacate the premises on legal grounds that she is illegally carrying on the business and accommodating the tailors and the student as a guest. Ultimately left alone to carry on the burden of her life, she now is forced to take refuge at her brother Nusswan's, much against her will. Mistry's comment:

> Independence came at a high price; a debt with a payment schedule of hurt and regret. But the other option under Nusswan's thumb was inconceivable (473).

'The evolved' Dina Dalal finally finds refuge with her brother. Her story is of the Indian women yearning for the almost impossible independence. Facing a life of misfortunes with dignity, refusing to give into debilitating memories, the female protagonist Dina leads a life finely balanced between hope and despair.

In contrast, the life of the minor women characters belonging to pre-independent India in the novel is very pathetic. Rohinton Mistry presents a very realistic and dehumanizing portrayal of various forms of torture that the women of lower castes are subjected to in spite of any number of rights that free India sanctioned to women. Despite new laws of untouchability passed by the government, nothing has changed. Exploitation of the low castes by upper castes continues unabated. The human history bears witness to the occurrence of violence against women on account of sex discrimination. Of all the violence against women, rape is one of the most violent. Rape as a violation with violence, of the private person of women, is an outrage by all canons.

> Rape in conflict is a weapon to terrorize and degrade a particular community often to achieve a specific political end. The rape of one person is translated into an assault upon the community as a whole through the emphasis placed in every culture on women's sexual "virtue." The shame of rape humiliates the family and all those associated with survivor.[4]

Women of low castes, including tribal women, are more prone to rape as in the case of Buddu's wife or Roopa in the narrative. The refusal by low-caste Buddhu's wife to go to the fields with the zamindar's son results in the shaving of her head and being paraded naked through the square. Again the way Roopa, Dukhi's wife, is raped by the watchman of the orchard, tells its own tale of helplessness. The heart-touching episode of Roopa, the self-obliterating mother of Ishvar and Narayan losing the chastity of her mango-like breasts and the rest of her charming young body to the lascivious watchman of the rich man's orchard in exchange for a few oranges she covets for her sons (120) throws light on the exploitation of low-caste women who willy-nilly have to succumb to the machinations of their very upper-caste seducers. The tragic irony is that a high-caste lust-perverted man who is likely to be polluted even by the shadow of a low caste, still covets and sleeps with impunity with a desirable woman of the cobbler caste. This shows the irrational travesty of justice in Independent India, that guarantees fundamental rights, irrespective of caste and creed.

The narrative here highlights another perspective of Indian reality, i.e., gender discrimination and asserts that every aspect of Indian society is 'gendered', conferring specific advantages to men and disadvantages to women. Women are relegated to a subordinate status in family and society. They are expected to be dutiful daughters, loving mothers, submissive daughters-in-law and faithful obedient wives. After marriage, women become the property of their husbands, and if daughters are born, are ordered to discreetly get rid of the newborn who gets strangled, poisoned or starved to death. When a son was born to Radha and Narayan, sweets were distributed. However, when daughters were born to them, no sweets were distributed. When Shankar's mother was born, her drunken father slashed off her nose in his rage, disappointed with the mother for giving birth to a daughter instead of a son. Avinash's three sisters were aware of their father's sad plight at not being able to afford dowries for them. In order to spare their parents the shame of three unmarried daughters, they commit suicide by hanging from a ceiling fan. This is an indictment of the vicious norms of the society which reduces woman to a commodity rather than recognizing her as an individual.

All these acts highlight the injustices done to women, interrogate the marginalization of women in the male-dominated society and prove that inequality between the sexes is caused by the cultural construct of gender. Dina's life stands as an example of gender disadvantage. In the village too the women are seen totally at the mercy of the upper caste landlords and their servants who exploit them sexually or even immolate without any questions being asked. Whether one sees the village Roopa or Radha who are raped or burnt or Dina Dalal, whose every effort is made to break her spirit, the story is one of gender oppression by a sexist male society. The recognition of women must be evident at every stage of the transitional process so that women can rebuild their lives with confidence, and that their human rights abuse has been addressed to with the necessary respect and appropriate protection.

Works Cited

1. Belliappa, K.C "Rohinton Mistry's A Fine Balance". *The Literary Criterion*.Vol.32, No.4, 1997. pp.20-30.
2. Barucha, Nilufer E. "From behind a Fine Veil: A Feminst Reading of Three Parsi Novels." *Margins of Ensure. Purdah in the Sub-continental Novel in English*. Ed Jasbir Jain and Amina Amin. New Delhi: Sterling, 1995, pp. 174-85.
3. Barucha, Nilufer E. "When old tracks are Lost: Rohinton Mistry's Fiction as Diasporic Discourse." Journal of Commonwealth Literature. Vol.30, No.2, 1995, 127-35.
4. Barucha, Nilufer E. "Repossessions and Appropriations: The case of the city by the sea", *New Quest*, No141, July-sep 2000, pp. 261-286.
5. Ball, John Clement. "Taking The Measure of Indias Emergency", A review of *A Fine Balance* by Rohinton Mistry, *The Toronto Review of Contemporary Writing Abroad*, Vol.14, No.2, Winter1996, pp.83-87.
6. Dangwal, Surekha. "Image of India in Rohinton Mistry's Fine Balance and Salman Rushdies Midnight Children: A comparative Study towards Diasporic Consciousness", *The Common-wealth Review*, Vol.15, No.1, 2004.pp. 67-77.
7. Fundamental Rights in India—Wikipedia, the free encyclopedia.htm
8. http://www.un.org/overview/rights.html
9. http://www.hrweb.org/legal/cdw.html
10. Kapadia Novy, "The Politics of Survival and Domination in a Fine Balance." The *Fiction of Rohinton Mistry: Critical Studies*. Ed Jayadipsindh Dodiya. New Delhi: Prestige, 1998.127-35.
11. http://legal-articles.deysot.com/constitutional-law/judicial-interpretation-of-article-21-of-the-indian-constitution.html
12. Mantel, Hilary, "States of Emergency". India: A Mosaic. Ed. Robert B. Silvers and Barbara Ebstein: *The New York Review of Books, Vol.43*, No 8, June, 20, 1996, pp.4 &6.
13. Nayar, Pramod K. "The text of cruelty: Power and Moving Portrait of life during the Emergency", Review of Rohinton Mistry's *A Fine Balance, India Today*, 15 March 1996, pp. 169.

14. RIGHTS AND PRIVILAGES OF WOMEN.htm
15. Ross, Robert L. "Seeking and Maintaining Balance: Rohinton Mistry's fiction." World Literature Today 73, No 2, Spring199, pp.239-44.
16. "Sexual Violence." http://www.un.org/womenwatch/daw/public/cover.htm
17. The Universal Declaration of Human Rights.htm

6

Middle Class Modern Indian Woman's Woes in Shashi Deshpande's *The Dark Holds No Terrors*

—Arjun Jadhav & Sujata Bamane

Shashi Deshpande, born in Dharwad, a small town in the state of Karnataka in Southern India, is a Sahitya Akademi award-winning novelist who writes in English with a sense of social commitment. She has carved her niche in Indian Writing in English due to her exceptional skill of presenting women characters taken from Indian background in a lively manner. Her novel *The Dark Holds No Terrors* covers the protagonist's life-story from her childhood days to her married life. It makes the protagonist brood over her 'past', and compare and contrast her 'past' with her 'present'. This technique of retroversion plays a vital role in strengthening her search for identity. The flickering of the story helps the reader to examine the development of the protagonist's character as an 'individual being'. The present research article is the discovery of modern Indian woman's woes through the character of Saru.

The events selected are mainly those which contribute to the psychological study of the female protagonist. In order to study the development of heroine's mental ups and downs, the analysis is made according to the chronological order of events that happened in her life. The analysis considers all the thematic aspects, reinforced by different structural features. The analysis begins with the analysis of the preface to the novel, as it introduces the writer's thematic concern. Finally, the contribution of the whole content to the projection of woman has been judged.

The narrative pattern adopted by Shashi Deshpande in *The Dark Holds No Terrors* is idiosyncratic. Though the novel is woman-centred, the whole story is not told in a 'First Narrative' style. The predicament of the modern Indian working woman is made authentic with an unusual narrative novelty. The presentation of her achievement is made realistic and interesting with the shifting of the narrative from first person to third person and vice-versa. The narrator of Chapter I of Part I can be called in the words of Gerard Genette as an 'extradiegetic narrator' referred by A.V. Ashok (1998:79). To trace the growing intensity of male-brutality and sexual assault, the 'preface' is given in the first person narrative style. The subjective and objective perception of the heroine's character is made possible with the wavering narrative technique. Though the alternate narrative pattern is not Shashi Deshpande's deliberate creation, it is maintained very well in the Part II. It begins with the third person narrative and ends with the first person narrative. In order to make the objective perception of heroine's last compromising step possible, all chapters of Part IV, except Chapter II, are presented in the third person narrative. Shashi Deshapnde herself explains her narrative technique in an interview by Holmstrom Lakshmi (1998:245):

> The present is in the third person and the past is in the first. I was doing it throughout in the first. But that's often a perspective I use in my short stories. I wanted to be more objective. So then I tried it in the third. But it wouldn't work at all. Yet I really needed to distance myself from the narrative in the present, otherwise it was going to be far too intense. And then I read an American novel by Lisa Alther where she uses this method. And the minute I came across her novel I thought – let me admit it freely – Oh god, this is how I am going to do my novel.

A Marital Strain between Saru and Manu

In this episode, a journey of Saru and Manu's married life is narrated. In spite of her mother's inimical attitude, she joins the medical college and finally marries a man out of her caste and class. She has no feelings left behind with her parents. Initially, she is impressed with Manu's caring stand when he thinks of her cutting off from her parents. Being a medical student, she explains her separation from her parents clinically and compares it with the cutting of the umbilical cord to separate the baby from her mother:

> ... it is to cut the umbilical cord and separate the baby from the mother? Ligate, cut and its done. There's scarcely any bleeding either. It's as if nature knows the child must be detatched from the parent. No, Manu, for me there will be no trauma, no bleeding. (p.39)

The initial years of their marriage are full of happiness, which later on are contaminated and resulted in Manu's indifference and Saru's withdrawl. One day an explosion in a factory gives her an opportunity to show her medical talent. And she does it successfully by curing the bodies wounded in the explosion. People start coming to her. It increases her social status. Her interview is taken as a successful lady doctor. Her success becomes irritable to Manu and hurts his male ego. As a result, he starts harassing her, sexually. Unable to bear the mental and physical harassment, she leaves her home and retreats to her parents' home. She herself admits the pleasure that she gets in the initial days of her marriage. She recalls the first moment of apprehension. She says:

> I became in an instant a physically aroused woman, with an infinite capacity for loving and giving, with a passionate desire to be absorbed by the man I loved. (p.40)

A feeling of being loved gives her an intense joy. In fact, the freedom that she enjoys in Manu's company gives her a heavenly experience. Her feeling being fulfilled in love shows when she thinks, "Each act of sex was a triumphant assertion of our love. Of *my* being loved. Of *my* being wanted" (40). Her feeling of being "wanted" by Manu takes her away from the taboo-ridden world of her mother, where her existence was "unwanted". Her hasty marriage with Manu is based more on her escape from the unprotected world of her mother promoted by her father than her love for Manu. Her initial ectasy signifies her desperate attempt of searching a "substitute" in Manu, who will bridge the emotional gap in her life. Her happiness is hidden behind her autonomous status that she has achieved after marriage. She finds her residence "heaven in spite of the corridors smelling of urine, the rooms with their dank sealed-in odours, women with inquisitive unfriendly eyes and men with lascivious stares."

Very soon, Saru realizes that the victory of her emotional autonomy is overshadowed by the rational world. The excitement caused by the autonomy gradually disappears when they are left "severely alone" by the "soundless, invisible" "grey ghosts" in the outside world. Her discovery of the happiness-as "unreal" mere "an illusion" and "so evanescent"—makes clear the unfavourable change in her life. At the same time she becomes aware that "It is grief that has a bulk, a weight, a substance and stays real even after years." In addition to this her parasitic position adds to her grief. But their alienation from the outside world no longer remains. She remembers the incident of the explosion in the factory that happened to be the turning point in her life, "It was the day there was an explosion in a factory. Burnt mutilated bodies poured in, in a horror so vast that it seemed meaningless." The first person narrative of how she handles the "burnt mutilated bodies" reinforces her devotion to her duty. She narrates:

> The world consisted of bodies into which I drew blood, bodies on which I transfused blood, bodies on which I did venesections, bodies to be dressed, bodies in agony, bodies blessedly, quietly dead. (p.41)

Thus, the incident of fire in the factory turns Saru's life completely and gives a new direction to her life. It provides her an opportunity to prove herself as a successful doctor. After helping out the wounded people, she returns home. While walking through the "refuse -lined avenue", people smiling at her at the first time indicates that the distance maintained earlier has vanished all of a sudden. Women calling her, "lady doctor, lady doctor" automatically gives her recognition and makes her aware of her own "self". The frequent visits of people with their miscellaneous complaints make her a centre of attention. Gradually, her social status goes high. In a state of exhilaration, she notices Manu's "an affected indifference" but she doesn't react to it. The "nods and smiles, murmured greetings and namastes" by people make Saru feel honoured. Her growing social status goes beyond Manu's endurance. A sense of being ignored hurts him a lot. The growing intensity of his humiliation is seen when he declares, "I'm sick of this place. Let's get out of here soon"(42). His own declaration reveals his own self and his feeling of being victimized. He tries to escape from the fact of life. As a result, a love between them gets affected, and Saru finds herself "shrinking from his love-making" (42). A gradual change in Manu due to a continuous rise in Saru's status focuses on his typical male-chauvinistic tendency. His malicious aggression causes the unfortunate condition in their married life. On the contrary, her professional life blooms with her intellectual performance. She comes to the conclusion "...that the human personality has an infinite capacity for growth" (42). But her rational thinking of her "self" as "human" is discarded by male ideology, where woman is not treated as "human" but "other". She is not supposed to enjoy mental, physical, economic or intellectual independence. In spite of her recognition as "a lady doctor" and Manu as "her husband", she appears to be a trained Indian woman, who withdraws from her struggle for independent identity. She can't feel herself free from the fear of hurting the ego of her husband. She comes to the conclusion that it is not a woman's personality that has infinite capacity for growth.

In one more incident, Saru marks the growing strain in her married life caused by her working outside. She remembers the night, when she comes back home late from her clinic; she is welcomed by Manu's "brooding expressions". She feels her heart "painful with quivering little jumps". The pain in her heart indicates the lack of emotional support by Manu. She deliberately tries to keep the conversation going with him. Her meaningless conversation signs her "penitence" and "contrition". Her feeling of deep regret on her coming late is intensified by her serious attempt of making him normal so that he won't take his revenge by harassing her sexually in the dark. To avoid the impending terror in the dark, she says:

> Manu, I want to stop working. I want to give it all up ... my practice, the hospital, everything. (p. 79)

She expresses her agony by comparing herself to the devotee rolling over and over on the hard ground in a temple. Like the devotees in a famous temple, she tries to show her "devotion", her "penitence" "in a multitude of agonizing ways".

In another incident, when Saru is being interviewed as a career woman, Manu finds his position low. The girl asks him:

> How does it feel when your wife earns not only the butter but most of the bread as well? (p. 200)

Manu takes the question casually at that time. But the experience leaves him with a feeling of deep hurt. He drives out his feelings in bed by attacking Saru like a wild animal. At another time, her high status causes the strain in their married life, when the wife of one of the colleagues of Manu gives almost all credit to Saru for their luxurious life. Out of humiliation once again on that night he lets out his frustration on her. She is left physically and mentally bruised. On the contrary, he appears to be normal the next morning with his usual question, "Morning Saru, slept well?" In short, it is Saru once again experiencing "the depths of humiliation" experienced in her childhood days with a complete understanding that "success and humiliation inextricably linked together." Manu rejects her status as a human being. The unequal treatment given by him makes her realize her deteriorating marital status. She thinks, "It became a monstrously unbalanced equation, lopsided, unequal, impossible " (42). The tendency of Manu can be judged under Simon de Beauvoir's (1997:726) observation of the male tendency:

> He is very well pleased to remain the sovereign subject, the absolute superior, the essential being; he refuses to accept his companion as an equal in any concrete way.

In course of time, due to the strong impact of Manu's invasive behaviour, Saru starts dreaming of a man in a brown scarf trying to strangle her. She finds no way out from the nightmares, and to escape herself from them, she withdraws to her parents' house.

The above analysis brings out the initial bliss of marital union transforming into an unbearable marital strain. The marital dispute basically emerges out of the wife's occupying a central position in society. Her segregation in later period of her life serves Shashi Deshpande's purpose of showing "aloneness of human being." The wife, though educated and financially independent, lacks the courage of expressing her suppressed and unsatisfied state of mind. Lack of communication adds to the stress in the marital relationship. The disapproval to the independent "self" of the wife gives rise to the "identity crisis". Neither the wife nor the husband is happy in the real sense. The episode brings out the victimization of both the sexes. The husband feels inferior due to his low-esteem and the wife gets agonized due to her high-esteem. The mute marital dispute between husband and wife indicates that their marriage is based upon an uneven ground. In order to intensify the submission of the wife to the imposed destiny, the episode is given in the first person narrative.

Saru's Stay at Her Parents' House

The episode describes Saru's reviewing her past life leisurely at her parents' house. The experience of traumatic married life reduces her to the state of submission. Her growing hatred towards the system of marriage and the husband-wife relationship is exposed while delivering a speech to girl students. By putting the ideals regarding the role of woman in society, ironically she exposes the complete control of man over society. With the awareness of male supremacy, she gradually realizes the static position of woman during her stay in her parents' house. The episode focuses on the cold relationship between Saru and her father. Her father's withdrawing support leaves her at a solitary stage. Thus being aware of her loneliness, she strengthens her mind to handle the situation. During her stay, she broods over her past memories in order to search for her identity. And at last she acknowledges her own power and strength under which she can take refuge.

In her brief stay at her parents' house, she receives many letters from Manu and her children that lie without any response. Her silent stay suddenly gets disturbed when the letter comes with the news of Manu's arrival to take her back. She hastens to leave home. Her refusal to meet Manu focuses again on her attempt of escapism. Out of fear, she refuses to meet him. Her father points out her fear by saying, "Are you scared of him?" (216). However, he tries to patch up the situation between Saru and Manu and does his duty as a father. He attempts to make their relationship transparent, when he tells Saru:

> Give him a chance, Saru. Stay and meet him. Talk to him. Let him know from you what's wrong. Tell him all that you told me. (p.216.)

But it is too late for Saru to follow his unexpected advice, as she keeps herself "behind the walls of negation". Not getting a positive response, her Baba blames her indirectly by holding her responsible for Dhruva's death. He reminds Saru of her part in the death of her brother, Dhruva: "Don't turn your back on things again" (216). It also shows his desperate attempt to persuade her to meet Manu. But his support remains limited up to his advice as he immediately withdraws his support. She feels terrified at the thought of his recession. His retreat makes her weak and senile. She feels vulnerable but for her the idea of suicide is not a way out for the crisis in her life. Her thought, "not to be labelled a coward" shows her positive and optimistic outlook on life. Baba's indifference to her makes her recollect the past memories to examine her contribution in losing her brother, mother and her husband. She says:

> My brother died because I heedlessly turned my back on him. My mother died alone because I deserted her. My husband is a failure because I destroyed his manhood. (p.217)

Saru's Baba appears to be caring and discards her guilty feeling. He advises her:

> I told you ... they're dead. They can do nothing. Why do you torture yourself with others? Are you not sufficient for yourself? It's your life, isn't it? (p.217)

But her anxiety is not over. Though her mother and brother are no more, for her "there's still Manu..." At the same time the "long", "shrill", "forlorn" whistle of the Mail confirms his arrival in her life. Her hands become cold. She finds her mental condition worse when her Baba leaves her alone without noticing her "panic". Her extracting a promise from Baba to not open the door to Manu reveals her lack of strength to face Manu. Baba's leaving her alone in the room symbolizes the bitter truth. Saru cannot realize, "A brooding stillness" in the house, which is intensified by the tick-tock of the clock. In that pin-drop silence, she regrets:

> It's my fault again. If mine had been an arranged marriage, if I had left it to them to arrange my life, would he have left me like this? (p.218)

However, she is left as an object of both, "the suffering as well as the guilt". She admits that she is segregated not only by the dead people but also by "the living as well". She finds her only and the last hope—Baba "pathetic" and a "defeated man". His support is termed as a "chimera". Her urge for the salvation from the plight caused by her husband is foiled. She realizes the truth:

> Perhaps the only truth is that man is born to be cold and lonely and alone. (p.219)

The knowledge of being "alone" guides Saru "to relinquish all hope forever." And the life without any hope brings her to "nothingness", hallowness and illusion around her. The knowledge of life full of "unreal" gives her a moment's relief and her body feels "insubstantial". "A feeling of weightlessness... made her almost euphoric. Even her fears faded into insubstantial ghosts". Her state of being comforted is compared to her "being cuddled in a soft warm blanket on a cold night". But she doesn't relinquish her all hopes as her thinking despairingly keeps her running right to the bitter end. And she finds a way out. Like Duryodhana in a mythological story, she accepts the reality, "knowing all the while it is only an illusion." Thus, she understands her solitary "self" and accepts the fact that neither her Baba not her husband can be her stronghold. The acceptance of her loneliness makes her search for the potential within. Instead of chasing chimera, she starts getting strength within herself. In his article, *My Life is My Own: A Study of Shashi Deshpande's Women,* P. Ramamoorthi (1991:116) observes:

> Loneliness, one of the concerns of modern society, is not a disease, but a symptom of man's condition and this awareness is the first milestone in one's journey into oneself.

In fact, Saru's brief stay at her parental home brings in her an awareness of the meaning of human life and human existence, especially the existence of a woman in the male-dominant world. She reflects on the condition of a human being:

> All right, so I'm alone. But so's everyone else Human beings...they're going to fail you. But because there's just us, because there's no one else, we have to go on trying. If we can't believe in ourselves, we're sunk. (p.220)

Saru's serious thinking on the condition of human being helps her to gain her confidence and will power that she had lost due to her following unsuccessful roles in her life, that of "the guilty sister, the undutiful daughter, the unloving wife...persons spiked with guilts". (220)

Saru accepts these selves and starts her journey towards the quest of her own "self". Her journey indicates her desire for autonomous being, free from her own fear and guilt. Her trust on herself removes her earlier fear of proving her mother right—that love marriages always fail, as her mother is dead. The fear of losing her "self" in the "areas of darkness" is dispelled by the understanding that the dark holds no terrors.

However, when the door is knocked, she finds her legs trembling but with the "cold" and "clammy" feelings she opens the door for Manu. But she finds Ravi at the door. The "perceived absence" of Manu gives her relief but boosts her confidence to face the reality.

A close examination of the above episode reveals a different image of a female protagonist. Her brief stay at her parents' house, away from her husband and children, brings out certain realities, like a woman is never welcomed at her parents' house once she is married off. In case of a married woman, her "alone return" to her parents' house is considered as an impending calamity. Her father's withdrawing support at the last moment proves to be a motivating factor for her. Her "aloneness", "feeling of being insecure" and "fear" provoke her to search for strength within her. Her determination makes her overcome the initial stage of hovering between anger and remorse, and moves towards the stage of understanding of life and her role as an individual in it. Simon De Beauvoir (1997:726) throws light on the way woman struggles:

> Today the combat takes a different shape; instead of wishing to put man in a prison, woman endeavours to escape from one; she no longer seeks to drag him into the realms of immanence but to emerge, herself, into the light of transcendence.

Conclusion

Thus, the female protagonist represents the new modern Indian woman, who, after a long struggle against the tradition-bound society, basks in the glory of her womanhood. No longer does she feel the need of a man's support for her existence. She follows the teaching of Gautama Buddha and "sees truth as a refuge." She realizes the need of co-existence with them but not necessarily on the condition of emotional or mental dependence or the inferior status. She has not shunned the existence of men from her life nor she has attached herself to them. She appears to be clear about her own needs and priorities, and takes pride in her achievements; she is ready to take responsibilities of her shortcomings. From them onwards her role would no longer be of a passive mute spectator but that of the person involved with individuality, identity and assertion of her own.

Works Cited

Ahuja, Ram. *Indian Social System*. Jaipur and New Delhi: Rawat Publications, 1993.

Altekar, A. S. *The Position of Women in Hindu Civilization*. 2nd edn., Delhi: Motilal Banarsidass, 1959.

Ashok, A.V. *Narrative: A Student's Companion*. Chennai: T.R. Pubiications Private Limited, 1998.

Beauvoir Simon, de. *The Second Sex*. Trans. H. M. Parshley. London: Vintage, 1997.

Bhatnagar, K.C. "Realism in Modern Indo-English Fiction." In Dwivedi A.N. ed. *Studies in Contemporary Indian Fiction in English*. Allahabad: Kitab Mahal (1987) 36-60.

Deshpande, Shashi. *The Dark Holds No Terrors*. 1980; rpt. New Delhi: Penguin Books, 1990.

Dwivedi, A.N. *Indian Writing in English, Part II Generes Other than Poetry*. Delhi: Amar Prakashan, 1991.

Holmstrom, Lakshmi. "Shashi Deshpande talks to Lakshmi Holmstrom." In Pathak R. S. ed. *The Fiction of Shashi Deshpande*. New Delhi: Creative Books (1998) 242-250.

Indira, S. *Anita Desai as an Artist: A Study in Image and Symbol*. New Delhi: Creative, 1994.

Iyengar, K.R. Srinivasa. *Contemporary Indian Literature*. New Delhi: A Sahitya Academy, 1957.

Madhusudan, Prasad. *Anita Desai: The Novelist*. Allahabad: New Horizon, 1981.

Naik, M.K. *A History of Indian English Literature*. New Delhi: Sahitya Academy, 1982.

Ramamoorthi, P. "My Life is my Own: A Study of Shashi Deshpande's Women." In Singh Sushila, ed. *Feminism and Recent Fiction in English*. New Delhi Prestige Books (1991), 115-127.

Reddy, Sunita Y. S. *A Feminist Perspective on the Novels of Shashi Deshpande*. New Delhi: Prestige, 2001.

Roy, Anuradha. *Patterns of Feminist Consciousness in Indian Women Writers*. New Delhi: Prestige Books, 1999.

Sharma, Tripat. *Women in Ancient India (320 A.D. to 1200 A. D.)*. New Delhi: Ess Ess Publication, 1987.

Shirwadkar, Meena. "Indian English Women Novelists." In Naik M. K. ed. *Perspectives on Indian Fiction in English*. New Delhi: Abhinav Publication, 1985.

7

The Theme of Woman's Search for Self-identity in Shashi Deshpande's Selected Works

—Vishwanath Bite

In the modern society the place of woman has been rapidly changing. She has her own realms to wander. Formerly education was not given to a woman. Husband, children, home-duties were her whole world. She was known only through her relationship with man and had not an independent identity. With the spread of education and because of the wind of women's liberation movement she became aware of her rights, self-respect, economical independence and individual identity. Though the woman is aware of her identity her position in society is still secondary. The Indian woman is a victim of patriarchal society. In the male-dominated society the position of woman is always secondary.

Because of the basic biological difference a woman is supposed to be inferior to man. Nurturing, love, caretaking are considered inferior works of woman, and power, success, competition—these issues are superior works of man. The masculine activities are always considered superior than feminine activities. The Indian society depicts woman as a symbol of sacrifice through the image of Devi, like Sita, Savitri, and Gandhari. A girl child in the Indian family is treated partially. The first preference is always given to a boy child. From her childhood a woman is taught to suppress her wills, desires. She is taught to become a good wife, mother, daughter-in-law and so on. She has no identity her own. In the Indian society the honour of the family depends upon the behaviour of the woman. The woman has to sacrifice herself for the family. According to Jyoti Singh, "Goodness of woman is in self-abnegation and self sacrifice that is by the patriarchal community."[1] Tolerance, nurturing, adjustment, self-sacrifice are the good virtues expected from a woman. Men are not bound to fulfil these expectations.

Even today the woman is regarded as a sex object. Though she is highly educated, economically independent, she is still considered to be inferior to man. A housewife's work is not valued. Though she is an equal earner, cooking, house-keeping are supposed her basic works and of primary importance. The society wants that the woman must think about her career after completion of her primary duties. Though she earns equally with man her income is always secondary or considered as extra money. The income of man is basic or primary income. If a woman tries to escape from the overload of the responsibilities she is called 'selfish'. If she complains about her inferior situation she becomes a black mark on the ideal womanhood. Even today society is not ready to give an equal status to women.

The quest for identity is an important search that each human being feels at a certain stage in life. "Identity is a subjective sense and an observable quality of personal sameness and continuity. It can only be realized by a process of examination in to the past incidents and the personal experiences. These experiences are different almost in every way: emotional, physical and social."[2]

The theme of a woman's search for self-identity is reflected beautifully in the short stories of Shashi Deshpande. Her women struggle to search for the self-identity not only as women but also as human beings. Though her protagonists struggle to search for their self-identity they are not family breakers. They always give priority to their family. Deshpande, through her stories, states that self-negation does not give happiness. The following stories are taken for study: *It was the Nightingale*, *The Inner Rooms*, *Lucid Movements*, *Death of a Child*, *I Want...*, *A Man and a Woman*, *The Awakening*.

There are two characters in the story *It was the Nightingale*, Jayu and her husband. Jayu is an educated, careerist, modern woman. She is torn between ambitions and her love for husband. The story portrays the wife who sacrifices her conjugal bliss for preserving her identity.

Jayu and her husband love each other. There is good understanding between them. The husband is not a dominating male. He respects his wife and her career. Besides his objection Jayu is firm on her going abroad for two years to get a bigger salary when she returns. He thinks that it is unnecessary to work hard for the young wife. He does not want her to go away. Though she feels his regret to leave her she is not ready to sacrifice her identity for him. Jayu's mother lived her all life through her husband and daughters. She had nothing of her own. Jayu says, "who (mother) tortured herself and tormented us. Who made her own hell and gloried in it. And so, for me each step out of home had been a battle, each success a treachery towards her"(67). She does not want to become like her mother. She fears that will shackle her. To preserve her identity, she feels, is necessary. Formerly for men the ideal woman was always totally selfless and totally loving. The protagonist accepts that the lives of both of them are intertwined, yet they are two distinct strands. She gives an example of two lights which shine more brightly together, but to keep her light burning is totally her responsibility. Jayu knows that if she surrendered to her husband's will, she would walk the road of self-abnegation forever. And her life would end up like her mother. And she does not want to do that. Finally she decides to go abroad. But all her life she would carry the burden of the guilt. She feels guilty for not fulfilling her role of an ideal wife.

Though Shashi Deshpande shows that "women have the capacity to determine their priorities for self discovery and still continue to weave the fabric of family harmony"[3] man always wants sacrifice from his woman. He is ignorant about the fact that self-respect for a woman causes happiness to her and to all.

The Inner Rooms is woven around the legendary character of Amba in *Mahabharata*. Bhishma, Salva, Vichitravirya are other characters in the story. The story is Amba`s feeling of resentment. Bhishma abducts Amba, Ambika and Ambalika for his brother Vichitravirya`s marriage. Amba has already decided to marry Salva, the king of Shaubha. Vichitravirya refuses to marry her after knowing this fact. Her lover Salva two rejects her. Amba helplessly and piteously questions herself. "Who is she?"(92). She is not a daughter, a wife, a mother, but only a woman.

It is dishonourable for each of them to accept Amba. No one feels it necessary to thing about her honour, because she is a woman. There is no place for a woman in the male-dominated society. The honour of a woman is an unacceptable term. Her honour is only concerned with the honour of man. She has no individual identity. With the wrong decisions taken by males the life of Amba becomes meaningless as she cannot become anyone's wife or mother. The princess of Kashi, Amba is even ignored by the 'black people', the ignorant and the lowest. Loss of identity causes intense pain and agony in her. She decides to end her life and she does so. She has no control on her life but death is only her decision. "At least this one thing would be for her choosing, the way she wanted, at time she chose" (93). The men destroy her identity for which she was fighting.

The pathetic story of Amba states the situation of women in India. Thus, the theme becomes universal. The rooms in the palace are called inner rooms. These are for women, their whole world. They never think to come out of it. The inner rooms are symbolic. If a woman tries to get self-respect, honour and identity she gets dishonour and a kind of punishment in the male-dominated society. The scholar of Shashi Deshpande's short stories. T.N. Geetha says, "The Inner Rooms signify the chambers of passivity which stifle the voice of protest for the sake of social and moral security. Indeed she has to suppress her individuality and even suffer a loss of self identity for fear of being socially ostracized."[4]

In another story *Lucid Movements*, Sujata, her dying mother Sumati, her sister Shilpa, her father, brother and sister's daughter Karuna are the characters. The story is about a dying woman's search for her mother's name—the identity and the process of ascertaining her individuality.

The mother is ill and has a very short life. She continuously asks her daughter about her mother's name but she is unable to give the answer. The old lady tries hard to find her mother's name but fails. She dies in the sorrow of her mother's name being unknown. The narrator calls her mother Akka. She also tries to find the name of her grandmother.

The story portrays the fear of a woman that her name, i.e., identity will be wiped out from the memory of the coming generation. According to Madhumalti Adhikari, "Obliquely, Shashi Deshpande provides the reader with an insight to probe into a social condition that condemns a woman to die unnoticed, unremembered and muted as an individual."[5] The dying mother wish is fulfiled when her granddaughter, Karuna, is taught that her grandmother's name is Sumati. For the grandmother, at least there is no identity crisis. She is saved from being wiped out from the memory of her granddaughter by her daughters. Deshpande here suggests that it becomes easier for women with the help of each other to find their own identity.

Death of A Child runs around the mother. The woman, her husband and unborn aborted child are the characters in the story. The mother takes a stand against the traditional norms of motherhood. The protagonist in this story, by asserting the woman's right to be an individual, affirms her selfhood and rejects the definition of motherhood pronounced by the males for their convenience. The struggle is between the role of a mother advocated by the patriarchal society and a desire for self-identity.

The mother in the story wants to get rid of her child, third in four years because it is unwelcome. The motherhood forced upon her makes her feels like an animal trapped and confined. She feels that marriage and child-birth destroy the reserve, secretiveness, innocence in a woman. She does not want to destroy herself. She wants to preserve at least some part of her self and her life. She cannot imagine that the main purpose of her life is only to breed. So she wants to abort the child. But her husband tells her that they will manage it somehow.

To a father an unborn child rarely has the same reality as it has to a mother. Though the child is her own product she has no right on that at all. After listening to his wife's decision the husband asks her, "Your life is that all that matters to you? How can a mother be selfish?" (62) Like any other Hindu male he wants another son. The mother in the story has already played her role satisfactorily by having two children and nourishing them with love and care. In all these situations many questions are articulated: Is the mother only a breeder? Can a woman not ask to reserve some part of herself, her life? Why should a woman be made feel guilty if she decides to deconstruct the stereotype image of a mother to preserve her identity and the welfare of her unborn child? At least the mother aborts the child but she feels extremely guilty for sacrificing the unborn baby's life for avoiding the pain involved in bringing it up. She expresses her feelings, "I feel heaviness in my breasts. There is a hollow feeling within me. I am filled with strange thoughts. Where have I heard that, after an amputation, a person continues to feel the amputated limb, my child seems to cling on me. Now when he does not exist, he asserts himself. I am conscious of a piercing pain in the place he had filled. Grief becomes real"(68). When she and her husband leave the hospital she feels fear. She thinks that she is not alone. The ghost of her dead child walks with her.

According to Madhumalti, *In Death of A Child*, Deshpande takes a revolutionary stand against the conventional norms of child-beading and motherhood[6]. A woman is always expected to sacrifice for her husband, children and others. If she tries to reserve something for herself it is not a selfish act.

Another story I want... is about Alka, an unmarried girl even though she is twenty-seven. She is worried about her fiancée who never thinks about what she wants. And her father too does not feel it is necessary to ask her what she wants. For the sake of so-called security in life, she sacrifice her career. A woman is forced to sacrifice a part of her.

In the Indian patriarchal society women are treated as objects. Men never consider women's point of view, and dictate terms. They have to do nothing with the expectations of women.

Alka and her parents are made to feel ashamed because she is unmarried even at twenty seven. Alka tells herself, "I was twenty-seven. My face had lost its youth. It had personality, I told myself. But I knew I regretted what I had lost"(143). Alka feels uneasiness, helplessness at the time of arranging her marriage. She says, "The woman in me is out aged and protested. I crushed her. She had no place there. Not at all"(145). She feels like she has no shape of her own. As if she is capable of taking any shape. No one feels it is necessary to ask her what she wants. She feels that she is never there at all.

Alka's fiancée takes her granted and behaves in an authoritarian manner. He wants a wife who should be able to manage everything. She stays at home when he returns. She must like people. She must get on with everyone. He is a man of selfish, self-assertive type. He wants her to resign her job and confine herself to home. Her father too wipes out her reluctance to do so by stating her position as a girl who has crossed her marriageable age and has no chance of getting married. Alka is a woman of consciousness and wants to discover her integral identity. She does not want a husband of four-figure salary, bungalow, a car; she wants a man who can hear her voice when she speaks and understands her even when she does not. But she is sure that people will call her crazy. It does not matter again a is she has good job, family and no bad habits.

In the end Alka accepts the reassurance of her father. She sacrifices her economical independence and becomes a slave of the patriarchy. "Alka thus becomes a wife by compromise, not by choice."[7] The problem of Alka is the problem of all Indian girls. There is no value to their opinion.

The Awakening is a story of a young girl, Alka. She compromises with the situation after the death of her father. Alka sacrifice her own wishes, life, ambitions for the battlement of her family.

Alka is a girl of ambitions. She wants to take higher education and get a job with a good salary. But because of her father's poor economical condition she has to sacrifice her dream of getting higher education abroad. She wants to come out of the chawl and to live a luxurious life. She does not like her sister Rekha's attitude to accept the life as it is. She does not want to become a clerk like her father. She has to take up a job of a typist after her father's death. She has to sacrifice her dream for the family. She hates her father because there are only incomplete duties left behind him. She thinks his life and death are both a failure. On reading the letters of her dead father she feels her father's love for her, his faith on her abilities. He is sure that Alka will become successful in her life. The letter awakens the feeling of responsibility and her ability to achieve her aim. She feels that she can achieve her aim now. She can realize her dreams. "The letter restores her faith and give her courage to continue working not only to share her fathers burdens and responsibilities but also to realize her own dreams."[8]

There are three characters in the story, *A Man and A Woman.* Lalita, a youthful and beautiful widow of thirty, her brother-in-law and Manu, her dead husband's friend. Lalita's education is not enough to secure a job. She is banned to participate in any social programme. She has to control her emotional and physical needs. Various questions come to her mind related to existence and self-identity. She wishes to fulfil the sexual need that arises in her search of identity. She satisfies that hunger by keeping illicit relationship with her seventeen-year old brother-in-law, Ajit. She feels guilty for this act. She feels a loss of morality and loss of respect in society. She confesses her guilt to Manu. She says that it is madness. She is disgusted with herself. She says, "So I have to live, with this weakness. A slave to my body. I disgust myself, I am dirty abnormal" (212). Sex is a natural desire like hunger and thrust. One should satisfy one's basic needs. But society does not think it is necessary for a widow though she is a human being.

Self-identity becomes inevitable for her. Manu relives her of his guilt. He says to her, "You can keep an animal in cage till it dies, but you cannot blame it for trying to escape"(208). He proposes to her to marry him. But she rejects it by saying, "What will people say?" Though she is willing to marry him she rejects his proposal for the false sense of prestige of Jayanta's family. She, thus sacrifices her happiness, her individual identity.

Shashi Deshpande portrays a realistic picture of Indian women's life. "Deshpande's strength lies in portraying uncertainties and doubts of women, who can not see themselves as heroic but who want to make life possible."[9] She shows that a woman has to play a dual role, as a breadwinner and as a traditional wife, mother and so on. The woman can be happy and will give happiness to others if she maintains a proper balance between the two roles. Deshpande stresses that self-respect for a woman is essential to give happiness to her and to others. She also says that the loss of self-identity in a woman causes many problems.

Shashi Deshpande, in the above stories, deals with women's search for self-identity. She shows that even in the modern context there has been no change in the situation of women. There are seven stories and they deal exclusively with women's search for self-identity.

References

1. Singh, Jyoti, "Validating the Self", *Indian Women Novelists. A Feminist Psycholoanalytil Study*, Jaipur:Rawat Publication, 2007 p.133.
2. Sondkar, M.D., "The Fiction of Shashi Deshpande, A Study", A Ph.D Thesis submitted to Shivaji University, Kolhapur, 2007, p.160.
3. Adhikari, Madhumalti, "The Female Protagonists Journey From Periphery to Center in Shashi Deshpande's 'The Intrusion and Other Storie.'", *Indian Women Novelists* (ed.) Dhawan,. R.K. set III, Volume 4, New Delhi: Prestige Publications, 1995 p.72
4. Geetha, T.N., The Short Stories of Shashi Deshpande", *Indian Women Novelists* (ed.) Dhawan, R.K New Delhi, Prestige Publications, 1991, p.172.
5. Adhikari, Madhuimalti, "The Female Protagonists Journey From Periphery to Center in Shashi Deshpande`s *The Intrusion and Other Stories* ", *Indian Women Novelists*, op.cit, p.79.
6. Ibid p.77.
7. Geetha, T.N., "The Short Stories of Shashi Deshpande", *Indian Women Novelists* (ed.,) Dhawan R.K., op.cit. p.173.

8. Abha, Shukla, Kaushik, "Mother-Daughter Relationship in the Stories of Shashi Deshpande", *New Perspectives on Indian English Writings* (ed) Agrawal, Malti, New Delhi: Atlantic Publications, 2007, p.84.
9. Adele, King, "Shashi Deshpande: Portraits of An Indian Woman." *The New Indian Novel in English. (ed)* Viney Kripal, New Delhi: Allied, 1990, p.167.

8

Journey from Anonymity to Recognition: A Study of Kamala Markandaya's Women

—Sahab Uddin

Man for the field and woman for hearth
Man for the sword and for the needle she
Man with the head and woman with the heart
Man to command and woman to obey.

Quoting these famous verses of Alfred Lord Tennyson one may say that woman, the fairest creation of God, is expected to mould herself in the pattern of the family into which she is married. She is expected to become the shadow of her husband by whose name she is identified, losing her own individual identity that she had before her marriage. She is called 'ardhangini'; chastity and devotion to her husband are her precious ornaments. Kitchen is her shrine in which she remains confined. She observes several fasts to ensure her 'pati parameshwar', a long life so that she does not have to suffer the pangs of widowhood.

This is the traditional image that a woman develops in her mind in girlhood. She is taught to be subservient and forbearing not only to her husband, but even to her in-laws. Marriage is considered a woman's adventure and with it she loses her freedom of mind. She then wishes to give birth a son to continue the ancestry and to get rid of her from the curse of infertility. S.C.Dubey has significantly analyzed it:

> The infertility of a woman was considered as a curse, in patrilineal groups she is expected to produce a son to

> continue the line. In matrilineal societies, this was not considered a necessary, though it was desirable. But even among them, as in patrilineal societies, procreation is a social necessity and a value. [1]

But there is a considerable ambiguity about the nature and status of woman in Indian society. The concept of Indian womanhood is as divergent as the country itself, and has undergone a far-reaching change in course of time. India has travelled from her glorious past to disintegration, from spiritual pre-eminence to communal clashes, from agrarian revolution to cyber technology. Simultaneously, the image of Indian woman has changed from that of 'diety' to 'devdasi', from 'shakti' to 'abala', from 'kitchen queen' to the 'head of the country'. Gone are the days when people used to think that man is for the outside world and woman only for the hearth. Women today are half the world's population, do two-thirds of the world's work hours, receive one-tenth of the world's income and own not less than a hundredth of the world's property. Woman is now no longer less important than man. In the developing countries, she is responsible for 50 per cent of total food production. A recent survey in Tanzania, for example, shows that a woman works on an average of 2,600 hours a year in agricultural field as opposed to only 1,800 hours for man. In Africa, as a whole, 60 per cent of agricultural work, 50 per cent of animal husbandry and 100 per cent of food processing is done by women. In India, mostly all the tea labourers are women, and many religious and linguistic minority women still work in the field and support their family does more than a man.

Indeed, a woman is doubly burdened of bearing and bringing up children as well as working outside the home. As the climate changes and takes various forms according to its nature, speed and velocity, so does a woman receive different names—daughter, sister, beloved, wife, mother—which, are though different in nature, yet are of the same woman. Many Indian English woman novelists have analyzed these variations in the socio-cultural context to their texts. Kamala Markandaya, a post-independence woman writer who ranks with Mulk Raj Anand, R.K. Narayan and Raja Rao, took the great initiative of transformation of the traditional woman to the 'new woman' in her sacred texts. The 'new woman' that she has shown a new face of her woman who seeks self-fulfilment through self-expression. Her new woman is a wonderful improved race of the traditional woman. S.K. Arora rightly says:

> The new woman, clinging to her basic values and changing herself according to the changing circumstances, goes ahead on the way seeking for her own identity with new depth and getting recognition. Kamala Markandaya has realistically presented emotional, moral and spiritual problems of new woman. The new woman in her novels is not in 'proper' but in the 'making'. [2]

Kamala Markandaya, being a woman novelist, has brought mostly woman characters into being. She left behind her eleven novels and almost all the novels depict an Indian woman's journey from the womb to the tomb, from anonymity to recognition which pass through different stages as said earlier, playing familial roles. Through them, she reveals the virtues and potentialities of a woman reflecting that a woman is in no way inferior to man. Her woman gives a ray of hope and a goal to those who live the dark and frustrated life. It is not possible at all to present a detailed analysis of all the spheres of her woman protagonists in this short essay; yet I hope that this may highlight a true image of woman the past and woman the present showing Markandaya's feminist moral concern.

To begin with, Markandaya's novels basically mirror a new awareness of fulfilment of feminine identity without losing their traditional individuality. The woman, in her novels, is gifted with depth and basic principle thinking and is aware of value system. There is a deep longing for 'self fulfilment through self expression'. They are able to make their own way of living despite constant suffering, dominance, poverty, etc., in order to project the image of a new woman as 'person'. Rukmani and Irawaddy in *Nectar in a Sieve*; Mira, Roshan and Premala in *Some Inner Fury*; Sarojini in *A Silence of Desire*; Annabel in *Possession*; Nalini in *A Handful of Rice*; Helen in *The Coffer Dams*; Mrs. Pickering in *The Nowhere Man*; Lalitha in *Two*

Virgins; Usha in *The Golden Honeycomb*; Valli and Mrs. Lovat in *Pleasure City* and Mrs. Rao in *Bombay Tiger* (posthumously published novel). These women survive out of hardships and discover their own identity sometime living inside the norms of the society and sometimes even escaping the society. For them, living is important.

Rukmani in *Nectar in a Sieve* holds her image of a new woman even without breaking the norms and values that society has laid down upon her. She works in the field to lighten the burden of her husband, Nathan. Besides being an astute and prudent housewife, she is amiable and kind-hearted in nature. Markandaya has presented a picture of tradition and modernity through the painting of Rukmani's character. Tradition reflects while she gives birth to seven children one after another, sows vegetables at the back of her cottage and sells them at a higher price. She even collects cowdung in the morning to save fuel as a common rural poor woman does to support the family. Despite her poverty, she does not lose faith in life. Having faced the brutal blow of her son and husband's death, she returns to her village with a renewed faith and reconciles to life that truly reflects the modern view of life. Sharad Srivastava aptly remarks:

> Like the traditional woman, the new woman, too, tolerates, makes adjustments for the family and the husband, understands him and even forgives him but nowhere do we find her changing or moulding her basic personality. [3]

Irawaddy, the first child of Rukmani, is married at fourteen but unluckily she proves to be barren. She leads a life of a deserted wife and breaks the so-called norms of the society in search of her own identity. She sells her body to save her starving brother, Kuti, and makes up her mind that she will neither go hungry herself nor allow her brother to do so. She feels that it is not she but corruption and hunger responsible for Ira's such immoral act. The narrator heroine says:

> 'Whose to blame then?' I thought wearily. Blame the wind and the rain and the sun and the earth: they cannot refute it, they are the culprits.' [4]

Ira learns never to yield, musters up courage and defies the social norms giving birth to an illegitimate child at the time when her barrenness has gone and her husband has taken another woman. She proves to be a reflection of today's modern and desperate women who set their own parameters of life without bothering about the morality of the society.

Similarly, Mira, Roshan and Premala in *Some Inner Fury,* take different paths in search of their selfhood, the one and the same goal of their lives. Kamala Markandaya portrays the image of liberated women of modern India through these women protagonists. Mira makes up her mind to marry Richard without her mother's consent. She thinks that she is the mistress of her life and has full freedom of taking decisions concerning her life. Roshan feels at home in whatever situation she finds herself. She wishes to mould her personality in her own way. In search of her identity, she breaks the bond of her marriage. She very clearly says, "My husband and I have parted company," and "We haven't lived together for years" (70). S.K. Arora rightly says:

> She exemplifies the eternal woman who has to assert her inner being and bear the consequence of doing so. She attempts to create herself a space in which she can strengthen her being and claim that which is lost with dignity. She represents the symbol of the woman's psyche, which considers woman to be helpless and dependent. She becomes a role model for Premala and Mira and shows them the spirit of freedom with a flaming torch. [5]

Premala, too, makes her husband realise that she is not a property at his possession but a woman who has her own identity. She does not care for his approval in bringing up an orphan girl while enjoying the pleasure of unfulfilled motherhood. This makes their conjugal life unhappy and Premala does not yield. She finds in her a new woman and gets recognition as a social reformer with her own way of choice.

Sarojini in *A Silence of Desire* realizes in her a new woman when her husband doubts about her chastity. She is a very simple, pious lady and her faith in the healing powers of the Swamy is irrefutable. She believes to the extent that the tumour in her womb will liquefy if Swamy keeps his hand on her head. She is the representative of the religious-minded Indian women who prefer to Swamy's healing power than medicine. But her faith in him makes her swami (husband) distrustful. She is deeply hurt at such suspicious behaviour of her husband, Dandekar. She breaks the silence and opposes boldly like a modern woman:

> But you have eyes, if you wish to see, you can. See for yourself—there is nothing to stop you. [6]

It is true that silence sometimes represents doubts and anonymity; and when one speaks, silence disappears and gets recognized. Sarojini thus fights the decay of her self within the marital relationship, and ultimately peace is restored and the couple emerges wiser than before.

Annabel, a slim and ordinary looking girl of eighteen, in *Possession,* represents the liberated girls who bid goodbye to the tradition and develop their own identity. Nalini in *A Handful of Rice* emerges as a new woman attracting her husband from his irregular movements to herself. Helen in *The Coffer Dams* represents the sensitive women of the new generation. She believes in bridging the gap of misunderstanding. She is the true image of a modern woman. She is a believer of not tradition, but religion—religion of humanity. She does not hesitate to scold her husband for his indifference towards the tribal people. Markandaya's Helen does speak against male dominance instead of remaining silent, and creates and identity of her own and establishing the right to speak even in an adverse circumstance.

Lalitha, one of the sisters in *Two Virgins*, gives a lesson to young girls of beauty on the one hand, but represents the views and ideas of the present generation women. She is beautiful and her beauty cheats her. She becomes a victim to narcissism, becomes pregnant and wants to commit suicide. But her sister prevents her from doing so. She develops an enchantment for the city life and leaves her village in spite of being deceived and exploited. She finds in her a new woman who considers the present-day amenities not as a luxury but a necessity. Like

Ira in *Nectar in a Sieve*, Lalitha makes her own identity to lead a successful life without considering the parental suggestion.

The journey from anonymity to recognition grows complete in Usha in *The Golden Honeycomb*. She emerges with her feminine cry: "Whoever heard of a revolution for men only? No, it is everyone. They belong to the same species." She stands as a symbol of independence. This reveals her strength in facing the world outside. She does not limit herself within the four walls of home, and believes that a woman can change the destiny of her nation through dedication and active participation in all the spheres of life.

Valli and Mrs. Lovat in *Pleasure City* are the two women who have great admiration for art and are conscious of their status in the society. They go beyond the four walls of home and work independently, proving them not being inferior to men. One is devoted to painting and the other is to writing. Both of them believe in the life of activity and wish to live in their own worlds.

Bombay Tiger, posthumously published, is Kamala Markandaya's eleventh and last novel. Set in the 1980s, the novel is about the rise, fall and the ultimate redemption of her protagonist, Ganguly. Now coming to the woman characters in the novel, Markandaya seems to develop a close familiarity with the urban Indian women who were able to overcome the crisis of identity and evolve a force to reckon with. Mrs. Rao fits well into the frame of the new Indian woman. Like Rukmani, she is the earth figure—"serene, steady, helpful, supportive and without malice."

Thus one may draw a conclusion from the aforesaid image of various woman characters that feel the pulse of the changed time. Markandaya has created a new race of women who are neither very loyal and committed traditionalists nor ultra-modern but who honour the customes and welcomes modernity to the best of their competence and responsiveness. Such a woman has rediscovered, redefined and reasserted her identity as a new woman. It is she who initiates the lead of woman's makeover and journey from anonymity to recognition. Such a women has opened a new panorama for the innumerable women who are groping in the dark, and living in seclusion and dissatisfaction. In fact, her novels reassess what today's women in the Indian context aspire for.

References

1. Sudhir Kumar Arora, *A Study of Kamala Markandaya's Women*, Atlantic Publishers and Distributors, New Delhi, 2006, 36
2. ibid., the cover page.
3. ibid., 74.
4. Kamala Markandaya, *Nectar in a Sieve,* Jaico Publishing House, Mumbai, 2003, 120.
5. Sudhir Kumar Arora, *A Study of Kamala Markandaya's Women*, Atlantic Publishers and Distributors, New Delhi, 2006, 82.
6. Kamala Markandaya, *A Silence of Desire*, Penguin Books, New Delhi, 2009, 73.

9

Tradition to Post-Modernism: *The God of Small Things*

—Neerja Sachdev

Of all the genres of Indian English Literature, fiction is the most developed and well received one in the post-modern period, both at home and abroad. With Arundati Roy's Booker Prize Award-winning novel *The God of Small Things* (1997), Indian English novel has won international recognition.

Before taking up individual Indian English novelists for a discussion, let me examine the characteristics of Postmodern Indian English fiction. The first thing that strikes us is the broadening of the thematic range of the Indian English novel. There is a shift in emphasis – we have moved away from the Gandhian era of village centrism to the city centrism of the Post-Emergency era. The 'locale' has shifted from the village to the metropolis of our country and then abroad. The East-West encounter which is explained in terms of hybridity in relationship by post-colonial critics, takes 'a space' in Postmodern Indian English fiction. When the world has become 'a global village, no culture, or society is pure or insular today. That is why Indian English fiction now takes character, situations both from inside the country and abroad, into its orbit, and develops them.

In the post–1980 era love, sex and marriage or the failure of it are some of the leading themes in Indian English novel. The description of love sex is very bold and rather unconventional. Arundhati Roy's *The God of Small Things* contains chapters which, to speak the least, are outrageous, and

Shiv K. Kumar's *A River with Three Banks* depicts love and sex without any inhibition. So is the case with Manju Kapur's *Difficult Daughters*. Marriage as a social institution has lost its sanctity and relevance in the post–1980 era.[1]

Lack of faith in religion and declining moral standards and behaviour are some of the predominant themes in post-modern novel. Corruption in public as well as private lives of individuals too appeals to our novelists and they write novels on this theme. Apart from love and sex, women novelists voice their feminism by asserting their rights to live in their own way.

The plot of the novel is complex and it moves both ways – backward and forward – and thereby makes the narration difficult and complicated. Thematically it centres round Ammu, her two children Raphel and Esthappen, her parents, brother, Chacko and his wife, Margaret and daughter, Sophie Mol and above all, Amu's low caste lover, Velutha, the parawan. The novel opens with Raphel's coming back to Ayemenem after a failed marriage, to see Estha, her twin brother ('They were two-egg twins', 'dizygotic') who was sent to his father after Sophie Mol's funeral and now returned to their native place after twenty–three years. The whole family has been personalized in retrospection.

The twins (Estha and Raphel) lived with their divorced mother, Ammu and their blind maternal grandmother, Mammachy and their maternal uncle Chacko, once a Rhodes scholar at Oxford and lecturer in Madras Christian College. He helped his mother run their paradise pickle business, and their maternal grandfather's youngest sister, Baby Kochamma. Chacko was married to an English woman, Margaret (who divorced him married Joe) and had a daughter, Sophie Mol who died later by drowning. Ammu's love for Velutha forms the core of the novel and makes the novelist's preference crystal-clear. The traditional society was not only conservative but authoritarian for it laid down who should love whom. It happened long ago and it is against this concept that the novelist protests vehemently. The right to love a man of her choice is a woman's birth right and should not be scuttled in the name of religion, caste, colour and class. It is in this sense that the novel could be read as a feminist novel or a postcolonial novel for both feminism and postcolonialism aim at destroying the old power structure. Roy wants to break this age old tradition to uphold the right of a woman to marry a man of her choice. Thus, she says:

> ....it could be argued that it actually began thousands of years ago. Long before the Marxists came. Before the British took Malabar, before the Dutch Ascending, before Vasco da Gama arrived, before the Zamorin's conquest of Calicut. Before by the Portuguese were found floating in the sea, with coiled sea serpents riding on their chests and oysters knotted in their tangled beards. It could be argued that it began long before Christianity arrived in a boat and seeped into kerala like tea from a tea bag. That it really began in the days when the love laws were made. The laws that lay down who should be loved, and how. And how much (1997:33)

'Things can change in a day' is used as a kind of refrain in the novel. It suggests that Roy is determined to break the tradition.

Who's the God of Small things? is it Velutha, the parawan, the maker of fine things with his superb sense of detail? who could have been? we are told:

> "The God of Loss? The God of Small Things? The God of Goose Bumps and Sudden Smiles? Of Sourmetal Smells like steel bus-rails and the smell of the bus conductor's hands from holding them? (Ibidem 217)

The liberation from old bondage and tradition needs not only courage but a new language. Arundhati Roy describes Ammu's (a high caste Syrian Christian woman) love for Velutha (a Parawan, a low caste man) in poetic prose. Roy fashioned a new language for fiction. Take, for instance, Ammu's parting from Velutha after the consummation of love. Roy writes:

> She moved closer, wanting to be within him, to touch more of him. He gathered her into the cave of his body. A breeze lifted off the river and cooled their warm bodies.

> It was a little cold. A little wet. A little quiet. The Air. But what was there to say? An hour later Ammu disengaged herself gently. I have to go'. He said nothing, didn't move. He watched her dress. Only one thing mattered how. They knew that it was all they could ask of each other. The only thing. Ever. They both knew that. Even later, on the thirteen nights that followed this one, institively they stuck to the small things. The Big Things ever lurked inside. They knew that There was nowhere for them to go. They had Nothing. No future so they stuck to the small Things. (Ibidem 338)

The above-quoted passage also explains the title of the novel. While trying to give a historical perspective to Estha and Raphel, Chacko say:

> We're Prisoners of War, Our dreams have been doctored. We belong no where. We sail unanchored our sorrows will never be sad enough. Our joys never happy enough. Our dreams never big enough. Our lives never important enough to matter. (Ibidem 53)

This kind of prose at once gives a made-in-India stamp to Indian English novel.

Arundhati Roy can be credited with creating, a new idiom and phrases like 'biological father', 'dia-able age', 'Sea-secrets', 're-Returned', 'non-elect,' 'death coiled like an angry spring', 'touchables', 'Rice-Christians', 'Clean children, like a packet of peppermints', 'as lonely as a wolf' etc. She impresses readers, as a writer of impulse rather than premeditation. Figures of speech are departures from the direct way of writing or speaking. Every writer like Arundhati Roy has his/her own style and says in his/her own way.[2]

Besides taking up cudgel for women's right to property and to choose their lovers, the novel also makes references to communist movement in Kerala and allusions to the *Mahabharata*. Those interested in politics can claim that it is a satire or politics—communist establishment, to be specific. One can call it a protest novel which is radical, subversive and taboo-breaking. Still another view may be that it tells the story of a family. This can be taken as a representative postcolonial novel for it seeks to restructure the power centre by giving right to women to live their lives in their own way, and fashions a new language for fiction by creating a new Indian English idiom.

As Jasbir Jain (1996) has rightly pointed out "Women have been kept in kitchens and parlours in purdah and in luxury but deprived freedom." (p.3)

Let there be a change and let more Roys come out and give expression to their passions and feelings which will certainly be welcomed by the literary world. We should be able to agree with Virginia Woolf (1995) when she argues that all activity of the mind should be so encouraged that there will always be in existence a nucleus of women who think, invent, imagine and create as freely as men do, and with as little fear of ridicule. It is a bold venture as a postcolonial novel because it gives an excellent indication of what the novel can do when it breaks those shackles and constraints of the bygone days.

Works Cited

1. Roy Arundhati, *The God of Small Things* (New Delhi, India ink: 1997)
2. Das – Bijay Kumar *Post-modern India an English Fiction*, Atlantic Publishers and Distributors.
3. Shukla – Dr. Suresh A Carnival from Kerala: The God of Small Things. Contemporary Indian writings in English edited by Jayadipinh Dudiya. Atlantic Publishers and Distributors.
4. Jain, Jasbir (ed) *Women's Writing: Text & Context*, Jaipur, New Delhi: Rawat Publications 1996.
5. Virginia Woolf, *Killing the Angel in the House*, Harmondsworth: Penguin Books, 1995.

10

The Image of Modern India in Aravind Adiga's *The White Tiger*

—A. Ramesh Babu

> Stories about rottenness and corruption are always the best stories, aren't they? (50)

Aravind Adiga's Man Booker Prize-winning novel *The White Tiger* deals with exploitation, injustice and discrimination between the poor and the rich in India. He is the fourth person who got Man Booker Prize from India after the eminent novelists Salman Rushdie, Arundhathi Roy and Kiran Desai. The novel deals with a man's journey from the darkness of poverty to brilliance and riches. The representation of dark India is also traced in Amitav Ghose recent novels *The Glass Palace* (2000) and *Sea of Poppies* (2008). Michael Portillo (2008) says: "The novel undertakes the extraordinary difficult task of gaining and holding the reader's sympathy for a through going villain. The book gains from dealing with pressing social issues and significant global developments with astonishing humour." As it is a very aggressive novel on corruption and injustice, Deirdre Donahue (2008) says: "*The White Tiger* is an angry novel about injustice and power which creates merciless thugs among whom only the ruthless can survive."

Adiga focuses on a man's ruthless exploitation of the system even as it deals with sub-themes of corruption, crime and illiteracy. He thinks that today's politics is degraded, and the poor people are dominated and humiliated by the politicians and elite sections. As he visited many northern places, he came to know the problems of poor people. He says that "In northern India politics is so corrupt that it makes a mockery of democracy. This is a country where the poor fear tuberculosis, which kills 1,000 Indians a day, but people like me—middle-class people with access to health services that are probably better than England's—don't fear it at all. It's an unglamorous disease, like so much of the things that the poor of India endure" (Stuart Jeffries, 2008). Though the novel deals with politics internally, Adiga says that he never intended *The White Tiger* to be a political or social statement. "It's a novel—meant to provoke and entertain its readers...but there is something I'd like my readers to think about. I'm increasingly convinced that the servant-master system, the bed rock of middle-class Indian life, is coming apart: and its unraveling will lead to greater crime and instability. The novel is a portrait of a society that is on the brink of unrest" (Aravind Adiga, R, 2008). He says that he was inspired to write this novel by the three great African-American twentieth-century novelists—Ralph Ellison, James Baldwin and Richard Wright. He says about them: "They all wrote about race and class, while later black writers focus on just class. Ellison's *Invisible Man* was extremely important to me. That book was disliked by white and blacks. My book too will cause widespread offence. Balram is my invisible man, made visible. This white tiger will break out of his cage" (Stuart Jeffries, 2008).

The White Tiger is an epistolary novel. It was written in the form of letters to the Chinese Premier Wen Jiabao who was going to visit India. Balram Halwai, the protagonist and who introduces himself as half-baked person and who represents that of the entrepreneur of modern India, narrates the story in over seven days and nights. He is born in a remote and small village to a rickshaw puller. After the death of his father, he searches for a job. Finally he gets the job of a driver to a rich family. The rest of the story depicts how he ends up being an entrepreneur. The novel is a brilliant social commentary on the poor and rich divide in India.

Balram, the protagonist of the novel, introduces himself as a Bangalore-based entrepreneur, reveals the secret of entrepreneurs which come from half baked clay and calls himself as half-baked Indian. He lives in the village of Laxmangarh, a fictional village in a community deep in the 'Darkness' of rural India. Though he is clever, his financial crisis impels him to work in a teashop in Dhanbad. His parents christen him Munna which means 'boy' in Hindi, whereas his school teacher Mr. Krishna gives him a new name Balram which refers to the brother of the Hindu god Krishna. As a half-baked person, he observes corruption in his school and says that "There was supposed to be free food at my school—a government programme gave every boy three *rotis*, yellow *daal*, and pickles at lunchtime. But we never saw *rotis*, or yellow *daal*, or, pickles and everyone knew why: the schoolteacher had stolen our lunch money.... Once, a truck came into the school with uniforms that the government had sent for us; we never saw them, but a week later they turned up for sale in the neighbouring village" (33).

Balaram want to become a unique person and a white tiger. When his father, Vikram, is unwell, he takes him to a hospital where he cannot find any doctors. His father dies of T.B. in the hospital. After a few days, he leaves the tea stall and wants to learn driving to get more money. After some upheavals, he gets a job as a driver to a rich family and moves to New Delhi with his master Mr. Ashok. He lives in a new apartment called Buckingham Towers A Block, which is one of the best in Delhi. Ashok likes to visit new places and spends his time in visiting malls, along with Pinky Madam, his wife. Balram's job is not only to drive the car but also to carry all the shopping bags as they come out of the malls.

In Delhi, Balram is surprised to see the clean roads and big buildings but he does not like the apartment which is very congested. He is very much fascinated by a magazine *Murder Weekly* which contains stories of murders, rapes and revenge. As other drivers read the magazines, he is habituated to read it and says that "a billion servants are secretly fantasizing about strangling their bosses—and that's why the government of India publishes the magazine and sells it on the streets for just four and a half rupees so that even the poor can buy it" (125). The mean and stingy behaviour of the rich is shown through the lost coin episode where Ashok's brother Mukesh, (throughout the novel he is called Mongoose), insults Balram for not having retrieved a rupee coin he lost while getting out of the car. He is bothered about the rupee coin after bribing someone with a million rupees: "Get down on your knees. Look for it on the floor of the car"...'Don't think you can steal from us just because you're in the city. I want that rupee!' 'We've just paid half a million rupees in a bribe, Mukesh, and now we're screwing this man over for a single rupee. Let's go up and have a scotch.' (139).

As Balram belongs to the sweet-makers' family, he is asked to prepare tea and sweets at his master's home. He is humiliated by them many times. He recalls how the poor people in rich areas are humiliated. Ashok and Pinky usually look down upon him for he mispronounces words in English. On Pinky Madam's birthday, he is made to dress up like a maharaja with a red turban and dark cooling glasses and serve them food. The lady deliberately asks him to repeat PiZZa as Balram always pronounces it as piJJA.

In the morning and evening hours in Delhi, many vehicles jostle on the road. The traffic grows worse day by day which makes Balaram a little bit of nervous. It is an eye-opening experience for him. He is degraded as a human being and not allowed to enter a shopping mall. A poor driver cannot enter a mall as he belongs to the poor class. If he walks into the mall someone would say "Hey, That man is a paid driver! What's he doing in here? "There were guards in grey uniforms on every floor—all of them seemed to be watching me. It was my first taste of the fugitive's life" (152). As he drives his master and his wife to shopping malls and call centre, Balram becomes increasingly aware of immense wealth and opportunity all around him, while knowing that he will never be able to gain access to that world. Through these experiences, he learns much about the world and later states that the streets of India provided him with all the education he needed, but he is trapped in an accident case to save Pinky Madam who kills a man on the road in drunken driving. He is forced to sign a statement accepting full responsibility for the accident.

When Ashok knows that his wife has left, he scolds, humiliates and beats Balram who drops Pinky Madam at the airport. Pinkey's absence throws Ashok in a nervous state. After a few days, he tries to forget Pinky by visiting the malls and enjoying life with girls. He is witness to all the things that Ashok does such as visiting the red-light area in search of a prostitute and bribing politicians. Balram does all menial jobs like carrying cash to ministers and politicians, bringing liquor and women for the men, and entertaining people by serving liquor while driving with one hand. He searches for strands of golden hair of women who frequently travel with Ashok in the car and has sex.

Balaram as a driver knows how to deceive his master. He gives out the way enterprising drivers make a little extra money by:

i) Siphoning of petrol and selling it.

ii) Repairing the car under a corrupt mechanic who gives inflated bills.

iii) Studying his master's habits and capitalize on his carelessness.

iv) Risking to make his master's car as a freelance taxi.

Having been a witness to all of Ashok's corrupt practices and gambling with money to buy politicians, to kill and to loot, he decides to do the same. Adiga delves deep into his subconscious as he plans to loot Rs.700,000 stuffed into the red bag. Go on, just look at the red bag, Balram—that's not stealing, is it? I shook my head. And even you were to steal it, Balram, it wouldn't be stealing. How so? I looked at the creature in the mirror. See- Mr. Ashok is giving money to all these politicians in Delhi so that they will excuse him from the tax he has to pay. And who owns that tax, in the end? Who but the ordinary people of this country—you!" (244). The monologue makes Balram to think seriously to steal the money and kill his master. The writer brings out powerfully Balram's unexpressed thoughts in several conversations punctuated with soliloquies. The stream of consciousness leads him to justify his plans of murder with growing meanness of Ashok in treating him. He has planned to confess his criminal thoughts, but Ashok interrupts him thinking that he might ask him for some money to get married.

Balram finally decides to kill his master for money. Indeed, Ashok's participation in funding political corruption makes Balram to become an entrepreneur. One day as Ashok carries seven hundred thousand rupees in cash as bribes for politicians in New Delhi, Balram decides to murder him. As Ashok's throat is slashed, he dies on the spot. Balram steals the money and escapes from there to Bangalore with his cousin Dharam. With the seven hundred thousand rupees he stole, he creates his own taxi company and changes his name to Ashok Sharma. Thus he becomes a wealthy entrepreneur in India's new technological society, and emerges as a part of the upper caste in the Indian society of the Light, namely, the world belonging to rich people who live in large, urbanized cities.

Adiga wants to show through his characters how corruption has become a big menace to the country. Balram introduces himself as "Thinking Man/And an entrepreneur" (3) and later as "his Midnight Educator on Matters Entrepreneurial" (45). He is called the white tiger, Munna, Country-Mouse and Ashok Sharma. He refers to the village only as the darkness, because he thinks that India is two countries in one: an India of Light, and an India of Darkness. Whenever he understands that illiterate and poor people are crushed by elite section of the society, he comes to know that there are two kinds of India with those who are eaten, and those who eat, prey and are predators. He wants to eat and not be eaten. Akash Kapur says: "He is not only an entrepreneur but also a roguish criminal remarkably capable of self-justification. The background against which he operates is one of corruption, inequality and poverty" (Akash Kapur, 2008).

As an innocent boy, Balram, who represents the "downtrodden sections of our society juxtaposed against the rich," (Shobhan Saxena, 2008: 9) sincerely works as a driver and believes that Indian servants are so honest: because of what he calls the Rooster Coop. After a few months of driving his master around and overhearing conversations, he is determined to know, just for a day or for a minute, what it means not to be a servant. By making some immoral decisions, he becomes successful. But the social conditions drive him completely towards corruption. By the end, when he becomes a boss, he has learned to work the system too—which is largely about greasing the proper wheels. He is a representative of the poor in India yearning for their 'tomorrow'. As a driver, his journey to Delhi indicates his journey from darkness to light. He observes that his master gives bribe to a politician to get a good position. It is a commentary on contemporary Indian conditions. Finally though his master is not a bad person, Balram kills him for money. Through his criminal drive he becomes a businessman and runs a car service for the call centres in Bangalore. "Above all, it's a vision of a society of people complicit in their own servitude: to paraphrase Balram, they are roosters guarding the coop, aware they're for the chop, yet unwilling to escape. Ultimately, the tiger refuses to stay caged. Balram's violent bid for freedom is shocking" (Turpin, 2008)

Adiga shows the modern India which is brutal, totally corrupt and unjust, where people behave like animals and everything is for sale: far distant from the shining India that we discuss in our day-to-day lives. He critically mentions that India is suffering from a lot of problems. He tries to show the real India that we can see in the Oscar award Hindi movie *Slumdog Millionaire* which is based on the novel "Q & A" written by Vikas Swarup. The modern India is full of illegal activities, corruption, injustice, illiteracy, discrimination of caste, religion and race, and this is poignantly pointed out as the main theme of the novel. Adiga unfolds the difference between what India really is and what it appears to be. He states: "I tried to tell a very real story about India on the brink of unrest. I tried to challenge the assumptions that many in middle class India hold about the poor: that they are stupid, easily manipulated, excessively religious bound by caste and family." In an interview, he says, "At a time, when India is going through great changes and, with China, is likely to inherit the world from the West, it is important that writers like me try to highlight the brutal injustices of society" (Shobhan Saxena, 2008: 9). It is not an autobiographical novel.

He again adds, "I don't think a novelist should just write about his own experience. Yes, I am the son of a doctor. Yes, I had a rigorous formal education, but for me the challenge as a novelist is to write about people who aren't anything like me." (Shobhan Saxena, 2008: 9)

Adiga illustrates the modern India that does not have "drinking water, electricity, sewage system, public transportation, sense of hygiene, discipline, courtesy or punctuality" (4). The most important part of this novel is Balram's observation of the real and modern India; the flocks of drivers hanging out by their vehicles outside air-conditioned buildings, waiting for their masters to summon them; the beggars at traffic stops, who get money mostly from the poor; the petty manipulations among the servants of the house. He gives some salient features of India:

> Every traditional Indian village has a blue-movie (pornographic) theatre (23)
>
> No one can enter Indian malls without wearing shoes. Shoes are compulsory. (148)
>
> No low-caste man can ever enter an Indian mall. Even if he enters stealthily, he is then caught,
>
> beaten and publicly humiliated. (152)
>
> In India, if an owner runs over a man with his car, his driver has to go to jail instead (309)
>
> In Indian brothels, they take extra money from servants, called as "Working-class surcharge"(232)

Adiga illustrates how rich people live in Delhi and at the same time he conveys the problems of the poor people in India. "The main thing to know about Delhi is that the roads are good and the people are bad. The police are totally rotten. If they see you without a seat belt, you'll have to bribe them a hundred rupees" (124). The development we see is purely in the big towns. Though India got independence in 1947, the people really do not have it. There is no development in India. Balram gives the scenario of India that "... families of pigs are sniffing through sewage ... vivid red and brown flashes of feather – roosters fly up and down the roofs of the houses" (20). Many villages do not have hospitals though people have liquor shops and brothels. "...there is no hospital in Laxmangarh although there are three different foundations stones for a hospital, laid by three different politicians before three different elections" (47). He says that "People in this country are still waiting for the war of their freedom to come from somewhere else – from the jungles, from the mountains, from China, from Pakistan. That will never happen. Every man must make his own Benaras" (304). Nobody can curb India's problems such as corruption and inequality. Finally he labels, "There's no end to things in India, as Mr Ashok used to say. You can give the police all the brown envelopes and red bags you want, and they might still screw you. A man in a uniform may one day point a finger at me and say, *Time's up, Munna.*"(320)

Adiga does not spare criticism on religions also. Religion plays the most significant role in an Indian's life as it symbolizes tradition and honour. Adiga has seriously focused on how religion dominates people. Balram takes advantage of the limited knowledge of rural beliefs of the upper classes by making up signs of respect for various objects or buildings, like a sacred temple, statue or tree. He doesn't take his religion too seriously and often pokes fun at it, especially at the number of gods Hinduism has, which he quotes as 36,000,000. Adiga mentions that "a common Hindu is worse than an Islamic terrorist" (293-294, 311). There is also some debate on the tensions between Hindus and Muslims. There is not much love for Muslims in India. For example, Balram is able to get the other driver of Ashok's family, Ram Persad, fired because Persad is a Muslim in hiding. However, he feels sorry for Persad and feels some regret for his actions. He does not have anger against Muslims. In fact, he even respects them and says that they are good people. He makes plenty of references to the "the four greatest poets who have ever lived" who are all Muslims, and agrees with the meanings he finds in their poetry. Thus this novel deals with not only corruption and inequality but also caste and religions.

Works Cited

Akash Kapur, "Review," *New York Times*. http://www.nytimes.com/2008/11/09/books/review/Kapur-t.html 7 November 2008.

Aravind Adiga, "Review: *The White Tiger* by Aravind Adiga," *The Telegraph*.http://www.telegraph.co.uk/arts/main.jhtml?xml=/arts/2008/08/09/boadi109.xml.Retrieved 2008-10-16. 09 August, 2008.

_____. *The White Tiger* New Delhi: Harper Collins Publishers, 2008.

Donahue, Deirdre "Review," *USA Today*. http://www.usatoday.com/life/books/reviews/2008-04-23-roundup-debutnovels_ (2008).

Michael Portillo, "Aravinda Adiga wins Man Booker Prize with *The White Tiger*," *The Times* http://entertainment.timesonline.co.uk/tol/arts_and_ entertainment/books/article4944850.ece15 October 2008.

Shobhan Saxena, "Fact not Fiction," *Sunday Times of India*, (19 October 2008): 7-9.

Stuart Jeffries, "Interview with Aravind Adiga," *The Guardian* 16 October 2008. Turpin, Adrian. *Financial Times*.

http://www.ft.com/cms/s/0/886f92c4-09c8-11dd-81bf—0000779fd2ac.html 19 April, 2008.

11

Cultural Dynamics and the Contemporary Indian English Novel

—N. K. Neb

The unprecedented changes in the nature of the material reality have immensely impacted life around. The quick urbanization of the Indian society in recent times, the speedy growth of the means of communication and developments in the field of technology have resulted in the emergence of an altogether different kind of cultural scenario. The migration of a large number of people to foreign lands for different reasons, and the close and frequent interaction among the people belonging to different cultural backgrounds have resulted in the emergence of cultural mix on a large scale. These developments have destabilized the earlier concepts of home, nation, native, alien on the one hand and on the other they have challenged the concept of the purity of races and cultures. They have also caused demographic uncertainties and disturbed the traditional Indian social fabric almost beyond recognition.

The traditional standardized ethical values based on a unitary and centralized view about the world have suffered a severe blow. Along with the intervention of institutionalized form of democracy, these factors have resulted in a heightened sense of individual freedom and the assertion of rights by the peoples traditionally kept marginalized due to caste, class, gender, ethnicity and sexual orientation. The introduction of new laws for the empowerment and assertion of the rights of these people has brought a new awareness among them. It has resulted in a drastic change in these people's behaviour and thoughts.

All these factors have brought a notable change in the content and form of Indian English fiction. A number of recently published novels interweave the Indian and the global, fact and fiction, the serious and the profane, and contest the canonical views about the high and the low forms of literature. It has transformed the very nature of the emerging forms of narratives. In this context, Gurupdesh Singh's observation is extremely relevant:

> The novel of the last two decades presents a liberated look. It is a denizen of the metropolis, a runaway globetrotter and a cultural crossbreed. Its fictional world stretches far beyond the bounds of India, and its producers are not necessarily the sons and daughters of the Indian soil. As consequence, this fiction pictures reality which is rootless, tentative and multiplex. (Singh, Gurupdesh, 2005:9)

The shift in the emerging nature of fiction can be ascertained from the major themes and the narrative strategies employed for their treatment in contemporary Indian fiction in English.

The depiction of traditional cross-cultural theme from a changed perspective forms a major concern in a number of contemporary fictional works. Earlier this theme was mainly concerned with the conflicting aspects of the East and the West. Indian life was presented to highlight its exotic features that had a specific appeal for the Western readers. The Western reason and scientific point of view juxtaposed against the Indian perspective governed by faith in spiritualism and highly emotional response to life formed the major thrust in the writings of earlier Indian-English fiction writers. It tended to create specific cultural stereotypes representing two major cultures coming in close contact due to political compulsions. The understanding that governed the depiction of this theme was usually based on the perspective that viewed life in binary terms. The two different cultures in question were seen from the consciousness of the colonizers. The essential qualities of both the cultures were considered to result in a conflict. The differences between the Eastern and the Western cultures depicted in this kind of fiction were treated to be fundamental, transcendental and eternal. Moreover, the interaction between the people related to these two cultures was shown to be taking place at a limited and specific level; either it was on the political level, or it was shown taking place at the individual level in particular situations. Consequently, the characters belonging to the Western culture were either political bosses or kind-hearted missionaries and social workers. The acceptance of an essential difference between the two cultures seemed to be the governing principle so far as the depiction of East–West encounter is concerned.

Instead of the depiction of essential difference between the two cultures, the constructed nature of this difference is highlighted in contemporary fictional narratives. Another significant aspect of cross-cultural encounter is presented by contemporary Diaspora writers. In the postcolonial times, these writers concentrate on the experiences of the displaced and exiled people. The sense of discrimination that the people from the erstwhile colonies experience particularly in the Western countries is different from what they experienced earlier during the British rule. In spite of the cultural interaction taking place more frequently and at a mass level the people who have to leave their home and settle abroad experience a different kind of dilemma. They may not be considered inferior in political terms yet their acceptance in an alien culture in a natural way remains a far cry. The contemporary fiction writers concentrate on the minute and subtle aspects of human behaviour that makes the Diasporas experience a sense of alienation and being kept at a distance. Different writers have tried to bring out multiple shades of this experience. On the one hand, there are writers who concentrate on the Diasporic experience at an alien place informing the supremacist attitude of the natives towards them. There are other writers who see this experience as an outcome of cultural interaction that facilitates the emergence of a universal civilization. Different shades of this theme can be observed in the fictional works of V.S. Naipaul, Bharati Mukherjee, Anita Desai, Kiran Desai, Jhumpa Lahiri, Hari Kunjuru, Kavita Dasvani, Rohinton Mistry, M.G.Vassanji etc.

A renegotiated and revised interest in the times during British Imperialism forms another thematic concern in the novels like Amitav Ghosh's *The Glass Palace*, Hari Kunjru's *The Impressionist, and* in the novels of M.G.Vassanji like *The Gunny Sack, Amriika, The In-between World of Vikram Lall*. It can be related to a common tendency in contemporary literature of the erstwhile colonies of the empire. According Neb:

> An awareness of and a particular attention paid to present the experience of the colonized culture vis-a-vis imperial powers has developed a common tendency in new national literatures marking a postcolonial understanding (Neb, 2005:19).

The fictional works dealing with this theme present a reinterpretation of colonial times to expose the subtle strategies adopted by the colonialists to extend their rule through military as well as civilizational imperialism. The difference in these writings from the historical fiction concentrating on the life during the British Empire is not in the themes they choose but in their attitude and positioning. Moreover, the concerns of these writers do not remain limited to British imperialism; they also offer a critique of colonial practices in the earlier colonies of the Empire much after their political decolonization.

The treatment of history has introduced another dimension to Indian English fiction. The fictionalization of contemporary political incidents having historical significance marks the insertion of socio-political positions in a number of novels like Shashi Tharoor's *Riot,* Manju Kapur's *A Married Woman,* Rohinton Mistry's *Family Matters*, Shashi Deshpande's *In the Country of Deceit*, Amrita Kumar's *Damage,* Githa Hariharan's *In Times of Siege* and *Fugitive Histories*. In these novels the writers seem to revisit the past due to some purposive stance of their own. The fictional discourse in these works, in particular, points out a post-structural attitude towards history explained in these words:

> A historian like a novelist includes and excludes, suppresses and stresses historical material depending on his prejudices, predilections and even prescriptions. S\He in this manner shares emplotting strategies' with the

> novelist. History thus is a construct made up by a historian. And like every other construct, it is necessarily a political act (Singh, Avdesh, 2005:133).

Such an understanding has also resulted in a reinterpretation of the past involving political implications. The novels like, Tharoor's *Riot*, Khushwant Singh's *The Burial at Sea*, Bapsi Sidhwa's *Ice Candy Man*, M.G. Vassanji's *The Assassin's Song*, Amitav Ghosh's *The Glass Palace* and *The Shadow Lines*, Rohinton Mistry's *A Fine Balance* and *Such A Long Journey* and Mukul Kesavan's, *Looking Through Glass* form some of the prominent examples of the works that tend to reinterpret history to highlight its fictional nature.

Another thematic aspect of contemporary Indian English fiction can be ascertained from the predominance of the treatment of the issues related to women's marginalized position in society and the ways they adopt to mark their protest. Their attempts to experience a decolonized existence forms one of the major themes. While presenting women's oppressed position, most of the women writers tend to explore aspects of female sexuality. It includes the expression of the ways women behave in the changed scenario and exhibit a changed attitude towards sex and the morality associated with it as these women show their defiance towards patriarchy-ascribed norms related to sexual behaviour, especially enjoined for women. Almost all the contemporary Indian women writers in English, like Anita Desai, Bharati Mukherjee, Namita Gokhale, Shobha De, Manju Kapur, Kusum Sawhney, Shashi Deshpande, Githa Hariharan and Amrita Kumar exhibit this tendency in their writings.

There has been a spurt of ethnocentric works of fiction treating experiences, thoughts, feelings and predicaments of particular ethnic groups or minority communities. This development can be related to the implications of granting privileges to minorities in the Indian democratic set-up and the emergence of a globalized world in recent times. The challenge from globalization to the fixed referrals and the sense of identity being plural and fluid has resulted in people's furious search for identity to define them for themselves and for others.

It has led to a quest for roots in the ethnic past. Consequently, writers like Rohinton Mistry, Firdaus Kanga, Bapsi Sidhwa, Amrita Kumar, and M.G. Vassanji concentrate on the themes related to specific ethnic groups or minority communities. These writings explore the complexities, tensions, problems and the cultural history of certain ethnic groups. The concentrated exploration of Parsee life in a number of recent novels, mostly by Parsee writers, is often being referred to as Parsee literature. Although there are writings concerning other ethnicities like Muslims and Christians the number of writings related to Parsee way of life is, no doubt, much more than the others.

Another thematic strain is related to the depiction of the forms of life traditionally understood to be inappropriate for literary expression. In the changed scenario, the difference between high and low culture, serious and popular art does not remain valid. Contemporary writers no longer hesitate in including deviant and bizarre forms of life into their writings. There are a number of fictional writings in contemporary Indian English literature which depict the experiences of the gays, lesbians and even the neutral gender. The presence of sexual freaks, underworld dons, drug traffickers, and the depiction of their wayward behaviour forms a major part in a number of contemporary fictional writings. The flashes of lesbian and gay sexual behaviour in Manju Kapur's *A Married Woman*, Amrita Kumar's *Damage*, Shobha De's *Strange Obsession,* Tarun Tejpal's *The Alchemy of Desire*, Kusum Sawhney's *Ayala* about incestuous relations and Raj Rao's *Hostel Room 131* form some of the examples of these writings. Similarly, Khushwant Singh's *Delhi*, Hari Kunzru's *The Impressionist*, Raj Rao's *Hostel Room 131*, include the experiences of marginalized groups of society like eunuchs. These writings provide expression to the forms of life traditionally kept at the margins of the mainstream society. It also marks an attempt of the writers to cater to the demands of the casual readers interested in easy, pleasing and enjoyable reading material.

In spite of the variety of issues and freshness of perspectives that inform the nature of themes and subject matter found in contemporary Indian English fiction, a study of contemporary fiction writers like, Khushwant Singh, Shashi Tharoor, Amitav Ghosh, Rohinton Mistry, Anita Desai, Shobha De, Shashi Deshpande, Githa Hariharan, Manju Kapur, Kusum Sawhney, Namita Gokhale, Gita Mehta, Hari Kunzru, Bharati Mukherjee, Jhumpa Lahiri, Kiran Desai, Tarun Tejpal, Amrita Kumar, Rupa Bajwa, R.Raj Rao, shows the limited nature of their fictional world that usually highlights the aspects of life limited to urbanized Indian society. No doubt these writers have been able to successfully explore the complexities, tensions, problems and multiple aspects of contemporary society. But the problems faced by the lower strata of urban society and the rural downtrodden finds negligible place in their fictional world. Similarly, the complexities and constraints of rapid urbanization and the problems faced by the emerging class of technocrats, professionals and the dehumanizing impact of technology-oriented jobs, the extreme sense of unbecoming due to the collapsing of traditional familial ties, commercialization of human relationships and the alienation felt by the elderly people due to the indifference of the younger generation, the impact of the migration of the children on lonely and deserted parents, all remain outside the fictional concerns of contemporary writers. In the same way, the traditional moral dilemmas, and economic problems are conspicuously absent from emerging fictional narratives. It may be a result of the shift informing predominant forms of reality. All these developments also relate to the fictional devices used by contemporary Indian fiction writers in English.

The question of narrative strategies or fictional devices is closely related to the thematic aspect of fictional works. The shift informing the subject matter and themes of recent Indian English fiction (discussed earlier) has also impacted its narrative design. Another factor that has influenced the formal features of the recent fiction, particularly novel, is the nature of the target reader in contemporary times. The contemporary reader of Indian English novel apart from academic, serious and critical ones includes casual readers like travelling-businessmen, rich educated, bored housewives, young men and women and the people who read novels as a pleasant pastime. Whereas the academic reader is interested in serious, moral social, philosophical, political and artistic issues, the interest of the casual readers is limited to have enjoyable reading material in the form of pleasing, sensational, romantic, titillating and wonderful details along with views on contemporary happenings having political, religious or social significance. For such readers as Raja Rao, Mulk Raj Anand, Bhabhani Bhattacharya or the writer like Munshi Prem Chand is hardly a choice. The expectations of the serious and the casual readers put heavy demand on the creative writers to experiment with the content and the form to make their works both, popular and artistic.

Apart from the implied readers the other factor that has impacted the nature of narrative in recent times is the shift informing the paradigms of understanding culture, literature and reality. The division between high and low, serious and popular culture is no longer treated to be relevant in contemporary times. Similarly, reality is no longer considered to be something transcendental, fundamental and unitary in nature. Therefore, literature is not considered to represent reality in an objective manner. Consequently, the narrative devices employed by contemporary writers include the use of magic realism, mixing of fact and fiction, and the methods that highlight the status of fiction as fiction instead of being a faithful picture of the external reality. The understanding that culture is not something always vertical and hierarchical but horizontal consisting of multiple possibilities provides much scope to include forms of life that earlier used to be kept at the margins. It marks the use of crude realism and multiple perspectives as a major narrative device. It adds the element of wonder to the fictional works.

The most prominent feature of contemporary fiction is the use of narrative voice that tends to disrupt the sense of acceptance of the authority of the writer or the narrator. The nature of the narrative that emerges now marks a shift from the traditional use of point of view expressed in the words of Patricia Waugh:

> In a realist fiction, a variety of points of view may be expressed, but as part of a controlled pluralism where no single voice is allowed to challenge the authority of omniscience recognized as the voice of commonsense or of the 'sensus communis (Waugh 1992: 57).

Earlier the authorial voice was considered all inclusive whereas contemporary narratives present the authorial views as one of the perspectives expressed in a work of art. It marks a challenge to the omniscient narrator and paves way for the role of the reader. Now a reader is no longer supposed to be guided by the author to make sense of the world created by him. The reader has to exercise his/her own critical faculty to award meaning to the world he comes across in a work of fiction. As the nature of the world and its meaning is no longer fixed, the emphasis now shifts from what kind of a world has been created to how it has been created and how it gains significance for different readers. It brings out a different nature of the emerging narratives that can be termed writerly texts in Barthes's terminology:

> A readerly text (or a readerly approach to a text) allows the reader only to be a passive consumer of a fixed, given meaning; a writerly text (or a writerly approach to a text) turns the reader into a producer (Krishnaswamy 2001: 41).

The inclusion of different elements of other art forms such as films, diary entries newspaper reports and factual historical details forms a part of the emerging modes of contemporary narratives. These elements contest the canonical view of literature and add to the variety and complexity of these fictional writings. According to Linda Hutcheon:

> The borders between literary genres have become fluid: who can tell anymore what the limits are between the novel and the short story collection, the novel and the long poem, the novel and autobiography, the novel and history, the novel and biography? (Hutcheon 1990 : 9).

The inclusion of anthropological research-oriented material in Amitav Ghosh's novels like *The Hungry Tide* and *The Sea of Poppies,* and the use of different narrative elements in Shashi

Tharoor's *Riot* and the details concerning historical research in Khushwant Singh's *Delhi* form the examples of such narratives. The disruption in the linear development of the fictional discourse through the insertion of these elements makes these writings a collage of different art forms and marks a rejection of the purity of genres. Different genres are viewed to form the fictional whole that adds to the complexity of these writings. Consequently, these fictional works develop in the form of an arrangement of different micro-narratives that tend to be individually significant apart from their relevance in the total scheme of the work. This aspect of contemporary fiction brings the narrative design close to the epic form of writing where we find story within the story.

The presentation of different images of life in sudden flashes like advertisements and media-generated images marks the proximity of fictional works with different forms of visual arts. There is a quick succession of images that appear in the novels like Khushwant Singh's *Delhi* and *The Company of Women* and almost all the novels of Shobha De except *Second Thoughts*. Different characters and incidents in these novels follow one another as series of scenes on a cinema screen. These narrative forms may seem simplistic and inartistic, yet they correspond to the variety plurality and complexity informing contemporary life. Instead of concentrating on the major happenings in the life of one or two characters, these writings express the diverse forms of life that one finds in contemporary globalized world. One consequence of the use of such narrative elements is that the reader neither does, nor is supposed to treat them as stable or representative forms of life and reality.

The fictional narratives concentrating on different aspects of contemporary happenings having political or historical significance mark a lack of temporal and spatial movement that informed the writings of earlier fiction writers. Instead of their progress like a Bildungsroman novel what we find is interaction and responses at the inter-personal and inter-ethnic levels or the multiplicity of responses to certain incidents. It is particularly so in the novels related to the incidents like Ram Janambhoomi/Babri Masdi conflict or the narratives concerning ethnic problems. Similarly, the novels by most of contemporary women writers register a gradual development in the awareness of women characters about their marginalized position in society instead of a temporal or spatial movement. These narratives involve internal development rather then externa!. Consequently, their fictional details often remain limited to inter personal relations, particularly of the women characters in different situations.

There has been a spurt of writings concerning the life and lifestyle of the peoples on the fringe side of the mainstream reality who remain oppressed due to gender, caste, sexual orientation or political reasons. The depiction of the forms of life related to these sections of society is carried out through the use of two types of characters: the oppressed and the oppressors. For example, the fictional works presenting women's marginalization involve men who are insensitive, arrogant, prone to violence and inconsiderate. The women are shown to be extremely passive, docile and gentle or aggressive and militant flaunting all norms of decent behaviour enjoined for them. The same is the case with the writings about the marginalization of gays, lesbians due to social norms. Similarly, the characters in the works involving postcolonial perspectives can be put into two neat categories: the colonizers and the colonized. Not only the characters, even the incidents presented in such writings indicate that the structure of these narratives is highly purposive and informs constructed nature of the narrative. The nature of this type of fiction has been rightly pointed out in these words:

> The novelist's business is no longer to render the world but to make one from language: fiction is no longer mimetic but constructive. (Woods, 1999:56)

It also contests the objective and representative nature of the fictional world.

The shrewd handling of the subject matter involves the use of the device that marks a deliberate blurring of the message or the authorial intentions. This device has been used as a potent tool by a number of contemporary Indian English fiction writers. These writers arrange the incidents and narrative details in their fictional narratives resulting in the confusion of the fictional message. Like Indian formula-films, a number of sensational, thrilling, romantic, striking and enjoyable incidents and details are interspersed with sudden and clever insertion of certain phrases or short descriptions that carry the message. The way these writers conceal the serious issues in the jumble of enjoyable reading material either keeps the message unnoticed or makes it look insignificant to the readers. To leave the fictional message in the form of signposts flashed for the reader turns out a useful ploy for the writers that serves their commercial ends also. For example, the sexual orgies one finds in almost all the novels of Shobha De, Khushwant Singh's *The Company of Women*, and Raj Rao's *Hostel Room 131, Kusum* Sawhney's *Ayala* keep the real message blurred.

The narrative strategy often deployed in the works concerning the problems of the people indulging in deviant sexual behaviour is related to the surroundings in which much of the action takes place. There are strange and striking places like dingy hostel rooms, film studios, street corners, parks, and isolated banglows away from the humdrum reality of life. It provides a sense of romance and mystery to the narrative details. The depiction of such scenes may suit the fictional design but such devices scuttle the very purpose of presenting the characters indulging in lesbian, gay and homosexual acts as normal and natural. The strange, shocking, fantastic and mysterious atmosphere created through the surroundings, no doubt, appeals the readers for creating the romance of the distant but fails to sensitize them to the problems of the people who remain strange, surprising and to a certain extent unnatural and abnormal to them. These writings seem to depict only the snapshots of a kind of reality instead of giving this reality a representative character. The novels like, Raj Rao's *Hostel Room 131*, Tarun Tejpal's *The Alchemy of Desire*, Kunjru's *The Impressionist,* Shobha De's *Snapshots, Sisters, Strange Obsession* and *Sultry Days* have employed these fictional devices to a large extent.

The Diaspora writers fictionalize situations and happenings usually in an alien land, where cross cultural interaction takes place. The details about the problems of the migrants and exiles, the discrimination these people experience, their mental journey to homeland, their own creation of a glorified view of their past, inability to find acceptance, and the ways these people adopt to settle in an alien land and their treatment as the 'other' by the host culture find recurring expression in diaspora Indian fiction in English. The depiction of these aspects of life involves the presentation of food habits, cultural traits, and social practices that pronounce the difference between the two cultures.

The variety, complexity and the shift informing thematic concerns of contemporary Indian English fiction and a corresponding development in the art of storytelling relate to the cultural dynamics impacted by globalized reality and changing perspectives of understanding reality.

Works Cited

Hutcheon, Linda (1990) *A Poetics of Postmodernism: History, Theory, Fiction.* New York and London. Routledge.

Krishnaswamy, (2001) Contemporary *Literary Theory: A N. John Varghese, Student's Companion.* Delhi: Macmillan.

Neb, Narinder 2005 *Culture in Transition: A Study of Contemporary Indian English* Fiction

Singh, Avadesh K. 2005 "The Re-Discovery of India: The Engagement of Contemporary Indian English Novel with Indian History" in *Narrating India: The Novel in Search of the Nation* ed.E.V.Ramakrishnan Delhi: Sahitya Akademi

Singh, Gurupdesh (2005) "Foreword" to *Culture in Transition: A Study of Contemporary Indian English Fiction* N.K. Neb Jalandhar: Nirman Publications

Waugh Fatricia (1992) *Practising Postmodernism Reading Modernism.* London Arnold.

Woods, Tim (1999) *Beginning Postmodernism.* Manchester & New York : Manchester University Press.

12

A Study of Globalisation and Changing Social Behaviour in Indian English Literature

—Anju Bala Agrawal

Globalization of literature and man has added new dimensions to interpretation of culture, location, relocation, exile, reinstatement of identity and their narration. It has emerged as an issue of concern to people from all walks of life. Indian writers with a re-ignited interest in their native culture retain the thematic and political connection with the national background and also establish fresh links with the Euro-American metropolies. Globalization strives to change the world through the market economy which in actual practice amounts to replacing the concept of society by the concept of the market.

Through the experiences of poor and middle class people, we may visualize the physical and psychic violence done to those who are minor to hegemonic languages of the nation and of globalization—by their class, gender, race or ethnicity. Many writers have revealed how the much celebrated global flow of human bodies and its associated tropes of empowerment can also be differently and violently abjecting processes-processes that empower the realization of equal citizenship. This paper focuses on the changing behaviour patterns of society especially in twenty-first century and their portrayal in the writings of new millennium. I have picked certain writers and their famous books specially those written in twenty-first century. Hari Kunzru's second novel *Transmission* (2004) carries forward the theme of uprooted individuals controlled and played upon by the global economy. Here, the novelist extends his exploration of assimilation and rootlessness by introducing an hopelessly ambitious outsider to a corrupt and corroding society. The novel is set in the ultra modern high tech world of computers.

Transmission moves along traversing the lives of three characters: Arjun Mehta (the computer programmer), Lila Zahir (the bollywood starlet) and Guy Swift (the high flier marketing executive) caught in the quagmire of contemporary emotions devoid life and tracing their respective misfortunes amid the collapse of the new economy. Most of the novel hinges around Arjun Mehta, the struggling computer geek, who finds himself lost in the jet-paced corporate world of America where he had come as a 'cyber-coolie'. He watches his "American-Dream" getting squashed under the pressing cultural forces of the ruthless corporate sector. He is one of the million Indian software engineers who dream to make big in the Silicon valley and get disillusioned.

Arjun too lands in America through a placement agency named Databodies which assures him a high profile programming job with an MNC. But the reality check takes him into a horde of many other unemployed Indian youths shown the same pipe-dreams.

After a year long enforced unemployment, he is transported to California where he is adjusted in a software firm named Viruginex, engaged in combating the computer viruses. The job is extremely low paid as against the promises made by the agency, none the less Arjun accepts it as a long-term prospect. But more so, due to his inability to return to India empty-handed. He enjoys the stint as an IT consultant for a while, gets enamoured of his bisexual colleague Chris, engages in a dispassionate bout of sex till the jolt comes. He is sacked by the firm as a strategic move to cut down on expenses.

Jobless and appalled Arjun decides to strike back and unleashes a virus named Leela (named after his heart-throb bollywood actress) into his employer's network computers in a bid to get his job back after a charade of fixing the problem up. But the tables are turned upon him as the virus goes berserk and infects the computers around the globe creating a tumult in the global order. Arjun suddenly becomes an international terrorist and is pursued by FBI and other crime taming agencies. Thus, the novel is a sort of forewarning for our excessive computer dependent world and our millions of abstractions attached to such a world.

Arjun fails to detach himself from this "virtual reality" and reaches his undue nemesis. Hari Kunzru's comments on Arjun and millions of others dreamers in an interview, "Arjun is somebody who prefers a highly controlled world of computers, one in which you can put a set of figures and get a definite answer out....in my works to come, I expect my interest in idealism and its disconnection with reality. Also in how people create abstractions of the world and tend to shoehorn the messy and unpleasant aspects of reaity."[1] Interweaving the themes of multiculturalism, modernity, globalization and its offshoots the novel sets the tone of life in a highly computerized age. Consequently, the novel becomes a critique of the postmodern society heading towards decadence of all sorts.

Thus, the novel shows that globalization in the form of information technology is invariably associated with the West and its values for which reason its agenda becomes imbued with fascist and racist undertones: fascist in the sense that the West in Orientalist fashion views the people of East as inanimate coolies who are superfluous and deserve to be exploited for their own good and racist in the sense that globalization re-evokes the idea of white supremacy in postcolonial societies. For an Indian, life becomes a stress-filled affair because there is no thought for the psychological havoc they create through mass unemployment. It also threatens to annihilate our identity and the humanitarian values that compensate in so many ways for the material deprivation that characterizes the majority of Indian lives.

Amitav Ghosh's *The Hungry Tide*, exposes the poverty, hardship and helplessness of those people who otherwise are rarely made of the stuff of any literary discourse. Besides it, environmental issues due to global pollution and its aftermath in the form of Tsunami has been depicted in this novel. Man is a part of environment, yet he does not act to maintain this ecological balance. The misuse and overuse of natural resources by man has resulted in disturbing the balance. They kill animals indiscriminately. This has badly disturbed the food chains. Now many species are on the verge of extinction. Plant and animal species are dying out at an unprecedented rate. The leading cause of extinction is habitat destruction, particularly of the world's richest ecosystems. If the world's rain forests continue to be cut down at the current rate, they may completely disappear by the year 2030. In addition, if the world's population continues to grow at its present rate and puts even more pressure on these habitats, they might well be destroyed sooner. The tall and upright trees act as breakers of destructive power and velocity of winds and water. It is necessary that there should not be any cutting of mangroves and other trees in Sunderban region. In the process of this novel, we see how Piya and Fokir become the prey of cyclone. It was only a tree which could save Piya though Fokir could not save himself as the tree was not so strong.

Human activity also plays a very important role in determining the environment of a region. The uncontrolled human activities constantly damage the environment. Forests have been cleared for accommodating people. Because of the huge growth in population, forests have been cleared not only to build houses but also for cultivation. One such historical event has also been mentioned by the writer. It comes through Nirmal's diary. On an island named Morichjhappi, many Bangladeshi refugees try to settle. They are making arrangement for their homes, societies and other means of livelihood and comfort. The government takes the decision to make these people vacate the island with allegation of unlawful subjugation of land. Social groups feel that the abode of the Royal Bengal Tigers has been encroached. The big men of the world who feel that the wonderful ecosystem of the Sunderbans is at risk from this group of hapless men, women and children. In this matter, Ghosh also sees the humanitarian point of view. The life and aspirations of Kusum and Horen, the two local settlers are an embodiment of Ghosh's reflections on this fundamental issue. On hearing the announcement of vacating the island as it has to be saved for its trees and that it belongs to a project to save tigers, Kusum rumainates:

> Who are these people, I wondered, who love animals
> so much that they are willing to kill us for them? [2]

Booker Prize winner, Arvind Adiga's *The White Tiger* is presented as an epistolary novel, a series of letters written over the period of seven nights. It's just an excuse, of course, for the narrator, Balram Halwai, to tell his story -- a supposedly creative approach that, at least initially certainly gets the reader's attention. The person Balram is writing to is the premier of China, Wen Jiabao, due to visit the city Balram is living in—Bangalore, India—in a week's time. What, one wonders, could possess an Indian entrepreneur living in Bangalore to write at such length to the premier of China?

Balram does have a story to tell, but unfortunately the connexion to his ostensible audience (the Chinese premier) is barely made. Sure, Balram explains that he can tell the premier all about Indian entrepreneurship—something he hears China is missing—and he makes the occasional comparisons between India and China, but it ultimately proves to be a feeble excuse for him to unburden himself, and because the premise is so poorly utilised undermines much of the novel. Balram does have something to get off his chest, of course, and his letters to the Chinese premier are a confession of sorts. Balram tells his life-story, recounting how he got to where he now is—a successful entrepreneur in Bangalore. And from early on we learn that he is a wanted man, as he writes about a poster describing him and alluding to his misdeeds. And soon he reveals what crime he has on his hands, too.

Along the long way Adiga does a decent job of describing the divide between the haves and have-nots, and the way the servant-class is treated. He's particularly good on Indian corruption, from the vote-rigging of the local elections, where the 'Great Socialist' candidate is unopposable, to the conditions at school, where the teacher steals the money for the school-food-programme and sells the uniforms meant for the students—but no one holds it against him, because he hasn't been paid in six months and that's simply the way the system works. Anyone in power abuses it for his or her own benefit. By the end, when he's a boss, Balram has certainly learned to work the system too—which is largely about greasing the proper wheels (and palms). His adventures in the big city and as an employee of a man who keeps having to pay bribes to politicians (and whose marriage falls apart) allows for some amusing observations and commentary on contemporary Indian conditions, and a nice contrast of poverty and wealth, but much of it feels a bit forced. Most of the narrative drive comes from the build up to the crime Balram commits, but that also distracts from Adiga's other purposes, making for a muddled mix where nothing—the crime, Balram's learning curve and then his business ventures, the state of modern India—is adequately presented.

The White Tiger 'says a lot' about contemporary India, but it tries to do so far too hard. Adiga has some talent, but leaves it at loose ends here. What suspense he builds up early on surrounding Balram's crime dissipates far too fast, while he tries too hard with his Indian panorama. And Balram isn't a fully realised or convincing character, either, even though he's talking (or telling his story) all the time, as Adiga's attempt to make him both a peasant-everyman (representative of so many Indians) and a white tiger confuses things.

It is a matter of sheer irony that women have always had a circumscribed existence across the cultures as well as literatures. Consciously or unconsciously, different male-centered studies have invariably depicted them in peripheral roles. Confined to a private space and condemned to live as non-actors, the women have rarely been portrayed as playing significant roles. Their contribution in giving a shape and substance to the society has largely gone unrecognized. They have to live under the "power of the fathers: a familial, social, ideological, political system in which men—by force, direct pressure, or through ritual, tradition, law, and language, customs, etiquette, education and the division of labour—determine what part women shall or shall not play and in which female is everywhere subsumed under the male."[3] Even in the twenty-first century and in this age of globalization, in most of the Indian families a girl child is accepted as a liability whereas a male one is welcomed as an asset. The contemporary

Indian women writers in English, by virtue of their experience and exposure, feel encouraged enough to dislodge this patriarchal dominance and appear to accept the challenges that befall their way in making a room of their own.

Namita Gokhale's *Shakuntala* is a novel about a woman's aspirations and romantic longings to cross the confines of tradition set by the patriarchy. In the novel, there are some obvious points of comparison and contrast against the mythical Shakuntala, a helpless nymph who dare not challenge the cruelty (though an unconscious one) of her husband, Dushyanta, who is guilty of deserting her. As though to set the things right, Gokhale portrays her Shakuntala with the qualities of boldness and restlessness, which would not allow the male chauvinism to rule over her. Rather, she would take delight in breaking the rules and customs of society apart from satisfying her lust for mental and physical adventures. Namita Gokhale presents the story of an adventurous and free woman against a backdrop of a historical period when Buddhism was on rise and even shaving the head and leaving home to join as a nun was considered an ultimate kind of freedom. 'New' Shakuntala has to pay for her freedom. Much against her mythical namesake counterpart's submissive attitude, this Shakuntala feels no qualms of conscience in questioning and defying the patriarchal dictates. As she muses:

> I knew there was more inside me than the limits of my experience dictated....A man's equal in bed, why could I not desire what men enjoyed: the freedom to wander, to be elsewhere, to seek, and perhaps find...something?[4]

The protagonist Shakuntala of Namita Gokhale's *Shakuntala: The Play of Memory* is named after the fifth century dramatist Kalidasa's heroine Sakuntala. While the original Sakuntala is a helpless nymph who is deserted by her husband King Dushyanta and needs her mother Menaka, 'the celestial apsara,' to put things right for her, Gokhale's mortal Shakuntala is bold and restless at a time when women are confined to the household. Shakuntala questions the rules and customs of society, and when the opportunity arrives, she goes out into the unknown to satisfy her adventurous spirit. Shakuntala is born into a poor 'vanvasi' family, hill people who live near the forests of the mountainous areas in India. She grows up roaming the woods, and spends her time watching clouds and birds. Shakuntala is married off to a wealthy man, and although they share a happy life, seeing traders and pilgrims and horses, Shakuntala feels there are 'thoughts and events and people' in far off lands that she is yet to see and experience. If men can travel and seek, why is it 'unseemly and inappropriate' for women? When her husband brings home a mysterious handmaiden from his travels, Shakuntala is consumed with jealousy. While praying by the Ganga (The river Ganges as goddess), she meets a Greek traveller and runs away with him, leaving her respectable home. Shakuntala wanders with him from place to place and gives up all her societal bindings to lead a life of pleasure. But this carefree lifestyle is not enough to satiate her restlessness, and she wanders off in the holy city of Kashi and then dies in an accident.

Anita Nair's *Ladies Coupe* is the story of a woman's search for strength and independence. Akhilandeshwari, Akhila for short, is a woman of forty-five and single, an income-tax clerk, and a woman who has never been allowed to live her own life—always the daughter, the sister, the aunt, the provider. Until the day she gets herself a one-way ticket to the seaside town of Kanyakumari, gloriously alone for the first time in her life and determined to break free of all that her conservative Tamil brahmin life has bound her to. In the intimate atmosphere of the ladies coupé which she shares with five other women, she gets to know her fellow travellers: Janaki, a pampered wife and confused mother; Margaret Shanti, a chemistry teacher married to the poetry of elements and an insensitive tyrant too self-absorbed to recognize her needs; Prabha Devi, the perfect daughter and wife, transformed for life by a glimpse of a swimming pool; fourteen-year-old Sheela, with her ability to perceive what others cannot; and Marikolanthu, whose innocence was destroyed by one night of lust. As she listens to the women's stories, Akhila is drawn into the most private moments of their lives, seeking in them a solution to the question that has been with her all her life: Can a woman stay single and be happy, or does a woman need a man to feel complete

Anita Nair's engrossing *Ladies Coupe* raises what many readers might consider taboo questions about to the role of woman in contemporary postcolonial India. Nair's India suffers from a system of sex-role stereotyping and oppression of women that exist under patriarchal social organization. Of course, patriarchy, in its different forms, has tried in many ways to repress, debase and humiliate women—especially through the images represented in cultural and traditional forms. *Ladies Coupe* deals with such issues by asking fundamental questions that not only shake the ideological ground of man's patriarchal role in a traditional society, but also imply the existence of an alternative reality. Put differently, the novel questions whether the role of Indian woman—as a representative of other women living under oppressive patriarchal systems—in relation to culture resistance should be restricted only to their roles as wives and mothers. In such a world, woman's role is limited to reproduction regardless of her own desires and needs.

In this age of globalization women's aspiration for identity has been presented by Manju Kapur in her A *Married Woman*. This novel brings forth the issue of gender discrimination and the struggle of the afflicted Indian women under the oppressive mechanism of a closed social web. Astha has a big jerk in her mind and this cripples her married life. She is Kapur's New Woman, "conscious, introspective, educated, wants to carve a life for herself, to some extent, she even conveys a personal vision of womanhood by violating current social code."[5]

In this novel Kapur has made a meticulous sociological cram in Astha-Aijaz- Pipelika relationship. Astha and Pipelika are impressed with the community as they are good friends, partners and human beings in spite of oblique references, "four wives, large families, instant divorce, inter community marriages, the religion of babies from such unions"[6] dating from Babur's time to the present day. While Astha's miniatures contain socio-political matters of time with an ethical touch, Aijaz has a radical view with his ready impact on social web through his theatre activities. Astha forms many relationships with different people, all the while searching for her identity. Her quest for identity is a "whole new look at women – not as the property of father, husband or son, and dependent on their bounty, but as valuable human material to be brought to full flower and full participation in her life and events."[7] Definitely Manju Kapur voices the implicit idea that man always expects sacrifice from woman and he is always callous enough to overlook the need of her fulfilment. The lack of self identity is the root cause of many conflicts; an endowed cry for self hood is prerequisite for all round mellowness and contentment.

To conclude, above mentioned writers and other writers are raising several issues that are vital in this century. In this technological age, some age old issues are raising the voice of protest while new issues are coming forward. Literature as a mirror of society focuses these issues to create consciousness in the masses. As in our constitution, there is equality, so there is a need of raising voice against injustice towards each and every person of Indian society. I hope this paper of mine has presented several issues that should be raised for the betterment of society.

Works Cited

1. Mukund Padmanathan interviews Hari Kunzru in *The Hindu,* July 4, 2004.
2. Amitav Ghosh, *The Hungry tide*, New Delhi: Harper Collins Publishers, 2004, p.262.
3. Rich Adrienne, *Of Women Born: Motherhood as Experience and Institution*, London: Virago, 1977, pp. 57-8.
4. Gokhale, Namita, *Shakuntala: The Play of Memory*, Delhi: Penguin Viking; 2005, p.48.
5. Seema Malik, "Crossing Patriarchal Threshold: Glimpses of the Incipient New Woman in Manju Kapur's Difficult Daughters", in *Indian Writing in English*, Rajul Bhardwaj, ed., Jaipur: Rawat, 2002, p. 171.
6. Manju Kapur, *A Married Woman*, Delhi: IndiaInk, 2003, p. 132.
7. Sahgal, Nayantara, "Woman's Liberation – The Indian Way"', *Sunday Standard*, 21 March, 1971.

13

Indian English Short Stories: A Comparative Study

—Aju Mukhopadhyay

Indian English Fiction

Of the fiction writers in Indian English, Raja Rao, Mulk Raj Anand and R.K. Narayan were the pioneers. Though Indian writers writing in English are scattered throughout the globe, their mental makeup and thought process are Indian.

Neel Mukherjee, fiction writer settled in London, chose to settle abroad. He feels that "Nostalgia, which is nothing more than a spurious, confected sentimentality, has ruined the migrant novel" [1] (Interview). He is more attracted to miscegenation of cultures than harmony. This is something which regularly happens with the second generation migrants. This is one aspect of their life.

To writers of Indian origin India is a subject; the theme they regularly utilise. Nostalgia they will have which is only natural but sometimes it is more than an emotion. Besides this, for them who are settled abroad writing as such has certain advantages over their counterparts living in India. Besides their stay in a foreign country their attitudinal expression also counts. Often their creations are mixed product.

Tabish Khaire, in a write up in *The Hindu* opines, mentioning such writers as Salman Rushdie, V.S.Naipaul, Hari Kunzru and Zadic Smith, that "They are the mirror images that make the liberal West feel comfortable with itself, because it feels that in gazing on them (and their works) it is reading and championing the Other."

He further mentions, "But unfortunately even an Indian who writes about India in English is not likely to be made visible by agents, clubs and book chains in the West: she has to write about India in certain approved ways, ways that very often depend on a celebration of the 'multicultural' West either as actual presence or enabling possibility." [2]

India bashing is an approved way, as we have seen in the Booker or Oscar ways of selection recently. Agents may take up such cases on special considerations.

As their pioneer, we may perhaps add the name of another veteran writer settled in England, Nirod C. Chaudhury. And then there is the publicity hype by the media to make men mad, to make one the celebrity. With discerning readers the scenario could be different. In their absence publicity is the only judge as in political field.

With this background of Indian English literature, Emigrant literature in particular, we discuss below four bunches of short stories by four writers, three of whom are settled in the West; one of them visited the countries referred but came back to settle in the capital of India. Her stories with Indian characters take place abroad, as if written from an emigrant status.

Jhumpa Lahiri: Bengali Indian writer, settled in America.

"I think that for immigrants, the challenges of exile, the loneliness, the constant sense of alienation, the knowledge of and longing for a lost world, are more explicit and distressing than for their children. On the other hand, the problem for the children of immigrants- those with strong ties to their country of origin- is that they feel neither one thing nor the other. This has been my experience...." Jhumpa Lahiri said in an interview. (Jhumpa Lahiri on her Debut Novel. An Interview with the author. A Houghton Mifflin Company Release; as reproduced by www.Hinduism.about.com)

In tune with this the critics have found a thread running through Jhumpa's stories—an experience of being foreign. She has written two books of short stories so far. Except two all other stories in *Interpreter of Maladies* are based on America, involving Indians who try to settle in a foreign land.

"Sexy" is a story of corporeal love between Miranda, an American and Dev, a Bengali married man. Inside the Mapparium, at the Christian Science Centre, Dev whispered back to Miranda, "You're sexy" (p.91), in response to her "Hi!" She relished it then but later in a tale-tell situation a small boy **tells** Miranda, "You're sexy" and in reply to "What did you say?" he repeated, "You're sexy." (p.107)

Hearing through the conversation between his parents he learnt as much a child can, as to what transpired between his father and the lady with whom he settled, leaving his mother for good. Being vigorously pursued by Miranda to explain his assertion, the boy said, cupping his hands around his mouth, "It means loving someone you don't know." (p.107)

This worked. She realized that there was no point dragging it on.

In "When Mr. Pirzada came to Dine" as in most other stories, Lilia's parents loved to mix with Indians, specially Bengalis, in a foreign situation. They found out the name of Mr. Pirzada, a resident within their compound, from a telephone directory and called him to host him daily, almost throughout his stay there. There was no problem that he was a Muslim from East Pakistan, in revolt against the Government there, so long as he remained a Bengali. They ate the same mango pickles, fish and rice with hands, gossiped over the tea cups which is real adda and had almost the same habits of walking bare foot or with flipflops in the rooms. He was invited to dinner every night and the ten year old Lilia, child of the hosts, would observe him eating and gossiping with her parents up to late evenings, sometimes up to midnight when she slept.

It is a brief eventful story involving families across the seas.

In "The Third and Final Continent" the narrator and his wife became veterans in American culture but they always renewed their love for the life they left behind. When their son became a Harvard University student, the father tells, "We drive to Cambridge to visit him, or bring him home for a weekend, so that he can eat rice with us with his hands, and speak in Bengali, things we sometimes worry he will no longer do after we die." (p.197)

In "Mrs. Sen's" Jhumpa has shown that most of the immigrant wives accompanying their husbands to America feel everything about them foreign, feel lonely and helpless, fish out of water at the beginning. Some of them struggle all the remaining years trying to fit themselves in their surroundings as did Mrs. Sen, a typical representative of such women, who accompanied her professor husband to New England and took up the job of babysitter of an 11-year-old boy.

She wears sari elaborately, vermilion powder marks the parting of her hair and she wears flipflops as does her husband and exerts herself too much to secure fish daily. Frankly she asks, "Eliot, if I began screaming right now at the top of my lungs, would someone come?" At home in India, she explains, "Just raise your voice a bit or express grief or joy of any kind, and one whole neighbourhood and half of another has come to share the news, to help with arrangements." (p.116)

"A Temporary Matter" is about the separation of a young couple because of the still-birth of their first child. Little unusual though, the story has progressed step by step, confirming their parting at last like a plaintive song. It is very touchy.

Shoba and Shukumar (Usually Shobha and Sukumar in Bangla), the young second generation Bengali couple, settled and dated in America before their marriage. They were habituated to American ways of life.

Finally a question hangs in the air: If for the cause of not giving birth to a child, specially male child, the husband remarries or rejects his housewife, as happened in India some years ago, would the people not blame him now for such an act of cruelty? But here in a different cultural milieu it happened the other way; the earning wife separates herself from the househusband who still is a student, mainly for the still-birth of their first child.

In *Unaccustomed Earth*, the second book of her short stories, immigrants continue to occupy the pages of her book.

The forces of globalization have shifted more Indian intellectuals- professors, students and professionals as in her stories- across the countries. Sense of alienation and rootlessness has spread more. All the eight stories here have North America as the essential place of enactment of the dramas of life. Disease and death, frustration and desolation have occupied more space. Cultural dissonances too have become more prominent. A sense of pessimism prevails in most of these stories for which critics have linked her work to Hawthorne and J.D. Salinger, fellow New England writers.

In "A Choice of Accommodations", Amit Sarkar studied in America and after some other affairs settled with Megan, an American bride.

"His daughters looked nothing like him, nothing like his family"—he repines and regrets that his parents had passed down nothing physically to his children. Both Maya and Monika had inherited Megan's colouring without a trace of Amit's deeply tan skin and black eyes, so that apart from their vaguely Indian names they appeared fully American.

"'Are they yours?'—people sometimes asked when he was alone with them, in stores, or at the playground in the park." (p.94)

"Only Goodness" is a story of parents settled in Penn, America and their children—a daughter and her younger brother—grown up there from their childhood. It tells that when middle class people go there, while their habits remain almost the same, socially or otherwise, their children with new-found freedom and acquired habits and customs prevalent there, which are taboos here, sometimes reach their adulthood like an image of worries and anxieties to their parents.

Rahul, a drunkard with bad habits and thoughts, said, "No one dragged them here, Baba left India to get rich and Ma married him because she had nothing else to do." (p.138)

"She thought of her parents, who had believed their children were destined to succeed, had fumbled when one failed. After everything Rahul had put them through they never renounced him, never banished him. They were incapable of shutting him out." (p.171)

The title of the story is "Hell-Heaven". It is a real love story; love, not only of the Bengalis for Bengali culture, Bangla language and for each other as other communities too usually feel the same way, but unexpected, shameless and triangular love between men and women. Bengali woman's love for cooking and serving, sitting and eating together, are often described in detail in Jhumpa Lahiri's stories, as here.

Pranab Chakraborty, a brilliant student, was gasping for proper food and company. Desperately at last he found out a suitable family; Aparna, a married woman, her husband and their daughter, Sudha. He became almost their family member. Though he never felt as such, Aparna was head over heal in love with him. "It is clear to me now that my mother was in love with him," the daughter said long after their hobnobbing was over. (p.67)

When afterwards Pranab was in love with Deborah, Aparna became jealous, a crestfallen woman. That Deborah became so jealous of her was known later by the former's confession. There was enough clashes of ideas and customs, surfaced between the two communities during the marriage ceremony. After years he broke with her, in love with a married Bengali woman resulting in the break up of both the families. But Sudha grew up to settle with an American, though not in marriage, after series of dating with others as it is their wont in the West. "My mother and I had also made peace; she had accepted the fact that I was not only her daughter but a child of America as well." (pp.81-82)

Pennsylvania, America, is the scene of "Unaccustomed Earth", the titled story, where the first generation settlers, Ruma and Romi's parents came to strike their roots. Ruma and Romi grew up to adulthood. Romi lived separately without almost any connection with his parents. Ruma settled with her husband at Seattle. After the expiry of their mother, her father sold their spacious house carrying the nitty-gritty of their memories and shifted to a small apartment. He took to travelling places in Europe. Eventually he was much drawn towards Mrs. Meenakshi Bagchi, a Bengali widow and a fellow traveller. With her he would travel again in the next trip.

"Once in a Lifetime" is told by Hema in the first person and "Year's End" is told by Kaushik in like manner. "Going Ashore" is the third story linking the lives of Kaushik and Hema, their parents and friends, told by the narrator but the closing chapter is reminisced by Hema again. The three stories are independent but linked too, carrying Hema and Kaushik from their childhood to their adult years. It seems to be the best creation of Jhumpa Lahiri, so far.

In the first story Kaushik and Hema first meet in a farewell party thrown by Hema's parents, given to Dr. Chaudhury and his wife, Parul with their son, Kaushik, who after years' stay at Cambridge, were leaving for their native place, Calcutta, in 1974. Hema was six and Kaushik nine years old then. After seven years they came back to the house of Hema's parents at Boston to live for sometime. It was the time when love first sprouted in Hema but Kaushik did not pay much attention. Then Kaushik's mother died.

"Year's End" begins with, "I didn't attend my father's wedding." (p.252)

When Kaushik was in the final year, his father visited Calcutta and married Chitra, a widow with two teenager daughters. He utterly disliked his new mother. Almost without notice he left driving in his car to the north almost hitting Canada, all by the unforgiving sea route in desperation and depression. His father moved to Boston.

"There were other Bengalis nearby and an Indian grocery in the town, things that were more important to Chitra than the proximity of the ocean and Modernist architecture had been for my mother. "(p.292) Kaushik recorded.

"Going Ashore" is the end piece of the trio. After many vicissitudes of life, after mixing with many men and women intimately they met by chance in Rome. They loved each other hungrily, living together for some days. But after a few days they departed out of pride and frustration with life, not being able to surmount all the obstacles on their way.

Susan Visvanathan, a Malayalee Indian and a University teacher, has settled in New Delhi.

She has written novels and short fictions. There are a bunch of linked immigrant stories in her *Something Barely Remembered*.

Remembering her childhood days the story teller tells us:

> I grew up by the river Pamba. It was broad and still, and its face was different from morning to evening. Kingfishers flew low across, their wings taking on the colours of sky, light and water. Across, on the other side were the green fields of paddy. And at the edge of the river were the swaying reed-like silhouettes of sugar-cane which reflected themselves dark and ominous in the water. ("Lukose's Church"; p.10)

> So I never went back. Sometimes in the dark green Roman street, ancient cobbles under my feet, I would think of the old house where I grew up. There were children, frogs, spiders, crows in the backyard, dark recesses, mangoes ripening in hay, and hens laying eggs in a chest of rice. ('River and Sea'; p.25)

Once when she was in Casablanca, a foreign place where it is not safe for woman to stray on the roads or to mix up with unknown face. But she ignored her husband and was allured by a pony-tailed girl of 13 to ride to the sea on her two-wheeler. Soon she was driven away from the beach road to the crowded city and then to the lonely highway. A boy warned her, "Don't go". Suddenly the eyes of the 13-year-old seemed to be of a hardened mercenary that could never have tasted a childhood. She asked her to stop but was being driven in maddening speed. And then suddenly a devil's strength visited her.

> I put my feet on the tarmac and dragged. I dragged with all the weight that I was capable and I was strong. All the brown unpolished rice, the different kinds of bananas, some a foot long which grew in father's yard, those flat white fish we ate at every meal, the raw green mangoes, those yellow ones with fibrous stones, those jackfruits with drunken smell about them which attracted tiny honey-

> bees, those sweet ant-run coconuts had given me strength which didn't show. (p.113)

And the mercenary kidnapper had to stop and she began abusing the stranger. But she walked and came back to the hotel in a taxi where lived her husband. ("Kidnappped in Casablanca")

Eli was in US for some research work after moving places on some errands. There she suddenly met Karan, her girlhood friend and fellow student. After some talks she asked if he was married and Karan showed her the picture of his American wife and children. In reply to "I missed you" he said, "You should have written." They met once again, Karen with family, but Eli did not accept their invitation, telling that she would move the next day. "Give me a hug", she said when alone with him, and Karan gave it but "It was so American, so casual and innocent, that I had to hold him."(pp.28-29)

With a sigh she was on her own again. Sometime after she remembered that she would be back to US in the fall for a teaching fellowship. "But meanwhile I would accept Benjamin's offer of marriage. I would go back to the old cardamom estate, and to my father's brother who would ask for Benjamin on my family's behalf, for me. Ben had waited too long." (p.31)

But alas, here too she heard that Benjamin had married last summer. "Oh hell!" She said and was too much disliked by her uncle for she did not write any card in the meantime.

> Just look at you. Dressed like a man. Pants. Even a belt. And your buttocks showing. Can't you pull out your shirt at least. And lipstick. Someone will think you've gone mad. (p.32)

Disappointed, heart-broken, dejected, she decided to leave forthwith for her foreign home, leaving her inherited estate. ("Waiting")

Here we remember a story by Rabindranath Tagore who was not only a poet but a good story writer too.

The narrator of the story, the protagonist and his companion, Surobala, were childhood friends. He had full command over her as he overheard his and Surobala's parents agreeing to marry them. Surobala became his obedient companion. As he came of age, he left for Calcutta for further studies and there he became one of the assistants of the freedom fighters, helping them and dreaming to be one of Garibaldi or Gladstone in future. His patriotism was so intense that he did not care to lend his ear when he heard that Surobala was married off to the village lawyer.

It so happened that he finally became a second teacher of a village school, living in a hut adjacent to the school, a part of the school building, and the husband of Surobala too came there with her to live as a Government pleader. Once there was a tremendous storm and tide. The sea roared and the river was swollen. Water was flooding every place except a small area near the school pond. For saving his life the teacher at night fled to that elevated earth and saw that Surobala too had come there to save herself. The pleader was out on business for a few days. They stood there for the whole night, sleepless, side by side, till the water did recede, remembering their childhood love but none could speak on any plea. At the end of the night the water abated and they left for their respective homes ("One Night").

This was one night but a fatal night. She did wait but her hero did not act at the right time like Eli, who forgot to contact anybody at the right time as she was in the heat of her studies and career. While we are busy doing things of our liking, time does not wait for us. The thing we postponed never happens again.

Bharati Mukherjee, a Bengali Indian settled in USA

Born and brought up in Calcutta, India, and further educated in the United States, she has settled there for long. Basically an academician and fiction writer, she had another collection of short stories titled *Darkness*, before *The Middleman and other Stories*. Both the books of short stories have been held in high esteem and prized in America. She has been held to be one of the most exciting writers of the world.

There are 11 short stories in *The Middleman and Other Stories*. Taking the book as a whole we find that it is an abnormal world of violence, sex, treachery and debauchery. No finer air of peace and tranquillity, of happy family life is found here. It is the underworld of the United States. We astonish how she has acquired mastery over the routine happenings of this world, not visible before the unaccustomed eyes. As an expert story teller she at once takes us in the middle of happenings and makes us see it in detail. Involved as we are as readers, we cannot come out of it without sharing the grief and sorrow, joy and petty happiness of the characters but we breathe a sigh of relief when we come out of it when the story ends.

"A Wife's Story" is the unfaithfulness of a Gujarati wife who lives in US for some years for study but defiles her married life by mixing with other men lecherously. Though the husband tells a lie about his position in his factory, it does not affect their livelihood. Finally he comes to US to be wired to be back for a severe labour trouble in his factory in India. In a few days the husband and wife would depart. The wife thinks:

> In ten days he has been here he has learnt American rites: deodorants, fragrances.... Tonight I should make up to him for my years away, the gutted trucks, the degree I'll never use in India. I want to pretend with him that nothing has changed.
>
> In the mirror.... I watch my naked body turn.... I stand here shameless, in ways he has never seen me. I am free, afloat, watching somebody else. (p.40)

In "Loose Ends" we find "Acapulco, Trijuana, Freeport, Miami— it doesn't matter where the pimping happens....

> It's life in the procurement belt, between those lines of tropical latitudes, where the world shops for its illicit goods and dump its surplus parts, where it prefers to fight its wars, and once you have settled into its give and take, you find it's impossible to live anywhere else. (p.50)

In "Orbiting" we find Renata, the daughter of parents who assist her live better, the daughter who had contacts with more than one man, has recently come in contact with an Afghan. She tells herself:

> He's ashamed that he comes from a culture of pain.... Ro's my chance to heal the world. I shall teach him how to walk like an American, how to dress like Brent but better, how to fill up a room as Dad does instead of melting and blending but sticking out in the Afghan way." (pp. 74-75)

In "The Tenant" wc find some names familiar with the writer's old world in Calcutta, India. But here Maya, the heroine from a respectable family, acts utter shamelessly, full of lustfulness, devoid of ethics and respectability though she, a doctorate, teaches comparative literature at the University of Northern IOWA. She perhaps covers up by being an India-basher: "All Indian men are wife beaters," Maya says.... "That's why I married an American." (p.99)

> Maya is known for her nasty, ironic one-liners. It has taken her friends weeks to overlook her malicious, un-American pleasure in other's misfortunes. Maya would like to finish Dr. Chatterjee off quickly. He is pompous; he is reactionary; he wants to live and work in America but give back nothing except taxes. The confused world of the immigrant- the lostness that Maya and Poltoo feel- that's what Dr. Chatterjee wants to avoid. She hates him. But. (p.106)

In an Indian newspaper she reads the news that a neo-Buddhist, a convert from an untouchable caste was stoned. While the editorial of the paper explains that the stoning was for several other reasons than caste, she firmly believes that the boy was stoned for his caste.

Finally she lives with an armless man, Fred, who is the owner of the building she has rented last as a tenant. He helps her by all means. She feels charmed that she has slept with all including an armless man. Now she is happy but she feels grieved when often Fred jokes that two wounded people live together. "It will shock her, this assumed equivalence with a man so strikingly deficient. She knows she is strange, and lonely, but being Indian is not the same, she would have thought, as being a freak." (p.112)

Does she want to say that India and a freak are falsely true? Is it a satire or an oxymoron?

But sometimes truth comes out. "Fathering" is a story that tells about the devastation carried out by soldiers in Vietnam. Sometimes soldiers marry some of the victims. In Saigon the man married a local and had two children. Now after ten years, back in his own country, he lives with another woman but he has affection for his sick children by his first wife though the present one is not at all sympathetic to them.

When the doctor tries to forcibly inject the teenager, she cries in desperation:

> "Get the hell out, you bastard!.... When they shoot my grandma, you think pills do her any good? You Yankees, please go home." She looks straight at me (the father). "Scram, Yankee bastard!" (p.124)

"Jasmine" is the story of Jasmine, an ambitious girl from Trinidad, who has come to America illegally to try her luck. She finds a lover in Bill at Ann Arbor when Bill's wife was not there. It was a quick passion. When Bill said that she was the flower of Trinidad, she corrected him: "Flower of Ann Arbor," she said, "Not Trinidad."

> She felt so good that she was dizzy.... She was a bright, pretty girl with no visa, no papers, and no birth certificate. No nothing other than what she wanted to invent and tell. She was a girl rushing wildly into the future. (p.138)

"Danny's Girls" is a tale of brothel business shared between Danny Sahib who once was Dinesh and Aunt Lini, the widow of a Gujarati gentleman, who "could turn a thousand dollars while frying up a bhaji".

> Aunt Lini's role was to warehouse the merchandise, as she called the girls, that couldn't be delivered to its American destination (most of those American fiances had faces a

> fly wouldn't buzz). Aunt Lini had spare rooms she could turn into an informal S.R.O. hotel. She called the rooms her 'pet shop' and she thought of the girls as puppies in the window. (p.143)

They came mostly from India and neighbouring areas. Episodes in Hindi cinema pleased the narrator of the story who would be pleased seeing the hero and heroine married without any caste barrier:

> "To that background I added a certain American equality. I grew up hating rich people, especially rich Indian immigrants who didn't have the problems of Uganda and useless father, but otherwise were no better than I." (p.146)

Kunal Basu, a Bengali Indian and university teacher, has settled in England.

Kunal Basu is another emigrant writer, living in England. He wrote three experimental, adventurous and speculative novels; *Racist*, *The Miniaturist* and *The Opium Clerk*, prior to the publication of the collection of his 12 short stories, titled *Japanese Wife*.

The subjects of the stories and the way of presenting them are somewhat outlandish and exotic, sometimes they are on the edge of fantasy. The author is said to have travelled well in various countries. His stories happen at various places and countries of the globe, including India. Each story begins with an element of stunt.

In the "Japanese Wife" the husband and wife marry through the channel of pen friendship but do not deeply feel the need to meet physically. Of the meeting, "They had toyed with the idea, then postponed it like a vacation." (p.8)

After 20 years of their married life, little they know of each other's country. But when the husband suddenly dies of fever, the wife comes instantly with a tonsured head wearing a Hindu widow's dress to begin to live the post-married life in India.

In "Grateful Ganga" the man meets a woman who just attained widowhood, in a plane and within minutes hug each other very passionately. Her husband never visited India but wished before his death that his ashes be strewn over the Ganges only because he believed that Ganga was "World's expressway to the stars." (p.20)

His wife begins to live with the man she boarded the plane, who offers her shelter in Delhi until she scatters the ashes in Ganga. The widow, "Evenly felt comforted, among strange people in a strange city"(p.22). She feels no urge to go until she is forced to. She feels a romantic charm for Yoginder Singh, her host, to such an extent that she is almost driven out of the house by the estranged wife of Yoginder.

"Tiger! Tiger!"—often borrowed from William Blake—is a story set on Sundarbans in India. Here the writer seems to know his place better with some details like the river Matla and weaves a delicate love story between rival parties. The wife of the rival, Anwar, a notorious poacher, falls in love with the forest officer but nothing happens even after intimate mixing to the forest officer or the wife as she is barren. Finally the forest officer is killed by a tigress which allures him, as if wearing the striped yellow and black sari of Amina, his lover and wife of the poacher, hiding behind a tree in a fierce field where bullets are exchanged between the poachers and the Forest staff. The tigress runs, instead of towards the man as usual, towards the opposite direction in an opening to allure her lover to chase and catch her. Instead of her the hero catches the tigress to be mauled and killed. Rowena, an American research student, is introduced as was Piya Roy introduced in Amitav Ghosh's *Hungry Tide*. She lives like locals and interferes in many forest affairs without fear. She too does not feel any discomfort in a foreign remote area, quite away from the city life.

"Lenin's Café" is about gathering and gossiping of Marxists and others at Zurich. It begins thus: "I met my father eleven years after his death, in Zurich at the Limmatquai where swans come to feed. After the first wave of disbelief, he said, 'Let's go to Lenin's Cafe.' "(p.37)

The story of "The Last Dalang" takes place in Indonesia and that of "The Pearlfisher", mainly in Chad. Actions in other stories too take place at different foreign countries and India.

"The Pearlfisher" begins thus, "During her birth, Mouttou Lachemy was half inside her mother's womb with only her head sticking out for one and a half days. The doctor had wanted to cut her up and her father had agreed, but God saved her and she came out." (p.191)

It is the story of a French soldier, Mouttou Sitaramane, native of Pondicherry, who arrived in Chad and within a short while married an Arab widow, Bouchara Adoum. After three years when Chad gained freedom from the French he was moved to other African countries and finally returned to India. In India he already had a wife and a son. Now his granddaughter writes from Africa to an editorial assistant at their Delhi office from time to time, requesting to find out Sitaramane and convey the news of his granddaughter. Though the letters do not seem to have been replied, though the staff is under no obligation to keep the request and such letters usually go unattended in newspaper offices, the staff undertake the journey to Pondicherry and finally with the help of some people and children find a hut on the shore where they say that Sitaramane had lived but recently died. They get no other information. Though the soldier moved to different countries, there is no mention of any cultural mix except the marriage and some trouble at the hands of the local people for saving a drowning man who he should not have saved as they believed that fate should be allowed to play its game. The drowning man's fate was to get drowned, they thought.

The Comparison

The nice ways of telling tales with all the details by Jhumpa Lahiri does not leave any scope for ambiguity. She is a true realist, writing without resorting to secondary ways of myth or symbol in fiction, ways of the one who usually does not know the details of the path he or she treads. Many of the characters in her stories mix up or marry within their community. They come back to that even after some misadventures somewhere else. Lahiri is nostalgic about the past and it seems that she strongly wishes to go back to that origin, in this life or later, for her unshakeable love for it. Maybe she is a harmonist rather than a miscegenist though she has undergone miscegenation and her subject is that.

In Jhumpa Lahiri we find an indomitable love for the country, heritage and family she was born in. She upholds it at any cost. She never belittles them. As a storyteller she delineates the true position of Americans and Indians in society, bringing out their respective drawback and qualities. Her broad areas of writing—cultural mix and clash among ethnic Bengali Indians and Americans—is a very interesting area of learning and study of people, race and culture, without any bias. It creates further understanding among the people leading towards peace.

Wherever Susan Visvanathan moves on earth she feels nostalgic about the tiny coastal village Puthenkavu, by the side or river Pamba in Kerala, a name long obliterated from the earth. Wherever the incidents of the stories take place, told in the first person, they are eventually linked up with the stories of her childhood days. Susan has affinity with Jhumpa. Both are surely nostalgic, feels pride of their respective places in India and move in places with their characters keeping a part of their heart in their native village or town in India.

Bharati Mukherjee's stories dazzle, as it has been claimed, but in another way. And above all, we find a special way of disposition of her thoughts and ideas about particular culture in her host country, in almost all her stories. She moves through the entrails of the lower world, the underground life of America. In doing it she brings in characters from different countries who feel grateful to her host country. In many stories Indians are neglected or ridiculed. The culture of her host country is upheld at the cost of India. "The Tenant" is the acme of her creation in that way, in the book under study. Hate comes out of Maya for India in the process of her lustfulness. We feel sorry for such an advantageable attitude at the cost of one' motherland. In contrast to the two former Indian writers, this too is a way of expression from the powerful pen of another Indian writer.

Kunal Basu's stories seem to lack reasonable substance due to absence of concrete description of the land and characters.

In "Japanese Wife" we find some touch of the Delta of Sundarbans but too sketchily. The development of the story of teacher's love for the widow could take us to an interesting man-woman relationship but it does not take any concrete shape and his meeting with the real wife in Japan never takes place. In "Tiger! Tiger!" human relationship is nicely weaved but the jungle position remains unconvincing. Though the characters of his stories are at some cultural cross roads, there is no effort to present Indian culture vividly. Nor is there any conscious effort to paint a superior culture of any foreign countries mentioned. Though nationals of various countries are involved in the making of his stories, there is hardly any effort to study the effect of one culture upon another; specially the position of Indians living abroad. It is a group of stories of adventure and imagination, of fancy and dream. They have their own charms, have different characters but lies apart from our expectation of touching the orbit of the foregoing stories. It has been included as a variety of contemporary Indian English fiction.

References

1. *The Hindu* dated 6.9.09
2. *The Hindu* dated 6.9.09

Work Cited

Basu Kunal. *The Japanese Wife*. New Delhi; HarperCollins India. 2008

Lahiri Jhumpa. *Interpreter of Maladies*. New Delhi; HarperCollins India. 2001

_____. *Unaccustomed Earth*. New York, USA; Alfred A. Knopf. 2008

Mukherjee Bharati. *Middleman and Other Stories*. New Delhi; Penguin Book India Ltd. 1990

Visvanathan Susan. *Something Barely Remembered*.

14

Anthologies of Indian English Short Story—A Survey

—M.G. Hegde

Of the different forms literary criticism can take, anthology is also one. Through selection and exclusion, through editorial preferences in presenting the selected writings in a specific order, through an introduction and annotated notes, as well as through, if indirectly, carrying on a dialogue with past anthologies, it plays the role of charting out/redrawing a literary map. A selected piece will have its own semantic content, carry the signature of its author and reflects the social, political and cultural forces of its age. But when it appears along with other writings selected on a particular agenda, and incorporated into a particular design, a change is seen in its mode of operation.

For instance, such writings in an anthology, throwing light on one another, invariably make some compromises in terms of their quality and in this process their semantic ambiance may get expanded or become narrower. It is here that the signature of the anthologist gets subtly inscribed. Further an anthologist invariably decides on the issues like the 'significance'/'representative-ness' of an author/ a text and contributes to the formation of a literary canon. The possibility of the map charted out by an anthology being accepted depends on how powerfully influential it is—which depends on the standing of its editor, the quality of the anthology, the status of its publisher and his marketing ability, etc.

Anthologies, attracting as they do both the common and the purely academic markets, have a greater commercial viability. In India in particular, owing mainly to the economics of book trade, anthologies, more than poetry or story collections, reach a wider spectrum of readers. Getting prescribed as text books they get discussed in the academic circles and lead to formation of critical opinion. From this viewpoint anthology becomes the most powerful of critical forms. Also, the literary politics it manages is prodigious. For instance, all the anthologies of Indian English Poetry which came out in the 1970s labelled all poetry from Derozio to Aurobindo as 'Romantic', investing the term with all its negative connotations and ignoring it totally, successfully convinced readers for nearly three decades that the modernist poetry of Ezekiel and his contemporaries alone is true poetry. It is this very attitude that, in a different context, Mokashi–Punekar called 'exclusionist tyranny' of modernism. However, the possibility of an anthology becoming 'exclusionist' is more only when it appears at a time of transition of literary sensibilities, when a new poetics is being formed or is to be promoted, motivated by varied feelings of concern, pressure and enthusiasm to escape the existing canon and make literary tradition acquire a new shape through re-affiliations. Also, in such periods of transition, more than one anthology of the same type normally come out. Thus an abundance of anthologies do become an index of a change in basic literary sensibility.

Before reviewing Indian English Short Story (hereafter IESS) anthologies against this background it would be necessary to have a comprehensive view of the history of such anthologies in India. Even before exclusive IESS anthologies were published, IESS had appeared in Indian short story anthologies. IESS found place in such an anthology for the first time in the 1940s. In earlier anthologies we find only Anglo–Indian short stories along with stories from the West and all these anthologies were meant only to serve as textbooks in educational institutions. Among the earliest anthologies *Modern Stories from East and West* could be taken as representative of such anthologies. Published in 1929 by the Calcutta branch of Macmillan, this was edited by R.K. Lagu. Tagore is the only Indian to figure in this anthology, while the others, Kipling, Steel and Bain are Anglo-Indians. These four represent the 'East' of the title while the 'West' is represented by Meredith, Gaskell, Doyle, Arnold Bennet and H.G. Wells who are British, and Tolstoy, the only non-British writer. It is not surprising that the anthologies of the colonial phase show a preference to the West.[1] But what is to be noted here is that at the back of this anthology we have an equation that the West means England. That a similar kind of faulty equation accepted at the beginning of the century prevailed at the close of the century too, we shall consider later. Suffice it to remember here that in this anthology Anglo-Indian writers represent India and the East, with Tagore being the lone Indian finding a place in it, and that the reading of our story writers was ineluctably England–centred.

As mentioned already, when in the 40s exclusive Indian short story anthologies (i.e. anthologies of stories translated from Indian languages) began to be published, the IESS began to get included in them. The understanding behind putting together translations of Indian stories in English and stories originally written in English was that even the IESS belong to the modern Indian story tradition.[2] The inclusion of IESS in Indian story anthologies signify that Indian English literature was gradually gaining official recognition. This is substantiated by the fact that around the same time, in 1960, the Sahitya Akademi began to consider literary works in Indian English for its annual award. A comprehensive view of Indian short story anthologies helps us easily to trace how Indian English literature, which acquired official recognition by the 1960s, grew from strength to strength.

In the anthologies of the 40s and 50s (like *Indian Short Stories* edited by Anand, another of the same title edited by Manmohan Saxena, and *Contemporary Indian Short Stories* series of the Sahitya Akademi) only Anand and Bhattacharya are Indian English writers. In anthologies which came after these we find R.K. Narayan and a little later Raja Rao and Khushwant Singh being included. And from this point on, the anthologists began weighting their collection in favour of fiction originally written in English. The most well known and representative of anthologies of this period is *Stories from India* edited by K. Natwar Singh, published around the middle of the 1960s. This has one writer each representing Hindi, Urdu, Bengali, Marathi, Telagu, Tamil and Malayalam while there are as many as five IESS writers. In the representative collection of the 1970s, *Modern Indian Short Stories* edited by Suresh Kohli for the OUP, we have ten stories translated from Indian languages into English, six transcreations and eight Indian English short stories. The process of IESS getting more and more representation in anthologies, which began in the 1940s completed in the 1980s. *Modern Indian Fiction* (Cowasjee and Shahane, 1981), *Modern Indian Short Stories* (Cowasjee and Shiv Kumar, 1982) and *In Other Words: New Writings by Indian Women* (1992) are anthologies which exclusively have stories by Indian English writers. Moreover, the "Indian" in their titles are, undoubtedly, equated with "Indian English". The logical end of this process is the anthology, *The Vintage Book of Indian Writing: 1947-1997* [3] edited by Salman Rushdie and Elizabeth West and Rushdie's claim in notorious forward to it:

> This is it: the prose writing—both fiction and non-fiction —created in this period by Indian writers *writing in English*, is proving to be a stronger and more important body of work than most of what has been produced in the 16 'official languages' of India, the so called 'vernacular languages', during the same time; and, indeed, this new, and still burgeoning, 'Indo-Anglian' literature represents perhaps *the most valuable contribution India has yet made to the world of books.* (p. x)

A review thus of IESS anthologies shows that Indian English literature, even when it had no official recognition, grew in influence gradually, and by the end of the twentieth century could establish its hegemony completely, and create an illusion that this marginally minor literature in the country represented the whole of Indian literature. In other words, Rushdie is only the logical conclusion of a historical process, and his anthology, or the claim he makes in it, does not, as his intolerant detractors believe, express his whimsicality. That Rushdie was not alone in this attitude is proved by over half-a-dozen anthologies of the 80s and 90s.

Among several reasons which enabled IESS in particular and Indian English Literature in general to establish their hegemony is the difficulty in obtaining good translations of stories from Indian languages. This is the immediate reason that all the anthologists including Rushdie offer. It is true that this deficiency was there till the 80s. For instance, the periodical *Thought* –generally kinder to translations and favoured them to the original stories in English – could publish over a period of 17 years, between 1945 and 1965, only 150 stories in translation as against 550 original stories in English. Also when all these stories were considered again for inclusion in the anthology *Call It a Day*, the editors felt that "compared with the material in English, many of the translations were wanting in many ways". But if one looks at the *Katha Prize Stories* series, Katha's other collections of translated stories, the two volumes of *Woman Writing in India* edited by Susie Tharu and K. Lalita, *Truth Tales* published by Kali for Women, etc. which appeared in the 90s, it becomes clear that the prominence acquired by IESS in the anthologies which appeared after the 1980s was not so much because of the availability of good translations but because of the cultural hegemony and of literary politics of Indian English Literature.

Against the background of the history of short story anthologies as we have noticed, if we consider those anthologies which clearly declare themselves as IESS anthologies, IESS anthologies which have come out purporting to be Indian short story anthologies, and those where half or more than half the stories are IESS as Indian English Short Story Anthologies, we may broadly divide them[4] into two groups:

i. Anthologies with a limited aim

ii. Representative and ambitious anthologies.

Of the anthologies with a limited aim, several sub-types could be identified. One of them is specifically to encourage new talent, as, for instance, the *Writers Workshop Anthology* (1967). The only criterion for the inclusion of all the eight short story writers in it is that none of them had published a collection of their own. Such anthologies encouraging budding writers are of course welcome. In fact, three of the writers appearing in the Writers Workshop anthology, Bharati Mukherjee, Melwani and Bunny Reuben, later published their own short story collections. Reuben and Melwani found a place in M.K. Naik's representative anthology and Bharati Mukherjee won international recognition. Some of the other anthologies which have been published specifically to introduce new writers are Sterling News Papers' series of new Indian fiction titled *Vox*, *I'm not Like That* and *Mosaic* of the British Council and *Many Rooms, Many Voices* of Katha Lok.

Another type of the anthology with a limited purpose is that which puts together select stories from the issues of a particular periodical. The earliest of these is the already mentioned *Call it a Day*, which is a selection of 29 stories from out of the 700 which appeared in *Thought* between 1949 (its year of inception) and 1965. Similar such anthologies like—the two volumes of *Namaste Book of Indian Short Stories* (a selection of stories from the annual issues of *Namaste*, the ITC–Welcome Group of Hotels magazine), *Indian Thought—A Miscellany* (containing stories and non-fictional prose selected by R. K. Narayan from the issues of *Indian Thought*), *Stories from India* (stories from out of the 260 stories published in *The Illustrated Weekly of India*, selected by Khushwant Singh and Q. Hyder), *Another India* (carrying stories from Vagartha between 1973 and 1979, selected by Nissim Ezekiel and Meenakshi Mukherjee) and stories from *Savvy* edited by Suresh Kohli—provide an index as to the inclination and attitudes and editorial policies of the periodicals which encouraged IESS writers as well as to the kind of stories which were popular at a given point of time. We can, for instance, observe that at the time when Khushwant Singh edited the *Weekly*, it published generally utterly contrived stories and those which gave to humour and black laughter; *Vagartha* encouraged those which concurred with modernist aesthetics; and *Gentleman* published entirely cosmopolitan, highly experimental avant-garde stories. These anthologies have to be gratefully remembered for extending the life of notable stories which otherwise would have remained buried for ever in the back issues of periodicals.

A third type of anthology concerns itself with stories from Diasporas, like the *Odyssey* edited by Divya Mathur. The only thing that connects the stories here is that they are all written by Indian women writers settled abroad. Similarly, especially abroad since the 80s, anthologies have appeared each putting together stories from Canadian writers of Indian origin, South Asian writers in America, and from writers of Indian origin in countries like Fiji, Africa and Singapore.

The fourth type of anthologies may be termed thematic anthologies. They provide opportunities to explore diverse attitudes towards the same experiences and to contrast formal treatments as well. That the tragedy of partition of the country agitated our writers deeply is evidenced by the maximum number of anthologies which have come out around that theme. The earliest of these is *Writings of India's Partition* edited by Allok Bhalla. The most recent anthologies on this theme have been *When the British Left* and *Orphans of the Storm*. As can be naturally expected, these collections have got together writings from North India. Ruskin Bond's *Indian Ghost Stories* and *Indian Railway Stories*, and Pritish Nandy's *The Vikas Book of Indian Love Stories* are also thematic anthologies. *Encounter* edited by Janaki Ram and Bruce Bennett has stories with the theme of encounter and interaction between diverse cultural backgrounds.

A variation of the thematic anthology is anthologies which focus on ethnic, gender and regional representations. Such anthologies have a clear political agenda and are highly polemic too. For instance, woman centred anthologies and those authored by women have a clear agenda of bringing to the fore women writers ignored by the main-stream, of tracing a history of women writers and establish a tradition, of offering a critique of patriarchal society and its gender discrimination politics and of pointing to the appropriate imaging and representation of woman. It is not accidental that such anthologies began to appear in large number simultaneous with the growth and influence of Women's Movement in India. *Odyssey* (1992), *In Other Words* (1992) and *The Inner Courtyard* (1991) are anthologies of stories by women writers while *Image and Representation* (2000) is an example of an anthology portraying the life of the Indian Muslim life. While the *Odyssey* is confined to women writers from abroad, *In Other Words* brings together stories by women who began writing in the 80s and 90s. *The Inner Courtyard* is a remarkable anthology in several ways. It has six translated stories and eleven writers originally in English. One of the English stories is by a woman of Pakistani origin. Of the remaining ten, four live in India and the other six either in America or in England. The choice has been deliberate—the point is to question the notion of a 'main stream' of women's writing from India. Thus, the anthology, albeit on a smaller scale, picks up a dialogue with the stupendous work of Susie Tharu and K. Lalita.

Anthologies reflecting regional culture have not been many. As early as 1965, Khushwant Singh had made a special compilation of stories written by Punjabis which appeared in the *Illustrated Weekly* (*Land of Five Rivers*, 1965). It has very few stories written originally in English. Some of the IESS anthologies focusing on regional culture are *Modern Goan Short Stories* (1971), *Ferry Crossing* (1998) and *Noon in Calcutta* (1992)

Of the IESS anthologies with a purely academic intent the most representative, and popular as a text book, has been Meenakshi Mukherjee's *Let's Go Home* (1975) which has remained continuously in print for many years. Mukherjee expresses concern in her foreword about how all literature expected to be read by an Indian student of English is "based on another cultural context... fairly remote from the life he leads". This very modern awareness regarding learning of a language has determined the choice of the stories as well as the title of the anthology. All the same, it is debatable as to how far this book contributes to the language teaching programme, for clearly the editor hasn't seriously considered the usage of contemporary English, evidenced by the fact that most of the stories in the book are set in pre-Independent India. Thus the anthology is more helpful in the teaching of literature than of language. From this point of view she has mainly chosen the eminently teachable stories—those with content amenable to sociological or thematic discussion in the class room. She also provides, along with each story, a biographical note on the author, a synopsis of the plot, a glossary explaining difficult words, and a set of questions on the story—often into which salient criticism of the story is woven. Mukherjee's model was followed in several later anthologies like *Lotus Petals* (1981), *A Portrait of India* (1983), *Short Stories* (1983) and *The Raj and After* (1986).

M.K. Naik's *The Indian English Short Story* (1984), Madhusudhan Prasad's *Contemporary Indian English Short Story* (1991), Shiv K. Kumar's anthology of the same title (1993) and the *Best Loved Indian Short Stories of the Century* (1999) are ambitious anthologies aiming to provide stories representative of the IESS in its entirety. Of these the anthologies of Prasad and Kumar are mere compilations without any particular editorial stance. Prasad seems to be content to select a story at random of all celebrated writers. The book exposes a lack of awareness of the short story form on the part of the editor. Shiv Kumar, on the other hand seems to have applied the yardstick of a story being published in a magazine abroad. Consequently, while those who have written only a couple of stories find place in his anthology, well known writers like Shashi Deshpande with several short story collections are left out. A few pages of R.K. Narayan's autobiography had been published under the title 'Green Sari' in the *London Magazine*, without a mention of its form. Shiv Kumar, perhaps even without caring to read it, includes it as a new story by Narayan. And then the *Best Loved Indian Stories of the Century*. How does one ascertain that a story has been 'best loved'? The editors say in their 'Introduction' that they have chosen those which have withstood the test of time. If so, how did Manjula Padmanabhan, Anjana Appachana and Gita Hariharan, who feature in the anthology, face this test? These are the writers of the 1990s. A look at the 'Acknowledgement' reveals that a different criterion other than the declared one has been applied in the choice made: debt is expressed to nine text books and anthologies. Which means that the editors have adopted the easiest way to determine what is 'best loved'. It's for this very reason that stories like 'Who Cares?' and 'Martand' find a place in this anthology. These stories were included in earlier anthologies which came out at a time when not many women wrote stories, perhaps only to see that women are also represented in them. And now they appear again as the 'Best Loved'. M. K. Naik's anthology is the only one which rejects simple criteria like celebrated writers, or contemporary writers, and offers a panorama of the IESS from its hesitant beginnings to 1980. His scholarly introductory essay traces the history of the IESS as well as offers a critique based on insights into the selected stories. It may also be said that through the selected stories, he recounts the story of the IESS.

The quality of the selected stories and significance of their authors in the history of IESS is indisputable. But what might be questioned is whether the anthology is truly representative. For, being an eminent formalist critic, Professor Naik has gone in search of stories which have a psychological drama revealing 'the mind's construction' although he does not say so explicitly. Thus a limitation of the anthology is he sacrifices the element of diversity. We may only say that he has the best stories from a formalist point of view, but not the representative ones. Also, Naik obviously has a project, which could be termed broadly as 'nationalist', of proving that the history of the IESS is inextricably linked with India's political and social history. Naturally he has chosen only those stories which substantiate his thesis and situates them squarely within the framework and rhetoric of emergent Indian nationhood. As a result of this agenda of Dr. Naik with a nationalist and formalist concern, IESS of a distinct type have been brought together and these build up one version of the nation's history. And we will have to take into account the exclusions made by Naik to know what were the formal preoccupations of IESS, to identify the variety in it and listen to the voices of dissent in the history of the nation.

Finally, when we compare all these four anthologies, another interesting factor strikes us. It concerns the canon of IESS. The writers who are common to all these four anthologies are Mulk Raj Anand, R. K. Narayan, Raja Rao, and Khushwant Singh. And those who are in three anthologies are K. A. Abbas,

Anita Desai, Arun Joshi, Manohar Malgonkar and Manoj Das. Thus, there seems to be a unanimity of opinion regarding these ten writers. But all these had consolidated the IESS canon as early as the 1960s. That this canon has been wholly acceptable to the anthologies of the 1980s and 90s and the fact that the stories of all these writers included in them were first published between 1940 and 1960 clearly indicates that these anthologies have ignored the evolution and development of the genre from the point of view of 'form'. In other words, we are yet to have a representative anthology of the IESS tracing the development of its form and content, shape and themetics.

References

1. This is clear in the 'Foreword': "Our students... have to be familiar with the life and manners of Western people."
2. In contrast nearly a dozen anthologies like *The Raj and After* and *Stories from the Raj* edited by Cowasjee consider IESS as continuing the Anglo-Indian story tradition. The same perception is at the back of Ruskin Bond's *The Indian Ghost Stories* and *The Indian Railway Stories* also.
3. Though this anthology has been called *The Book of Indian Writing*, with thirty of the thirty two authors here are Indian English Writers, the anthology may very well be called *The Book of Indian English Literature*; or as there is no poem in this, it could be called *The Book of Indian English Prose*; and all the writings here except four being fiction, it may even be called *The Book of Indian English Fiction* – thus limiting its scope.
4. This division is only for the convenience of evaluation. The possibility of overlapping and border crossing is always there.

Works Cited

Alexander, Cheriyan (2000) *Many Rooms Many Voices*, Bangalore: Katha Lok.

Alter, Stephen & Wimal Dissanayake (1989) *The Penguin Book of Modern Short Story,* New Delhi: Penguin India.

Anand, Mulk Raj (1968) *Experiments: Contemporary Indian Short Stories*, Agra: Karanchalson.

_____. (1968) *Grass Roots: Selected Short Stories,* Agra: Karanchalson.

_____. & Iqbal Singh (1946) *Indian Short Stories*, London: New Indian Pub. Co.

_____ . & S. Balurao, (1986) *Panorama: An Anthology of Modern Indian Short Stories*, New Delhi: Sterling Publishers.

Aziz, Hurjchan (1994) *Her Mother's Ashes and Other Stories by South Asian Women in Canada and the United States,* Toronto: TSAR.

Bhalla, Alok (1994) *Stories About the Partition of India* (3 Vols.) New Delhi: Harper Collins.

Bhushan, V. N. (1945) : *The Earthen Bowl: An Anthology of Short Stories in English by Indian Writers.* Bombay: Padma Pub.

Bond, Ruskin (1994) *The Penguin Book of Indian Railway Stories*, New Delhi: Penguin Books.

_____. (1993) *The Penguin Book of Indian Ghost Stories*, New Delhi: Penguin Books.

British Council Division, Madras (1987) *I'm not Like That and Other Stories*, Hydrabad: Orient Longman.

Balakrishna, A. S. (1984) *The Refugee & Other Stories*, Bombay: Orient Longman.

Butalia, Urvashi & Ritee Menon (1992) *In other words: New writings by Indian women*, New Delhi: Kali for women.

Cowasjee, Saros (1986) *The Raj and After* (Short Stories) Madras: Macmillan.

_____. (1988) *Stories from the Raj: From Kipling to Independence*, New Delhi: Indus.

_____. (1990) *More Stories from the Raj and After: Kipling to the Present Day*, New Delhi: Indus.

_____. & K.S.Duggal (1995) *Orphans of the Storm: Stories on the Partition of India*, New Delhi: UBSPD.

_____. & K.S.Duggal (1987) *When the British Left: Stories on the Partitioning of India*, 1947, New Delhi: Arnold Heinemann.

_____. & V.A.Shahane (1981) *Modern Indian Fiction*, New Delhi: Vikas.

_____. & Shiv K Kumar (1982) *Modern Indian Short Stories*, Delhi: OUP.

Dharmarajan, Geeta (1991-2001) *Katha Prize Stories*, Vols.1-12, New Delhi: Katha Association.

Ezekiel, Nissim & Meenakshi Mukherjee, (1989) *Another India: An Anthology of Contemporary Indian Fiction and poetry.* New Delhi: Penguin Books.

Gabriel, M.C. & Gwen Gabriel, (1968) *Call it a Day—A Selection of Modern Indian Stories*, Delhi: Siddhartha publications Ltd.

Gupta, M.R. (1966) *Home and Abroad: An Anthology of Short Stories*, Allahabad: Indian press.

Gupta, Rukhsana & Rahila Gupta, (1994) *Flaming Sprit: Stories from the Asian Women Writer's Collective,* London: Virago press.

Hagedorn, Jessica, (1993) *Charlie Chan is Dead: An Anthology of Contemporary Asian American Fiction*, New York: Penguin Books.

Hasan, Mushirul & M. Asaduddin, (2000) *Image and Representation: Stories of Muslim Lives in India.* New Delhi: OUP.

Holmstrom, Lakshmi (1991) *The Inner Courtyard: Stories by Indian Women*, New Delhi: Rupa

Janaki Ram, Alur & Bruce Bennet, (1988) *Encounters—Selected Indian and Australian Stories*, Jaipur: Pointer Publishers.

Kakar, Sudhir (1999) *Indian Love Stories*, New Delhi: Roli Books.

Khosla, G.S. (1991) *Punjab Short Stories: An Anthology*, New Delhi: Vikas.

Kohli, Suresh (1974) *Modern Indian short stories—An Anthology*, New Delhi: Arnold- Heinemann.

_____. (1977) *Savy* (Stories by Indian Women Writers), New Delhi: Arnold.

_____. (1983) *More Indian Short Stories*, New Delhi: Arnold Heneimann.

Kumar, C.Ravindranath (1981) *Lotus Petals* (An Anthology of Indian short stories), Madras: Macmillan India Ltd.

Kumar, Shiv K. (1983) *A Portrait of India* (A selection of stories), New Delhi: Vikas Pub.

_____. (1991) *Contemporary Indian Short Stories in English*, New Delhi: Sahitya Academy.

Lal, P. (1967) *The First Writer's Workshop Story Anthology*, Calcutta: Writer's workshop.

Mahindra, Anuradha (1994) *The Raymond Gentleman Collection of Short Stories* 1994, Bombay: Sterling Newspapers Ltd.

Mathur, Divya (1992) *Odyssey: Short Stories by Indian Women Writers Settled Abroad*, New Delhi: Star Publications.

Mathur, Ramesh & Mahendra Kulasrestha (1976) *Writings on India's Partition*, Calcutta: Simant Publications.

Mishra, G. (1972) *Modern Short Stories from Indian Authors,* Calcutta: Cuttack, Students Store.

Mukherjee, Meenakshi (1975) *Let's Go Home and Other Stories* (An Anthology of Indian S. S in English), Hydrabad: Orient Longman.

Mukundan, Monisha (1993) *The Namaste Book of Indian Short Stories* (Vol. I), New Delhi: UBSPD.

_____. (1994) *The Namaste Book of Indian Short Stories* (Vol. II), New Delhi: UBSPD.

_____. (1999) *Mosaic: New Writings from Award—Wining British and Indian writers*, New Delhi: Penguin.

Naik, M. K. (1984) *The Indian English Short Story—A Representative Anthology*, New Delhi: Arnold-Heinemann.

Naikar, B. (1989) *Sparrows,* Madras: Blackie.

Nandy, Pritish (1979) *The Vikas Book of Indian Love Stories,* New Delhi: Vikas Pub.

Narayan, R.K. (1997) *Indian Thought: A Miscellany*, New Delhi: Penguin Books.

Nevile, Pran (1995) *Love Stories from the Raj*, New Delhi/New York: Penguin.

Poonacha, Veena (1992) *Childhood that Never Was* (An Anthology of Short Story on the girl-child), Bombay: Research Centre Women's Studies.

Prasad, Madhusudhan (1993) *Contemporary Indian English Short Stories*, New Delhi: Sterling.

Ramakrishna, D. (1980): *Indian English Prose*, New Delhi: Arnold-Heinemann.

Robinson, A & K. Dutta, (1992) *Noon in Calcutta : The Short Stories from Bengal*, New Delhi: Viking.

Roy, Jalian Sunil Martin (1986) *Short Stories*, Vol.1, Calcutta: Roy Sumusti Publications.

Rushdic, Salman & Elizabeth West (1997) *The Vintage Book of Indian Writing 1947-1997*, London: Vintage.

Saksena. M. (1951) *Indian Short Stories*, Calcutta: OUP.

Singh, K. Natwar (1972) *Stories From India*, London: Hoddes and Stoughton, 1966, Bombay: BI Publications.

Singh, Kushwant (1965) *Land of Five Rivers*, New Delhi: Disha Books.

_____. & Qurratulain Hyder (1974) *Stories from India*, New Delhi: Sterling.

Shetty, Manohar (1998) *Ferry Crossing: Short Stories from Goa*, New Delhi: Penguin Books.

Srinivasan, Indira & Chetana Bhatt (1999) *Best Loved Indian Stories of the century* (vol. I), New Delhi: Penguin Books.

Srinivasan. K. (1983) *Short Stories*, Madras: Anu Chitra Publications.

Thayil, Jeet (1996) Vox*: New Indian Fiction*, Bombay: Sterling Newspapers Ltd.

_____. (1997) Vox 2*: Seven Stories*, Mumbai: Sterling Newspapers Pvt. Ltd.

Thieme, John (1996) *The Arnold Anthology of Post-Colonial Literatures in English,* London: Arnold.

Vas, Rita & Sohuis (1971) *Modern Goan Short Stories*, Bombay: Jaico Publishing House.

15

Social Realism in Premchand's Short Stories

—Beena V. Rathi

Premchand (1880-1936) was born in a small village near Varanasi. He was named Dhanpat Rai Srivastava by his parents, but adopted the pen-name Premchand. Extreme poverty and domestic problems marked his childhood and youth. He grew up in an environment where both Urdu and Hindi were commonly used. As a writer, Premchand was deeply influenced by Gandhi, Tolstoy, Gorky, Victor Hugo, and Romain Rolland. He resigned from his government job in 1920 when Gandhiji launched the Non-Cooperation Movement. Subsequently, he immersed himself in political and literary writings which accentuated his intimate knowledge of rural India. He had a progressive outlook and presided over the Progressive Writers Conference held in Lucknow in 1936. Premchand brought a new sense of social awareness to fiction.

Premchand is considered one of the outstanding short story writers of world literature, with more than three hundred short stories in Hindi and Urdu to his credit. His literary writings reflect with empathy and insight into the harsh life of the Indian peasant caught in the web of inhuman landlords and heartless moneylenders. The novels *Prema, Vardaan, Nirmala, Gaban, Rangabhumi*, and *Godaan* are some of his well known works. The present paper proposes to study social realism in two of his short stories.

'The Child' is the story of Gangu, a poor Brahmin servant who works for a rich man. Premchand has delineated Gangu as a typical Brahmin who does not bow to his master like the other servants. He does not touch used utensils and his master lacks even the courage to ask him to fan him in hot weather. If at all he has to do it, his attitude is one of doing his master a great favour. Being short-tempered, he rouses at the slightest rebuke and considers it below his dignity to sit with the syce or the bearer. He avoids going to fairs or public shows, and detests 'bhang' which is a common addiction with the people of his class. Even though an illiterate, he expects all the respects due to a Brahmin.

Gangu's Master avoids talking freely to servants and if at all they pay an unsolicited visit to him it is either to complain about other servants or ask for an advance against their salary. One day Gangu comes to his Master with a request to relieve him of his duties. The latter feels hurt for he is considered an ideal employer and any servant considers it his good fortune to be employed with him. On enquiring, Gangu tells him that he wants to leave so that people don't raise any fingers at his master on his account. Now the Master is bewildered and asks him for details. The reason given by Gangu is astonishing. He tells his Master that a woman named Gomti Devi has just been turned out of the Widow's Home and he wants to get married to her.

The Master is speechless for a few seconds and then asks Gangu if he knows about Gomti Devi's past. He remembers how this woman had created quite a stir in the placid atmosphere of their area. She had entered the Widow's Home some years ago. Twice the authorities there had got her married off but both the times she had returned after a week or two. Eventually she had been expelled from there. She had now taken a room in their area and was an object of great interest to all the lovelorn young men.

The Master tries to enlighten him but Gangu reiterates that all these stories about Gomti Devi are lies. Unperturbed Gangu tells him that she had left three husbands because it was they who had turned her out of their houses. He says with the zeal of a poet, "Where there is no love, you cannot expect a woman to stay on, you cannot win a woman with mere board and lodging. Those people who married her thought that they were doing her a great favour by marrying a widow and took it for granted that she would do anything for their sake. But to win someone over one has first to forget about oneself. And besides, Sir, she gets fits, sometimes, starts talking all sorts of nonsense and becomes unconscious. People say that she is under the influence of a witch."

His Master is more than surprised and asks him if he still finds her interesting and Gangu tells him that by getting her, he can change his fortune for the good. The Master accepts his resignation even though he is not a person who believes in old customs and meaningless traditions, he definitely considers it dangerous to keep Gangu as a servant who is intent on marrying a woman of such doubtful reputation.

After five months, the Master meets Gangu who earns his livelihood as a hawker. He always finds him very happy. His face has a glow which only comes with complete lack of worry. But one day Gomti runs away. The master is pleased for after all he has been proved right. That afternoon Gangu; who is completely shattered, cries to his heart's content. When the Master asks him if she has run away with his belongings too, Gangu puts his hands on his heart and says, "Don't say that Babuji, she hasn't taken a thing. Her own things are still lying with me. I don't know what lacks in me that she left me. May be I'm not good enough for her. She is educated and I am an illiterate Had she stayed a little longer she would have made a man out of me. Whatever she was for other men, she was definitely a goddess to me. It must have been surely my fault."

After this incident, the Master goes away to Nainital to return only after a month. He has barely taken off his clothes when Gangu comes to meet him with a newborn baby in his arms. He is bursting with joy. On enquiring about Gomti Devi, Gangu tells him that he has found her. She was in the Women's Hospital at Lucknow. She had told a friend of hers to tell about her whereabouts if and only if she found Gangu upset for her. He had gone to Lucknow to bring her back and had also got a child in bargain. Gangu shows the child almost with the pride of an athlete showing off a newly won medal.

The Master is surprised at Gangu's shamelessness. He had not been married for more than six months and he displays the child with great pride. The Master tauntingly asks him if he is sure that it is his own child. Gangu's reply is wonderful. He says,

> Sir, that question never bothered me. This was the reason perhaps why Gomti had left the house. I told her that if she did not love me she could leave me by all means and I would never bother her again. But if she did love me she must not let the child resparate us. I would love it as my own. After all, when one takes a harvested field one does not refuse the crop merely because someone else has sown it.

The Master is touched by Gangu's sentiments and feels like an utter fool. He extends his hands, takes the child from Gangu and kisses it. Gangu praises him and tells him how he has been telling Gomti about his good Master. But she is so bashful to take the initialive to meet him. The Master now feels ashamed for his middle class morality. He has great respect for Gangu's courage and sincerity. He goes with Gangu to his house to meet Gomti.

A lot of stories of Premchand deal with social realism. The other story to be taken into consideration is the story The Shroud, the story of Budhia, a poor labour woman. The story begins with Budhia lying in her hut, writhing and wriggling in the throes of childbirth. Her husband Madhav and her father-in-law Ghisu are waiting outside for her to die. Theirs is a family of cobblers notorious in the village. Ghisu rests for three days if he has worked for one and Madhav is such a shirker that every half an hour of work, he smokes for one hour, with the result that they barely ever secure work. They are so content with a handful of corn that they live on it for two to three days. Only starvation really compels them to gather firewood or twigs to be sold to live on.

There is no dearth of work in the village for in a peasant community labour is always in demand but these two float through their miserable lives suffering indignities, burdened by heavy debt, even beaten up when required. At harvest time, they pilfer potatoes and peas to bake and eat or dig up sugarcane to munch at night.

Ghisu has spent his sixty years in such precarious existence and Madhav has followed suit; like a worthy son. With Budhia bringing order in their household, these shameless creatures devour while she grinds corn or cuts grass for their livelihood

Now, she lies in labour pains and these two wait for her to die, so that they can sleep in pleace! Budhia goes on moaning. Next morning Madhav goes inside the hut only to find Budhia dead, the child dead in her womb and flies hovering all over her face.

The father-son duo wail loudly beating their chests to attract the neighbours who hasten to offer customary condolences to the unfortunates. With little time for weeping they hurry to the Zamindar's house to procure a shroud and firewood for cremation of the dead body.

Lying to the Zamindar of having spent the entire money they had on her medicine and treatment, Ghisu requests him to help him to perform her last rites. The Zamindar, who never received Ghisu's services when asked for, contemptuosuly throws two rupees at him. Trumpetting the Zamindar's favour, Ghisu extracts a two-anna piece, a four-anna bit from the moneylenders and shopkeepers. Within an hour he has collected full five rupees in cash, besides foodgrain here and firewood there.

At noon the two set out to the market to buy a shroud. Other helping hands begin cutting bamboo and other wood. In the market they roam from shop to shop trying to select a shroud as cheap as possible. They tell each other that she who didn't have a rag to cover her living body shouldn't expect a new shroud at death just to be burnt with the body. Moreover, it would be dark by the time the body was taken out so no one would be able to see the quality of the shroud.

Led by some mysterious power, they find themselves in front of a tavern and as if the visit is predetermined, enter it. They order for a bottle followed by snacks and fried fish. After several rounds in quick succession, they get into a state of exhilaration blessing Budhia for having fed them even after her death. Ghisu orders two seers of puris, chutney, pickles and meat. They sit and eat in great style with no one to answer to, no dread of public censure. They have got over such scruples long ago. Madhav enquires of his father what answer he would give to her in heaven for having swallowed all her money. After all he had put vermilion on her head and was answerable to her. Ghisu pacifies him by assuring him that the very people who gave her a shroud now would provide it a little later.

Maybe, they won't put cash in their hands, but give Budhia a shroud all right.

As it grows darker and the stars shine brighter, the two become livelier. They continue to sip and be merry. Having had their fill, Madhav gives away the leftover puris in the leaf-plate to a beggar who is standing and staring at them with hungry eyes. And for the first time in his life he feels the pride, glory and the thrill of "giving". He asks him to bless her with every hair of his body and let her become the queen of heaven.

Ghisu joins him and says, "She must go to heaven for she never harassed or bullied anyone here. And dying she met the biggest craving of their lives. If she doesn't go to heaven will these pot-bellied ones go there who loot the poor left and right and bathe in the Ganges to wash away their sins and pour oblations in the temple?"

Their mood of reverence slowly undergoes a swift change. Instability is a characteristic of intoxication. A fit of grief and despair overcomes them. Madhav covers his eyes and starts weeping and wailing aloud. Ghisu consoles him by telling him to rejoice because Budhia is freed from this web of illusion, escaping from this tangle of misery and breaking loose from the bonds of *maya*.

The two stand up and begin to sing loudly. Everyone stares at them bewildered. They begin to dance. They bounce and jump, reel and wriggle, mime and mimic. And in the end fall down—dead drunk. This is the story of a destitute family where the suffering caused by stark poverty brings the central characters to a situation that is at once comic as well as pathetic.

Premchand's keen observation of life and his knowledge of human nature made him create excellent characters like Gangu, Ghisu and Madhav—each one so true, so life-like. His realistic depiction of the social problems of our country has earned him the accolade of a prolific writer.

Works Cited

Premchand, *Laghu Kathaye*, Jaico Publishing House, 1987.

16

The Inheritance of Chaos: Crisis of Values and Ethics in Modern Indian English Poetry

—Kanwar Dinesh Singh

Indian English Poetry in the post-Independence period has shown a rapid change in the age-old value systems of India. The change or crisis of values can be seen more in the elite and intellectual circles, mostly with English education, than among the commonplace masses. The fundamental human values have also undergone changes with this turning point in the mindset and way of life of the Indian people under the influence of the West. Love, friendship, mutual respect, religious tolerance, compassion, pacifism, altruism, symbiosis and ecofriendliness are some of the most vital human values that have a bearing on each and every human being on the planet earth.

India is known for her lofty standard of human values and moral ideals, both in theory and praxis, as enshrined in the ancient Hindu scriptures such as the *Vedas*, the *Upanishads*, the *Puranas*, the *Ramayana*, the *Mahabharata* and the *BhagavadGita*. The most prominent example of the time-honoured human values in the *Vedas* and *Upanishads* include *Vasudhaiva kutumbakam* (The whole world is one family—*Rigveda*), *Sarve bhavantu sukhinah* (May all be happy!—*Rigveda*), *Ahimsa paramo dharamah* (Non-violence is the supreme religion), *Atithi devo bhavah* (The guest is God—*Rigveda*), *Shantih sarvam* (Peace be everywhere for everyone—*Yajurveda*), *Sarvaashaah mam mitram bhavantu* (May all directions be my friends!—*Atharvaveda*), *Yad bhadram tanna aasuvaah* (May we get whatever is good for all!—*Yajurveda*), among several other instances. All these are global values, as there is a wish for the well-being of all, irrespective of one's caste, creed, faith, colour, community, sex and nationality.

Human values, morals and ideals enshrined in the ancient Indian poetry that are today recognized and revered the world over are, indubitably, an upshot of the vision of the poets of yore. The values established, professed and practiced by poets of those times bespeak of their being astute seers. The term 'kavi' employed for a poet in Sanskrit is a synonym of sun as well as seer. Thus, a poet was deemed to be a 'seer' who was endowed with the prowess of seeing, that is, envisioning the verities of human life and existence vis-à-vis nature and environment. It is certainly because of those great seer-poets that the posterity takes pride in inheriting the inimitable and inspiring values of life.

The poet is, in the real sense of the term, gifted with a special sight which an ordinary person does not have. That's why observation and perception of a poet by and large conform to values that are extensive, widely-shared and universal.

Generally, values maintain a particular approach to life, a specific mode of conduct over a period of time and mould and lead the society in a specific way. Therefore, there are always newer values replacing, changing or improving the old or outmoded values. Poets have always been significantly instrumental in bringing about the required change in the value system in a society. The best example can be seen in the spate of devotional (*bhakti*) poetry in the medieval times dominating almost all major languages of the Indian subcontinent. It helped the masses get at their real self through devotion and love for their chosen deity and even through devotion to the absolute non-dualistic truth. It connected the worldly with the divine, and thus, the conventional love poetry acquired newer dimensions and newer meanings in all languages – Hindi, Awadhi, Braj, Maithili, Persian, Kashmiri, Tamil, Telugu, Marathi, Gujarati, Oriya, Bengali, Assamese, Manipuri and Panjabi among other languages of India. The devotional poetry revolutionized the Indian society toward awakening and understanding human existence with a fresh perspective. Hence, poets have the power to bring about a transformation in the society by amending the existing value systems.

The pre-Independence poets have also been greatly influential in bringing about renaissance of classic Indian values and beliefs. The poetical works of Henry Derozio, Swami Vivekananda, Sri Aurobindo, Rabindranath Tagore et al. have been really effective in transfiguring the outlook of the whole society of their times. But, the post-Independence generation of Indian English poets, however, tends to sacrifice the age-old sterling and universal human values at the altar of subjective or individual values, which may be of help to an individual or a particular group and not to the humanity at large. And the values these new poets adhere to have nothing to inspire the coming generations. These values are too individualistic and, therefore, are short-lived and of no consequence at all. It can offer no aesthetic delight, emotional solace, succour, contentment, inspiration or illumination what is expected from good poetry.

The modern, poet-Independence Indian English poets have in the names of modernism, realism, concrete experience and lucidity detoured from the real objectives of poetry altogether. As said earlier, the crisis of values is more evident among the so-called highly educated and intellectual class. The middle classes, albeit, uphold the long-established human values of India. The poetry of the new poets is replete with a range of psycho-sexual complexities, erotica sans love, emotional confusion, irreligiosity, debauchery, defiance of conventions, skepticism, cynicism, pessimism, immorality, sexual perversity and mostly individual concerns in the name of felt experience, realism and new humanism.

Nissim Ezekiel who is regarded as the pioneer of modernism in Indian English poetry fills his poetry with several indiscriminate descriptions of female body, nudity and lovemaking, which are often plain, blunt and devoid of emotion. At places, in an effort to create a work of erotic appeal, he even slips into the obscene. All the same, he finds himself still inhibited vis-à-vis his "poetic ancestors", the Sanskrit eroticists, as he conveys in "Passion Poems – 3: The Sanskrit Poets":

How freely they mention
breasts and buttocks.
They are my poetic ancestors.
Why am I so inhibited?
(Ezekiel: CC: 1989: 214)

Ezekiel perhaps forgets that mere mentioning of "breasts and buttocks" does not qualify the poem for the canon of erotica. The term 'erotic' is a derivative of Eros, the god of love in Greek mythology (identifiable with the Roman love-god Cupid and the Hindu love-god Kamadeva), thereby accentuating the vital element of love. Eroticism, thus, involves both the psychological and spiritual aspects of love along with the corporeal. Insofar as the fine points of amatory content and the spiritual dimension of love are lacking in Ezekiel's poems, he fails to come up to the standards of the Sanskrit eroticists. Ezekiel's poems suffer from the bane of trite, obvious, obscene, kitschy and crude effusions of sexuality. Similar effusions are marked in the excerpt below from his poem "Nudes 1978: 2", which even the Muse of poetry would decline to own up as her subject matter:

'I love undressing', she has to say,
as she undresses. The verbal
and the visual join in her.
'Is this a part of you?' she asks,
as she holds it, stares at it.
Then she laughs...
'... put your fingers there',
she pleads, as if
I need instructions. It's only
impatience, though, becoming frenzy
as I penetrate. 'Now', she claims,
'you are within me. Aren't you
within me?' And she makes me say, 'I am.'
(Ezekiel: LDP: 1982: 32)

It's clearly a plain, crude, oafish verbalization of the slush of his sex-ridden mind, and has no value – poetic, aesthetic / artistic, psychological, sexological or erotic. There is nothing earthshaking; nothing pleasing or gratifying; nothing enlightening or catharizing. His depiction of man-woman relationship is purely physical, merely deriving pleasure from each other's body without having any lasting emotion or deeper understanding or admiration for the individual. The following excerpt from the poem "Description" plainly manifests the poet's fondness for a woman's nudity: "... between your thighs a wonder/of hair, secret/in light and in darkness/bare, suffering with joy / kisses light as air" (Ezekiel: *CC*: 1989: 48). Heaven knows what "wonder", "joy" or "secret" the poet finds in the depiction of the trite and obvious and denuding the female without any potent symbolism to persuade the reader.

Values of love and lovemaking are completely jejune in the lewd and lecherous male gaze of the poet seeing woman merely as a body, a desirable body, an object of sex to be enjoyed by man, and nothing more than that. Nor is there any desire expressed to relate to her as a person. In his poem "Love Poem", he calls woman a "beast of sex" and sees her as "myth and dream". In poems such as "Progress", "Three Women", "motive", In India", "In Twenty-Four Hours" and "in Nudes", etc. he projects woman as seductress or whore or a mere sex object. He, thus, tends to commoditize and reduce woman to an object created for the pleasure and physical gratification of man just as "trees, waves, birds, buildings, stones, steam rollers, cats and clocks." In a country having an age-old value system prescribing to worship woman as goddess, Ezekiel out-and-out disregards and defies those values and makes several disparaging, crude and uncouth remarks on the womankind.

At places, Ezekiel seems to be too presumptuous about femininity and female sexuality. As, in the poem "On Giving Reasons", he presupposes a woman's "NO" as an approval:

> She gave me
> Six good reasons
> for saying NO
> and then
> for no reason at all
> dropped all her reasons
> with her clothes.
>
> (Ezekiel: CC: 1989: 215)

This is, no doubt, a vague, sweeping statement, taking woman for granted regardless of her inner feelings. It is only the poet's individual fetish and obsession with the carnal. His poem "Motives" conveys his so-called aesthetics of life: "My motives are sexual, / aesthetic and friendly / in that order, adding up / to bed with you... /... Your thighs are full and round, / thin and flat / I'd love them too. / There go my aesthetics" (Ezekiel: *CC*: 1989: 154). All meaningless and preposterous. Love, which is probably the root of all human values and ethics, has been altogether demeaned and derided.

Like Ezekiel, Shiv K. Kumar also shows obsession with sex and sensuality. His images, mostly drawing on sex and nakedness of female body without any genuine concern of love, are too insipid, dry and wry and have no aesthetic appeal of any kind. In his poem "A Mango Vendor", through the persona of an old woman, he gives voice to his own vision stuck at the naked body of a poor woman: "Through the slits / Of her patched blouse / One bare shoulder / Two white moons / Pull all horses / Off the track / This old man's eyes / idle birds pecking / at the mango-nipples" (Kumar: 1976: 36). Certainly, it is not the subject matter for a serious art like muse. Similarly, in the poem "Wife At Prayer", he scoffs at the religious sentiments of his wife:

> Who has tamed the raw wind
> around this grey room
> where stones are gods
> and musk-roses do not inebriate?
>
> Soft as the inside
> of a tender coconut, she weaves halos
> with joss-sticks that only
> incense my groins
> to break the truce.
>
> (Kumar: 1976: 30)

Like Ezekiel, Kumar also reduces woman to a mere sex object, desirable to satiate the carnal passions of man. A. K. Ramanujan, another noted poet, derides the religious devotion of a woman through a persona in the poem "Mythologies 3",

"And all he could think of was her round breast, / her musk, her darling navel and the rest" (Ramanujan: 1995: 228). The phrases fraught with carnality demean altogether the values of love and even treating woman as human being above anything else. Ramanujan does not resort to the first person singular and crude form of articulation as Ezekiel and Kumar do, but yet he has the similar subject matter, which shows decadence of human values and ethics.

Shiv K. Kumar is too pessimistic even about marital relationship. In his poem "Married Too Long", he states: "we wear each other / like soiled underwear./... / I see you hung / on every wall / like an *obituary*. / Now let me *entomb* you / in a gilded frame... / Till death do not us part." (Kumar: 1974: 46). In another poem, "To A Young Wife", he articulates his debility: "Ask me not to act / deed is now my perdition" (Kumar: 1974: 29). Thus, family values of sharing and mutual understanding and adjustment are giving in to personal preferences and assertions. In "Love Poem for a Wife 1", A.K. Ramanujan laments the breaking marriages and he sees rationale in child marriages and marriages between cousins which could develop better understanding between a husband and a wife: "Really what kept us apart / at the end of years is unshared / childhood...." (Ramanujan: 1976: 25-27). In "Love Poem for a Wife 2", he depicts how a connubial relationship, "happy for once / at such a loss of face" turns bitter and brings in unhappiness and disappointment and estrangement in marriage. In "Love Poem for a Wife and Her Trees", he talks about the disillusionment: "I forgot at night and remember at dawn / you're not me but Another, the faraway / stranger who's nearby...." (Ramanujan: 1995: 180-83). The reasons for bickering in marital bonds could be psychological or physical, but all these breakages can be well described as a crisis of values and ethics that are shattering bit by bit merely for the sake of subjective concerns and motives.

In Jayanta Mahapatra's poems also, one can find man-woman relationship totally devoid of love and only resting on physical need and encounter. In most of his poems, he seems to be obsessed with whores. For instance, in "The Whorehouse in a Calcutta Street", he depicts an encounter with a whore thus: "You fall against her in the dumb light, / Trying to learn something more about women—/ While she does what she thinks proper to please you" (Parthasarthy: 1976: 61). Images of crude sexuality can be seen intermittently even in his longer poems, such as in "The Twenty-fifth Anniversary of a Republic: 1975":

> In my dreams when I fondle Kamala's brazen breasts
> my hands encounter the blind flowers at a desecrated tomb.
>
> (Mahapatra: 1976: 32).

All associations and collations are weird. The images are gross and decadent and do not evoke any fine or tender emotion between a man and a woman. Love is altogether missing amidst purely carnal longings.

Kamala Das has been described as a bold and candid woman poet in the post-Independence phase of Indian English poetry, but the other side is that even she is shorn of all values and ethics as a writer. In the garb of feminism, she, in fact, writes with a stance of reverse sexism. One can find frequent male bashing and even denuding of male body in her poems, probably, as a reaction against the male denuding women in their poems. As, for instance, in her poem "The Looking Glass", she presents voyeuristically the "fond details" of the male thus:

> Notice the perfection
> Of his limbs, his eyes reddening under
> The shower, the shy walk across the bathroom floor
> Dropping towels, and the jerky way he
> Urinates. All fond details that make
> Him male.
>
> (Das: 1967: 25).

There is no erotic strength, no aesthetic sense or delight in Das' way with words and there is not even proper content for the muse. Such descriptions are recurrent in her poems. In "The Old Playhouse", she describes lovemaking thus: "You dribbled spittle into my mouth, you poured / Yourself into every nook and cranny, you embalmed/My poor lust with your bitter-sweet juices." And in "The Looking Glass": "Stand nude before the glass with him/So that he sees himself the stronger one / And believes it so, and you so much more/Softer, younger, lovelier" (Das: 1967: 25). She even advocates adultery or infidelity, as she herself tries extra-marital relationships:

> After that love became a swivel-door
> When one went out, another came in,
> Then I lost count, for always in my arms
> Was a substitute for a substitute.
>
> (*Das*: 1967: 7).

All this can be described as a mere kitsch, devoid of aesthetic and erotic value as it fails even to meet the objectives of verse. Bruce King remarks, "Rather than a poet of free love, she expresses the disappointments of sexuality. She describes a void to be filled with others or with alternative passions" (King: 1987: 150). However, she has been *flaunting* about all that as she confesses in an article "I Have Lived Beautifully": "I often walked with young man along the sea flaunting my unconventionality" (*Debonair*, 15 May 1975: 41). She prefers "the return of the social order that allowed woman to have more than one husband if she so desired" (*Eve's Weekly*, 6 May 1972: 35). Thus, she goes even against social ethics and human values, where one has to live with mutual understanding and respect and work out solutions with incisiveness and good judgment, and not impulsively or so passionately as to subvert the whole social system for personal grudge and dissatisfaction.

Mamta Kalia describes marriage as a trap and voices her anger thus: "I feel like crying all the time/Or running on the roads with an unwashed face./I want to smash a glass early in the morning/And wake up everybody with a start./I hate these people around,/Related to me" (Kalia: 1978: 19). Thus, the sanctity of marriage is breaking just because the marriage partners as well as all other family members fail to understand and respect each other. In actuality, values have gone wrong and people have forgone ethics and morals in favour of ego and self-interest. Kalia describes marriage as hazardous to keeping love alive and, therefore, cries in disenchantment:

I am a great fool
To think that marriage is bliss,
Was it last month or last year
That we exchanged a kiss.
(*Kalia*: 1978: 19).

But, all the same, she forgets marriage is not just an exchange of kisses. It's rather a huge collective responsibility of both husband and wife toward each member in the family as much as toward each other. And, according to the Indian tradition, it requires sacrifice of individual ego, attitude and personal interests, preferences and prejudices in favour of the common interest of the family.

Besides demeaning values of love, sex and marriage, modern Indian English poets, show equal change or corrosion in familial, social, interpersonal, religious and spiritual values. The modern day relationships seem to be mechanical and based on utilitarianism. The traditional concept of blood ties seems to be losing its significance, especially in terms of emotional bonding. These modern poets are too critical even of their parents. A.K. Ramanujan's poem "Obituary" on the passing away of his father is sarcastic, rather derisive and dismissive and fails to have any impact on the reader. The poet is too cynical in his cataloguing the family liabilities left in legacy by his father: ".. when he passed on,/left dust/on a table full of papers, / left doubts and daughters,/a bedwetting grandson...." (Ramanujan: 1976: 49). The poet feels concerned for the poor father's incessant "burning" on the catafalque of life, and finally being reduced to "ashes" at the decisive blaze of death:

Being the burning type,
he burnt properly
at the cremation

as before, easily
and at both ends,
left his eye coins
in the ashes that didn't
look one bit different,
several spinal discs; rough,
some burned to coal, for sons...
(*Ramanujan*: 1976: 49)

The non-fulfilment of family commitments by the father is resented: "everything he didn't quite/manage to do himself,/like his caesarian birth/in a Brahmin ghetto/and his death by heart –/attack in the fruit market." (Ramanujan: 1976: 49-50). Be it father's penury, incapacity, lethargy, reluctance, or inability to fulfill his duties, the son dismisses him as an incompetent father. The son expresses scorn over his ineptitude through pun, implying he did nothing by himself – when he was born, he did not come out by himself, he gave all the trouble and pain to his mother ("caesarian birth") and when he died of heart attack, he troubled others again.

The modern poets show no emotional attachment and obedience towards their parents. They rather question them for certain infirmities and inconsistencies. The prominent issues raised by them include a difficult-to-fill-up gap of communication between generations, a tough conflict between idealism and reality, tradition and modernity. But, in doing so, they become too curt and callous that they tend to forget all those long-cherished Vedic values that held parents identical with gods and accorded them all respect and high place: *Matri devo bhavah* (Mother is God); *Pitri devo bhavah* (Father is God). A.K. Ramanujan seems to be wedged between the sacraments and commandments of his father on the one hand and his impulses and social veracities on the other. An ethico-moral quandary grips him when he is caught up in the enticements of a beautiful woman as reflected in the poem "Still Another View of Grace", "Bred Brahmin among singers of shivering hymns," he shudders, but finally he yields:

> ... Commandments crumbled
> in my father's past. Her tumbled hair suddenly known
> as silk in my angry hand, I shook a little
> and took her, behind the laws of my land.
>
> (*Ramanujan*: 1976: 20).

While Ramanujan is seen turning away from his father and his values, Jayanta Mahapatra seems disgruntled with his "indefinable mother". Mahapatra's relationship with his mother was not very pleasant. There were strains due to her eccentric, rigid and unresponsive nature. She was unable to respond to the tender cravings and expectations of her child. As a result she became a misfit in his life. With his father he finds himself repressed altogether under the weight of tradition and commandments. Like Ramanujan, he finds himself sandwiched between tradition and modernity, dogma and reality, conventional values and individual identity: "Burden of your peace, Father / theme-song of my life that burns my tongue / voices of children always wronged" (Mahapatra: 1982: 18). His father's perfectionist values, ideals and purist commandments become cumbersome for Mahapatra. In "The Quality of Ruins", he mentions "of a father that devour you with terror / at the feeling of bringing perfectness to your life." (Mahapatra: 1983: 12). He is always on the horns of dilemma: "Thinking to escape his beliefs, / I go to meet the spectre of belief..." (Mahapatra: 1983: 12). Shiv K. Kumar has also not shown much attachment to his father. In "The Death of My Father", he recollects how his father scolded "a boy of five / for emerging from his shower, / draped only in his nudity, as though to show/that we shared something (besides our fierce dissents)/that had been denied to mother and sisters" (Kumar: 1998: 13). Kumar's idiom is too coarse and indecorous at places. He always seems preoccupied with sex and all vulgar stuff.

Mamta Kalia grumbles over the generation gap between her and her father. In her poem "Tribute to Papa", she rejects forthwith her father's values, ideals and thoughts:

> Who cares for you, Papa?
> Who cares for your clean thoughts, clean words, clean teeth?
> Who wants to be an angel like you?
> Who wants it?
> You are an unsuccessful man, Papa.
>
> (Kalia: 1970: 10).

The modern daughter dismisses her father's idealism and 'sacredness' and uses harsh words for him: "these days I am seriously thinking of / disowning you, Papa... / Everything about you clashes with nearly / everything about me" (Kalia: 1970: 10). So, these modern poets' disrespect for their parents and elders bespeak of the eroding human values and ethics. The sole reason is that they are too impatient, impudent, snobbish, selfish and inconsiderate. A. K. Ramanujan does not spare even his grandmother. In the poem "THE HINDOO: he doesn't Hurt a Fly or a Spider either", he presents her as an adulterous and sexually promiscuous woman who flits out of her coyness and enjoys an extra-marital affair with a passionate relish. The cuckold-husband, the poet-narrator's grandfather, is depicted as passive, overly patient and lax, even in personal matters. The poet casts an aspersion on his grandfather who, as an over-flexible "Hindoo", could not hurt even a "Fly" or a "Spider" either. The 'Fly' symbolizes the perverted woman who dodged her husband, and the 'Spider' is a symbol of the outsider who seduced and trapped someone's wife in his 'web' of intrigue: "Maybe it's once again my / great swinging grandmother, / and that other (playing at / patience centred in his web) / my one true ancestor, / the fisherman lover who waylaid her / on the ropes in the Madras harbour..." (Ramanujan: 1976: 23). In the following lines, the poet-narrator talks about the sex-starvation and sado-masochism of his grandmother who, with her lover, makes love in the manner spiders do (the female devouring the male): "one day, spider – / fashion, she clamped down and bit / him while still inside her, / as if she'd teeth down there – / they'd a Latin name for it, / which didn't help the poor man one bit" (Ramanujan: 1976: 23). The imagery, the phraseology and the thought-content – all are impertinent, unaesthetic, indecent and unpoetic and speak of a crisis of values and ethics in the modern Indian English poets.

It is not just man-woman relationship, love, matrimony and family relations where the modern Indian English poets show sheer lack of fundamental human values, but they mostly lack even social, patriotic, religious and spiritual values. No doubt, growing urbanization, careerism, materialism and consumerism in the modern world seem to be the major causes of tension, conflict and friction in human relationships, yet the poets under study by and large lack personal morals and ethics as well as interpersonal and universal values. Their lack of mutual understanding, emotion and respect certainly bring about a cataclysm of (human) values and all ethics and moral ideals. They forget that as poets they have certain obligations even toward future generations. They are too individualistic, egotistical and indifferent, and are too callous to their responsibility toward society, nation, posterity and humanity at large. They have nothing substantial to offer to their readers; they have nothing to inspire the young generations. In actual fact, they have left an inheritance of chaos for them. Therein lays their fiasco. The questions arise—What exactly they write? Why they write? For whom they write? Who are their readers? How many people buy their poetry? How many of thee poets are from professions other than academic, literary professions? Who are the people critiquing their poetry? What parameters are adopted for evaluating their poetry? Where do they stand in the light of classical Indian, and even western canons of poetry? How authentic or genuine they are? The answers to all such questions are disillusioning.

It's a fact that the poetry of these modern poets is not the poetry of the common masses and, thus, they have no common acceptability. The sole reason is that they don't conform to the basic human values, morals and ethics as writers. Their poems lack readability. They lack the warmth and pleasure one expects from poetry. Redundancy, obscurity, verbosity, exaggeration, over-candidness, over-indulgence and moral indiscipline come out as their weak points. Their concerns are too subjective, and not universal, and therefore, do not come up to the canon of classic literature. In *Waffle of the Toffs*, M. Prabha puts a question mark even on the Indianness of these poets. She declines to consider Nissim Ezekiel even as the starting point of the modern Indian English poetry as his *A Time to Change* (1952) bears "not a single reference to India". She calls him a "master manipulator" (Prabha: 2000: 184). According to her, Jayanta Mahapatra "invents a mask for himself" and "has poured out of his prolix tartuffery" (Ibid. 190); Shiv K. Kumar offers nothing but "libidinous, titillating stuff—the leftovers of the west" (Ibid. 193); R. Parthasarthy is "unethical" and now "a self-extinguished poet" (Ibid. 195); Keki N. Daruwalla shows "a pathological aversion to his milieu (Ibid. 213); and he wears "colonial cockade" that engenders all angularities (217); Dom Moraes has "distaste for all things

Indian" (Ibid. 221); and Kamala Das has offered "sex loaded poems" and such a stuff has been a "real change for the hungering Indian male" (Ibid. 224). Harsh, but it's true. The best odour of the soil is jejune in most of these "toffy" poets, though they are amply proficient in maneuvering the nuances of English language.

Today, the need is to look for and encourage some good poetry, which must be there somewhere in the margins within the country, so that the long established literary culture and value system of India may be saved from wearing away under the influence of alien ideologies, distorted realities and false and pretentious values.

Works Cited

Das, Kamala. *The Descendants*, Calcutta Writers Workshop, 1967.

_____. "I Have Lived Beautifully", *Debonair*, 15 May 1975: 14.

_____. "Why Not More Than One Husband", *Eve's Weekly*, 6 May 1972: 35.

Ezekiel, Nissim. *Collected Poems: 1952-1988*, New Delhi: Oxford University Press, 1989.

_____. *Latter-Day Psalms*, New Delhi: Oxford University Press, 1982.

Kalia, Mamta. *Tribute to Papa and Other Poems*, Calcutta: Writers Workshop, 1970.

_____. *Poems'78*, Calcutta: Writers Workshop, 1978.

King, Bruce. *Modern Indian Poetry in English*, New Delhi: Oxford University Press, 1987.

Kumar, Shiv K. *Cobwebs in the Sun*, New Delhi: Tata McGraw-Hill, 1974.

_____. *Subterfuges*, New Delhi: Oxford University Press, 1976.

_____. *Woolgathering*, Hyderabad: Disha Books, 1998.

Mahapatra, Jayanta. *A Father's Hours*. Calcutta: Writers Workshop, 1976.

_____. *Relationship* (New York: The Greenfield Review Press, 1980), rpt. Cuttack: The Chandrabhaga Society, 1982.

_____. *Life Signs*, New Delhi: Oxford University Press, 1983.

Prabha, M. *The Waffle of the Toffs*, New Delhi: Oxford University Press & IBH, 2000.

Parthasarthy, R. ed. *Ten Twentieth Century Indian Poets*, New Delhi: Oxford University Press, 1976.

Ramanujan, A. K. *Selected Poems*, New Delhi: Oxford University Press, 1976.

_____. *The Collected Poems of A. K. Ramanujan*, ed. Vinay Dharwadker, New Delhi: Oxford Univesrity Press, 1995.

Singh, Kanwar Dinesh. *Contemporary Indian English Poetry: Comparing Male & Female Voices*, New Delhi: Atlantic Publishers & Distributors, 2008.

_____. *New Explorations in Indian English Poetry*. New Delhi: Sarup & Sons, 2004.

17

The Metaphors of Conquest: Trends in Contemporary Indian Woman Poets in English

—Jaydeep Sarangi

With the ideological ascendancy of science, medicine, the formulation of the knowledge based society and the rapid spread of cyber space the notion of 'biology is destiny' has become a myth. Women's search for the self is invariably engaged in resistance to prevailing notions of women's 'nature'. Associated with that biological destination was a host of psychological attributes—acceptance, passivity, dependence, subordination—which further reinforced a growing emphasis on the gendered separation of the personal and the public spheres. Women's fixed role as caregivers was ideologically determined by their biological capacity to bear children and that was through a fixed set of codes represented by 'categorizers' as Kamala Das has expressed in her poem, "An Introduction". In women's poetry, there is anger at patriarchy that eloquently argues the woman's cause with the help of striking morbid and sexual metaphors, careful symbols and traditional Hindu allusions. "The Woman Question" is a sociological issue that incorporates myriad contemporary feminist questions and concerns regarding women's role in society and the domestic space. Women, in the first place, are the slaves of capital; their cause is man's cause. In addition to this burden of economic servitude they are subjected to the misery of being the property, tool, and plaything of man, and have neither power to protest against the use, nor remedies against age-old practice of abuse, of their persons by their male masters. 'Right' is a euphonious equivalent of 'might.' While the resistance to this view of sexual difference varies historically and culturally, it is against this backdrop that thoughts of modern and contemporary Indian woman poets in English must be understood.

India is shining with female voices in poetry. Indian woman poets writing in English from Toru Dutt to Kamala Das and from Sarojini Naidu to Sanjukta Dasgupta reveal the mind-boggling variety of themes that poetry is capable of offering. Each one of them has tried to speak in a distinctly personal voice, yet they form a part of chorus, a collective voice asserting the autonomy of women.

Kamala Das (Madhavikutty in her early days and Suraiya now as she has converted to Islam) is an image-breaker who has asserted her identity on the firmament of Indian English poetry by her honest poetical lines that breaks through the hypocritical veneer of man-woman relationships in Indian traditional society. She is an Indian poet, short story writer, novelist, playwright, essayist, non-fiction writer, children's writer, and autobiographer. Her poetry is not merely Indian like that of Toru Dutt and Sarojini Naidu, but a passionate expression of the universal experience of love, despair, anguish,failure and disgust against the traditional mode of gender manifestation apprehended through a feminine Indian sensibility:

> All I want now
> is to take a long walk
> into the sea
> and be there, resting,
> completely uninvolved.
> But,
> rest is only a childish whim,
> a minor hunger.
> Greater hunger lurks
> at the basement of the sea.
>
> ("Composition": Kamala Das)

The poem "The Invitation" by Kamala Das illustrates and explores on the struggle for power and autonomy by the women poets. This poem is a narrative of power—a creation of a self-affirming way of life for the female protagonist as an intelligent, self-aware, confident and integrated personality with the aptitude and ability to live life on her own terms. The central action in the poem revolves round an encounter between a seemingly irresponsible female protagonist and the sea. The combat between the woman and sea is presented in the poem in the form of a dialogue—argument and counter-argument follow each other in a persuasive battle of verbose expressions.

Kamala Das is at her poetic best a poet of private (confessional) sensibility. Her consciousness is firmly yoked to the world around her, a world characterized by ecstasy and pain, love and despair. At 42, she published her autobiography, *My Story*, baring the secrets of her heart. Her poems are gestures that counter the luridness of the world. Her first volume of poems *Summer in Calcutta* (1965) arises from the poet's agonized response to the external world about the traumatic experiences of her childhood and early married life. The next collection *The Descendants* (1967) not only explores the leading motifs like love, lust and disillusionment, but also shows a metaphysical concern with time, death and decay. *The Old Playhouse and Other Poems* (1973) continues the poet's concern with the deeper meaning of life, death, disease and decay. In her *Collected Poems* (1984) we hear Kamala Das with a more mature and talented poetic voice. Her poetry collection published under the title, *Only the Soul Knows How to Sing* (1996) is a touching account of a traumatic frustration in love and marriage. Irony assumes a tinge of social criticism in the short poem "The Fancy Dress Show," as the poet exposes the great fancy dress show, that is, our civilization.

> Every virtue requires today
> A fancy dress; the cassock is
> The priest's main virtue, the clever
> Politician dons a saint's mean
> Apparel.

Kamala Das's language question is her honest commitment as a postcolonial poet:

> I am Indian, very brown, born in
> Malabar, I speak three languages, write in
> Two, dream in one.
>
> ("An Introduction": Kamala Das)

In "An Introduction", Kamala Das goes on to describe her growing up to womanliness. Her 'Self' comes to the fore at the encroachment of her freedom of expression; her right to self-expression which is a prelude to her right to gender equality. "An Introduction" is her self-assertive statement attacking conventionalism. In her honest poetic lines in the poem she advocates the rights of women. Coupled with her exploration of women's basic needs is an attention to eroticism. For her poetics, restrained love seems to be no love at all; only a total immersion in love experienced in union of bodies can do justice to her experience. She becomes a feminist writer by making her women conscious. Her poetry shows a landmark in her female journey from victimisation to consciousness. The essence of her poems is struggle about her own 'Self'. As the self, female self, in her takes different sociological roles, the ultimate self in her cries out honestly which, in fact turns out to be a collective cry. It is a cry for constructing female space and identity: 'I too call myself I' ("An Introduction": Kamala Das)

Sanjukta Dasgupta, a professor and a poetess from Bengal, is known for her intellectual sophistication and emotional vigour that blends the world and the women motifs. Her poetic corpus candidly expresses the predicament of modern Indian woman's ambivalence in her verses that perplexes the minds of her readers with top-heavy theoretical speculations of philosophy. She deeply penetrates the inner pores of the feminine psyche, the postmodern shifting realities and brings out the residue of life:

> I am sangam and shakti
> Power of fire, water, air and earth"
>
> ("Identity", Sanjukta Dasgupta)

Dasgupta explores the infinite possibilities of the self constructed and integrated through the passage of time.

> I am a skylark
> Can't sing to another's tune.
> ("Identity", Sanjukta Dasgupta)

The poetess rises with the aesthetics of resistance and establishes her conscious intention in a seemingly changed social discourse by the traditional Hindu image of Durga:

> Albatross or tyrant
> I had to annihilate you
> Piercing your lying heart
> With the unerring trident
> Of furious Durga
>
> Forgive me
> I could not be Lakshmi anymore
> In calm composure
> Forgiveness
> Like a misty halo
> Shielding the cruel and callous.
> ("More Light" Sanjukta Dasgupta)

Haunting note of despondency mark Dasgupta's poetic lines. We may refer to her poem, "Nihilism" (*Dilemma*) to fathom the depth of her wounded self:

> It was something
> So intense and true perhaps
> That was a bit too much.

Dasgupta's felicity of phrasing, her delicate sensibility and the intelligent use of Indian mythology make her poetic lines impressive.

Ecofeminism links ecology with feminism; ecofeminists see the domination of women as stemming from the same ideologies that bring about the domination of the environment. Ecofeminism connects the exploitation and domination of women with that of the ecology. One of the representative poetess of Ecofeminist trend is Mamang Dai who is a writer and journalist. She was born in Pasighat, East Siang District, Arunachal Pradesh. Former President, Arunachal Pradesh Union of Working Journalists (APUWJ) Dai is currently the Vice-president of the North East Writers' Forum (NEWF), an organisation dedicated to the cause of promoting the literature of North East India. In her poems she searches for a bond between woman and the territory. For her poetic aesthetics of woman and the territory (Nature) have creative energy. Therefore, both are tied with a cemented bond:

> Footsteps.
> Silence.
> A twig breaks
> and thunder raises the canopy of trees.
>
> The tiger runs swiftly from my father's house
> calling my name.
> Brother ! Man brother!
> Have mercy for our destiny!
> ("Man and Brother", Mamang Dai)
>
> *I go where the forest is unknown.*
> Under the sacred tree I'll place my bow,
> the night will be long,
> the wild birds are restless,
> but I'll wear my disguise
> and wait.
> Green intoxication
> fading swiftly to darkness.
> Alone I wait, wearing my amulet,
> waiting where I can hear best
> instructions from my ancestors.
> ("Man and Brother", Mamang Dai)

Lakshisree Banerjee's collection of poetry, *I am the Woman: I am the World* is a celebration of womanhood which can be interpreted as an extension of the concept—'territory as woman and woman as territory'. Like as true ecofeminist by temper she thinks herself "Bred as a fire-girl/ a rhododendron / in ashes of cold heights..../ schooled for / the fire rites" ("Sita or Sati").

In the title poem of the volume she eagerly looks at "a new rainbow-sun" which can relieve her agony and trauma of living. Nostalgia and regret about days that are no more dish out poignancy and pathos in her poems. Laksmishree Banerjee (2004) in her "Preface" to *"I am the Woman: I am the World"* notes that her poems 'highlight the Woman-question as a fulcrum and a pivotal, humane point of the world at large.' Laksmishree Banerjee's poem "Lakshman Rekha" symbolises the woman's struggles and victories through an aesthetic mode:

> Why did Sita cross the Lakshman Rekha
> (or did she trip over it?)
> Between life and death (.)

Archana Sahani with her collection of poems, *First Fire* reveals uniqueness as an Indian poet writing details of feminine psyche that suggest the voice of a true insider who has seen life to the lees. She bitterly laments over the transitoriness of the physical fleshly attire that subjects to decomposition in the biological process of death, "the flesh fell away" and expresses desperation, "I lay pining/ for a mortal man's love." ('She Who Tears Apart Thought') Her poetic self gasps in darkness to search for her emotional root proclaiming it as, "Sap is my heritage." Sap is liquid in a plant that carries food to all its parts. It is a source of vitality for the poet to voyage within.

The use of private symbols and seemingly opaque images demand a thorough and close reading of her poems. She has consistently struggled with language to develop and use a human language in her poetry. Vilas Sarang in his 'Introduction' claims Arachna Sahani as "a worthy successor to the poetic mode developed by Kamala Das". We would like to go a step further to call Sahani as a pioneer in setting up the trend of celebration of the feminine self in her own way. Sahani scrutinises loopholes of traditional patriarchy and the modern society questioning concepts of gender and associated forms of power. There is a straddling of public and private spheres here, yet also a failure to achieve secure identity in either. Her poems encompass the struggles of women to secure their economic and political agency and an integrated as well as dignified journey to the self. *First Fire* points out a new history of feminine selfhood, or rather of a process of becoming, in which women re-think her story and rebuild her story. A woman writer is both the "inheritor" and the "originator" of the female literary tradition. Archana Sahani is candid and honest in her self-exploration. Her poetry shows a landmark in her female journey from victimisation to consciousness. As the awareness of the self; female self, in her takes different roles, the ultimate self in her cries out honestly which, in fact turns out to be a collective cry. It is a cry for freedom of all sorts. Her quest for identity is not the spiritual Odyssey; it is a human journey, a journey that dignifies the reader. Her poetic lines enrich all who follow the way through the "syllable/of sound" ("She Who Tears Apart Thought").

Archana Sahani's *First Fire* like other contemporary Indian English 'confessional' poets springs from her own private agony. Indeed, each poem in Sahani's *First Fire* is rich with varied dexterity that explore the states of mind and genuine feminine sentiments. Her poetic mode ranges from the meditative to sensuous where the metaphysical subtlety of arrivals and departures get confused. A feature that impresses and ultimately convinces the readers is the poet's readiness to allow conflicting voices to be heard from all contending perspectives. Her poems pose a tension that reaches out to the reader, arousing in one a sense of need that will not be satisfied. Sahani's poetic lines seem to echo from life itself, from the pauses of loss and vacuity.

Archana Sahani is an intelligent and insistent soul-maker. The depth of the oceanic sense of frustration eludes the poet. Sahani's poems show us the tangible spaces between objects which cause our hearts to nearly burst from moments of trajectory of sadness and the objective beauty immaculate by which we live our life:

> Something is born
> when something dies
> Something congeals
> when something is denied.
>
> ("The Tale of a Demonic Woman")

Sahani's quest for sincere love is her quest for searching the Self; her integrated psyche that is aware and free. Her poetry is poetry of complaint, discontent and restlessness.

Sahani's poem dedicated to His Holiness the Dalai Lama, "Passage to Tibet" is a stark postcolonial refugee reality in India which adds a new dimension in contemporary Indian Woman Poets in English. Sahani with wings of her poetic imagination touches the holistic height as symbolised by "Dhauladhars":

> I touched
> the roof of the world
> amidst the Dhauladhars.

"Dhauladhars" represent the Truth, the bitter sweet tyranny of the eye. Sahani predicts a sociological Truth—"Tibet Bill Be Free". She includes herself as a politically conscious journeyman in the quest for Truth, "I will come with you / when prayer flags wave."

Sujata Bhatt, born in India and educated in the United States, now living in Germany, has been shaped by her diasporic experiences as reflected in her three collections: *Brunizem* (1988) which won the Commonwealth Poetry prize (Asian Section), *Monkey Shadows* (1991) won a poetry Book Society Recommendation and her third anthology the *The Stinkin Roe* (1997) is the recent book with a selection from the first three books introduced by one new poem, the title poem. Sujata's poetry is the anguish of immigrants when they start to lose their first language, and she comments approvingly on the poet's attempt use Gujarati line interspersed with English ones for onomatopoeia effect, and because for her certain subjects cannot be described in English. In fact, her bi-lingual poems explore the conflict of the self crossing over between pulls of cultural forces.

Shanta Acharya, born in Orissa, has lived in England for about twenty-five years. His books of poems *Not This, Not That* (1994), *Numbering Our Days' Illusions*(1993) *Looking In, Looking Out* (2005) and *Shringara* (2006) eloquently argue the woman's cause. His poetry reflects the diasporic aesthetics, which reinforces the emptiness (for indigene cultural root) experiencing the exile in the space determined for 'identity' which is tinged with her quest for womanhood:

> We travel not to explore another country
> but to return home refreshed,
> bearing gifts rejuvenating our lives.
> ("Somewhere, Something")

Separation from the root haunts him like the dark shade of despair.

The metaphors and symbols of representations in her poems connect her essential fragmentation of exile identity with the suspended feeling for home. His diasporic voice is studded superimposing blocks of images:

> Our lives airports from which we fly forth
> days the journeys we make,
> Past the continents we leave behind
> We hope shattering our future.
> ("Somewhere, Something")

In his poem, "My Good Luck Home", Ganesha is but one of several gifts of fetishes from around the world in her poem:

> Even Ganesha travels with me in my handbag
> To help me over come obstacles in my adopted home.

Shanta Acharya's poems hint not at stable patriarchy, but modern society questioning and playing with concepts of gender and associated forms of power:

> You gifted me the Song of God
> blessed me with insight –
> Urging me to explore the universe
> find the sacred temple buried deep in us
> see the world as if for the first time,
> to fare well and fare forward.
> ("On First Reading the Bhagavad Gita",
> Shanta Acharya)

The use of illness as a 'conceit' seems to be rather unusual for a postcolonial poet as it is combined with the sense of space-bound displacement. Acharya is obsessed with the desire to be loved and to be accepted as she is. Her search for ideal lover remains incomplete.

A strange sense of personal loss pervades Acharya's poems. Inward-looking and at the same time deeply rooted in cultural and interpersonal realities, her poems speak to us in their own inexplicable intensity. For her, woman self life enjoys a promise between the outer world and the self. Acharya's poems reach across that specific space and we all feel when we pause and reflect what our lives mean. All that surrounds us is ready for the adventure and trust that accompany us on our journey. A worldwide realisation comes alive—we are huddled together; we share weaknesses and strengths; and a generous spirit finds rewards in available objects. Indian critics have disagreed about the significance of Sahani's choice to write of her experiences as an Indian woman in English; some scholars suggest that, in her shunning of traditional aesthetic form, she has created a new language for the expression of colonial contradictions. Despite disagreement over the aesthetic qualities and consistency of her body of poetry, scholars agree that Archana is an important figure whose bold and honest voice has re-energized Indian writing in English.

Dalit poetry in India is structurally alternative to the models prescribed by traditional Hindu aesthetics precisely because they are literatures of sociological oppression and economical exploitation. It is subversive, or assault to anthropomorphic practice of castism in India. Dalit poetry is that militant in texture and aggressively blunt in meaning. It challenges codified language (because it has so far been used and manipulated only by the dominant, discriminating powers), it challenges assumptions, it challenges age-old worldviews. Its temporal and political designation does not give justice to the artist whose intentions may subsequently be ignored. It is an aesthetics of pain, and a prolong longing; a powerful aesthetics of resistance.

For Meena Kandasamy, the young Tamil poetess, poetry is about empirical truth and experience and she writes and reflects from where she is. The poems in *Touch* by her amplifies, illustrates, and carries on this struggle for power and autonomy by the women poets. For her, the young Tamil poetess, poetry is about empirical truth and experience and she writes and reflects from where she is:

> We: their daughters,
> We: the daughters of their soil.
> We, mostly, write.
> ("Their Daughters")

Touch (2006), Meena's maiden collection, has a fascinating and thought-provoking 'Foreword' by Kamala Das where the senior poetess acknowledges the 'superiority' of Meena Kandasamy's 'poetic vision'. Meena follows the tradition of Gwendolyn Brooks, Sylvia Plath and Langston Hughes a 'fabric rare and strange'. Women's fixed role as caregivers was ideologically determined by their biological capacity to bear children and that was through a fixed set of codes represented by 'categorizers' as Kamala Das has expressed in her poem, "An Introduction". Meena Kandasamy regards her poetic corpus as a process of coming to terms with her identity and consciousness: her "womanness, Tamilness and low/ outcasteness", labels that she wears with pride. Meena has honed her sociological awareness of what it means to be a woman in a caste-ridden social groupism in Tamil Nadu (a Southern state in India).

Her poetic self gasps in darkness to search for her emotional root proclaiming it as, sap is her heritage. Sap is liquid in a plant that carries food to all its parts. It is a source of vitality for the poetess to voyage within. Her confessional mode is not as radical as we find in Mamang Dai, Archana Sahani and Kamala Das. She explores wide range of subjective possibilities and relates them to her own identity and sociological formulation.

Therefore, her poetry that arises not out of mere profound reading and knowledge, but out of active engagement. *Touch* is rich with varied dexterity that explore the states of mind and genuine feminine sentiments. A feature that impresses and ultimately convinces the readers is the poet's readiness to allow conflicting voices to be heard from all contending perspectives. Her poems pose a tension that reaches out to the reader, arousing in one a sense of need that will not be satisfied.

There is always a haunting note of despondency mark in Meen's poetic lines. We may refer to her poem, "Immanuel":

> Now, if there be any mourning
> Let it be for our heroes
> Yet to die, fighting...

Meena's poetic lines seem to echo from life itself, from the pauses of loss and vacuity in her sociological repression in a class-stratified Tamil society. She deeply penetrates the inner pores of the feminine psyche and brings out the strength and power of life. Meena's quest for identity is not the spiritual Odyssey; it is a human journey, a sociological journey that dignifies the reader. Debates over dalit studies in India have intensified studies of anti-colonial resistance in general which has been augmented and contested by a broad range of studies and research in several places. Through Meena's conscious poetic lines, dalits are hit back in the coloniser's tongue. Poems in *Touch* represent the indigenous lifestyle, that resist colonial acts of authority and oppression through their textual transmission.

The corpus of the contemporary Indian woman poets in English marks a strong self-expression; thereby conforming to a new (confessional) female literary tradition and the textual body liberates the suppressed voice that has been trying through ages to find its own identity. The indomitable gusto and interpretative autonomy of these 'confessional' poems make the reader sit and read the poems again and again. They women poets have chosen poetry as a genre of self-expression and there is a feminine sensibility and assertiveness in their poetry. What distinguishes the contemporary female poets from their male counterparts is their realistic attitude to love, sex, their social status and role-relationships; their poetry defines their fiery sensibility with the metaphors of conquest.

Works Cited

Kamala Das, 'Foreword', *Touch,* Meena Kandasamy, Peacock Books, Mumbai, 2006, 07.

Laksmishree Banerjee, 'Preface', *I am the Woman: I am the World*, UBSPD, 2004, vii-viii.

18

Compromise as a Survival Kit in Girish Karnad's *Naga-Mandala*

—Smita R. Nagori (Lakhotiya)

The paper is intended to reveal the human need to live by truth and reality and not by half-truths and fictions as the blurb of Girish Karnad's *Naga-Mandala* proclaims. In fact, living by half-truths and fictions is like a camouflage put on reality. Despite it being strange, bitter, engendering hatred, truth, under no circumstances can it be disregarded. Reality never arrives neatly wrapped. It may not make us free from troubles, but we cannot run away from it. It has to be confronted with compromise as a kit to survive. Half-truths and fictions please you only transitorily.

All the three major characters Rani—Appanna and Naga—weave fantasies. Appanna marries Rani, and so, Rani is his sole responsibility. But he escapes from this responsibility. For Appanna, Rani is his property, providing him with his domestic needs. He reveals his indifference towards her even when she is newly married. Her dismay and loneliness do not move his callous and barbaric behaviour. She is unaware of his philandering in the beginning. She confronts this colossal mental trauma mutely.

In the patriarchal society, a woman is virtuous only when she mutely consents to the subservience of her lord, her husband. She has to serve him unquestioningly; her strength is to do her duty even in the face of viciousness and suffering. She does not let the faults of her husband keep her from realizing her potential to be a consummate, devoted, ideal wife.

The Laws of Manu, state "Though destitute of virtue or seeking pleasure elsewhere, or devoid of good qualities, a husband must be constantly worshipped as a god by a faithful wife. If a wife obeys her husband, she will for that reason alone be exalted in heaven". Rani caters to all the norms of the Laws of Manu. But the Laws of Manu codified during the first or the second century cannot comply with the feelings of the liberating woman of the twenty-first century. The irony is that our Indian women live in the twenty-first century and adhere to the norms of the centuries-old ideals to retain their virtuosity. Rani is presented as this ideal in the beginning. Her subservience under Appanna's brutal and savage visage motivates him to subjugate her unceasingly and to continue to live with the concubine. On account of her slavish countenance, she becomes despondent. Her desolate appearance provokes the cobra, after consumption of the aphrodisiac root, to capture her physically as well as emotionally.

Karnad excels in his proficiency of art when he mixes human and non-human worlds and renders the form of Appanna to the cobra. Regardless of this, the cobra or Naga has to be considered as an individual. Shape-shifting is a strategy adopted by Karnad from myths and folk-tales. After all, the cardinal concept is to explore similar situations and ideas. Laximi Chandrashekhar, an academic and an active figure in Kannad theatre of the yesteryear opines: "Karnad has been accused of escaping into the past". But the present is nothing but the continuation of the past. The past is just a vehicle to peep into the present.

A cobra, taken as a symbol, can be interpreted in many ways. It refers to the genital organ, as God of fertility, also as God of protection and at the same time the cobra, naga, can put an end to one's existence through his poisonous bite. His phallic passions fascinate him towards the lonely Rani. Appanna is merciless. Rani is helpless. Naga readily comes forward to exploit the situation by captivating her with parental love. All the characteristic features revealed by Naga are that of a lover. His nocturnal visits make her yield to his love. His love blossoms her feminity and also develops the animus in her making her courageous. Owing to the mask of Appanna, Rani takes Naga to be her husband. But as time passes by, she finds drastic changes in the day-time and the night time husband. She, at times, senses utter difference between them. As far as nature is concerned, she can apprehend, but contrast in physical appearance makes her feel mysterious. She experiences Naga's blood to be very cold unlike human blood and like reptiles. Once, when she opens the mirror box, she is shocked to see the image of the cobra in the mirror in place of Appanna. Sylvia Plath, the great American poetess, in her poem "Mirror" says:

> Mirror do not have any preconceptions.
> They are exact; unmisted by love or dislike,
> Not cruel, only truthful.

This is an indication for Rani. Later, she sees that the day-time Appanna has no marks or scars of injury on his face while the nocturnal Appanna has scars of injury on his person. His absence for a fortnight perturbs her. When he turns up, his whole body is injured. The face in the morning unrelated to the touch at night baffles her. She does not divulge the willingness to contemplate on it lest her happy nocturnal world tumbles down. If she is so confident of the two Appannas being the same, she could have easily enquired regarding the absence of his visits at night when he visits for her lunch. Rani also takes due care not to connect the two Appannas in conversation. She never relates the incidents in the afternoon to those of the night. It is just impossible to have two extreme countenances in the same man. In spite of experiencing several traces, she does not want to probe into the details but pleases herself with the half-truths. But the great Greek Master, Plato, says: "A man is not to be reverenced more than the truth". In fact, "Truth is as old as God and will endure as long as He-a co-eternity" says Emily Dickinson.

This means that Rani cannot be happy for a long time, if she conceals the truth. Her happiness by half-truths is short-lived and transitory. Yet, she fosters these moiety-truths because she knows that if the truth is manifested or even if she tries to break the ice in this connection, she may lose the part of her life that is filled with ecstatic pleasures, passion compassion and freedom. She purposefully avoids discovering the whole truth. On the other hand, the spineless Appanna takes pride in binding Rani in his shackles.

In course of time, Rani's announcement of her pregnancy leads to an imbroglio, a mishmash for both, Naga and Appanna. The reaction of the two Appannas mystifies her. Naga's frigid reaction makes her cry. He tells Rani dully: "I am glad you hid the news from me all this time. Even now, try to keep from speaking about it as long as possible. Keep it a secret from me." The fact is, Naga metamorphoses as Appanna through shape-shifting. This transgressing may have unpleasant consequences once it is found out. It might also end in death, destruction or unhappiness. The transgressor has to pay a heavy price. Moreover, the lover is interested only in satisfying his phallic passions. He does not like to be burdened by a child. And so impregnated with fear, he insists upon her to undergo the Snake Ordeal.

The news stuns her husband, Appanna, and makes him thrombose. His temerity is shattered to pieces. Kicking Rani, he showers abusing words on her. He shouts:

> Aren't you ashamed to admit it, you harlot? I locked you in, and
>
> Yet you managed to find a lover! Who did you go with your sari off?

Dragging her out of the house, he takes a huge stone to kill the bastard child. But on the spur of the moment, Naga intervenes by a hissing sound, and paves the way for Rani to escape. He protects her. In magic, 'mandala' means protection. The very title 'Naga-Mandala' refers to it.

Rani, shattered to pieces, is unable to apprehend the situation. In our Indian culture, especially women, marriage means duty and devotion, and adultery is the highest crime when committed by a woman. It causes shame for both, her mother's family, and her husband's family and is punishable by death.

Appanna, a staunch representative of the patriarchal society, conveniently manifests his promptness to follow the footprints of the age-old example of Sita undergoing the Fire Ordeal to prove her chastity. The centuries-old example cannot give vent to the feelings of the contemporary world. It is Sita's subservience that helps Rama command the Fire Ordeal. Had Sita denied, things would have been different. These obsolete examples are very conveniently followed by the patriarchal society.

Appanna wants Rani to undergo the Chastity Test. Rani resolves to go for the Snake Ordeal and is not only successful but is hailed as 'Divine Being', a 'Goddess'. The reality is that no ordeal can prove one's chastity if one determines to speak against the truth. Rani is not chaste but the chastity test has elevated her to a Goddess. No one's chastity can be measured by any means, let that be holding of red hot iron rod or any other. All this is inhumane. Karnad seems to mean that women will attain equality only after undergoing a sort of ordeal. All this is simply a farce, creating a humiliating situation for women.

Our Indian culture projects the institution of marriage as a very pious and dignified one. Marriage is generally not a happy result of an accident of fate, which we call as 'Falling in Love'. The notion of marriage being made in heaven still holds good in our Indian hearts. The nuptials keep them bound to each other. They are not easily separable. During the wedding rituals, the priest makes the husband and wife committed to each other. If the husband deviates from his conjugal fascinations, the wife has the right to prevent him from the same and vice versa. They have to accept each other with all their weaknesses and strengths. Once Rani is married to Appanna, it becomes obligatory on her part to stay with him in spite of his harshness. The same norms go for Appanna also.

Despite Kappanna's opinion: "Appanna should have been born a wild beast or a reptile. By some mistake, he got human birth," Rani has to confront the reality that Appanna is her husband and she has to make a compromise. She will also be equally responsible for connivance at Appanna's weakness. But care should be taken, that it is in no way a justification to reinscribe the patriarchal sensibilities of a male-dominated society. Rani's mute subservience will now fail to have strength in our eyes where women are protesting against patriarchy. Rani's compromise is not for Appanna's continuing his routine with the harlot but to commence a harmonious conjugal relationship afresh. Rani accepting the concubine as a maidservant in their house is a big compromise in itself. Indeed, she has been compromising from the day she entered into wedlock.

Appanna too has to extend his cooperation in compromising with the situation. Though a world hails Rani as a Divine Being or the Goddess Incarnate, he knows that he is not the father of the child. But because he has sinned so much against Rani, he feels: 'Have I sinned so much that even Nature should laugh at me?' He has to accept her not only as as a wife, but also a 'Divine Being'.

Rani also realizes that it is Naga in a transgressed form who visited her every night. He commits suicide by strangulating himself in the tresses of Rani. Later, while combing down her hair the dead cobra falls down. This doesn't make her jump out of her skin. She simply utters in a sad tone: "Oh! Poor thing. It is dead." The young wife who shuddered at the very name of the snake and now reacts very coolly even when it falls from her tresses. This is something very surprising. The same is further confirmed when she picks up the dead snake and shedding tears, she presses it to her cheeks. What this reveals is that she knows that Naga is not Appanna, her husband. She goes to the extent of asking Appanna to perform the annual rituals in commemoration of the snake, in addition to the cremation to be done by their son. It, indeed, needs a mega heart to consent to all these demands of Rani. Yet, he shows great courage in accepting all this willingly because he knows that compromise is the only way to make their conjugal life happy.

Naga's giving up of his phallic passions makes way for Appanna and Rani's happy married life.

In fact, unlike what the blurb says, living by fictions and half-truths will only bring down the whole edifice of day-to-day living and finally lead towards the destruction of one and all. What is essential is mutual conjugal responsibility with compromise as a strategy to maintain the dignity of the institution of marriage. Ultimately, it is truth that triumphs and prevails.

Lord Byron rightly says;
It is strange, but true;
For truth is always strange,
Stranger than fictions.

Works Cited

Karnad, Girish *Naga-Mandala*, Delhi: Oxford University Press, 1990.

19

The Fragrance of Flowers: A Reading into Girish Karnad's Monologue

—Zinia Mitra

Girish Karnad's *Collected Plays* in two volumes (OUP) includes *Two Monologues*. *Flowers* is one of them. The play was premiered at the Ranga Shankara Theatre Festival in 2006 starring Rajit Kapur and directed by Rosyten Abel. In the monologue, we again have the familiar evaluation of human predicament presented within the characteristic framework of a folktale. The play questions duty and its complex correlation with human desire. This folktale from Chitradurga, centred on the life of a priest, devoted and pious, exploits the fantastic God's response to the devoted and the rise of devotee to sainthood. Within the scaffold, Karnad's surveillance points again at the conflicting norms of societal acceptance and questions the very cosseted position of sainthood, just as Nandikar in their recent presentation of *Madhavi* questions the very idea of sainthood that is ultimately conferred on Galab.

The monologue opens with a reference to the rising constellation of Scorpio in front of a temple. It is significant that the reference is to the visibility of the constellation not in the sky but as reflected in the water of the temple tank: "In a few moments from now, Scorpio will start creeping into the water from the south—eastern corner of the temple tank. There is a hollow there in the third step under the water, large enough to hold an unhusked coconut" (243). A priest of a Shiva temple reflects on his life and brings to the present an incident that occurred in his life in the recent past. It facilities a movement in the past and brings it to the forefront just like the movement of the constellation makes it visible. It introduces mystery and symbolism and brings it to the core of the play. The priest's deep thoughts swim out in a continuous flow just as the constellation, as reflected in the temple tank and affirmed by the priest, would seem to swim out of the cavity moments later. Later, when the end of the play meets the beginning in a circular structure, it would also be the point of the 'swimming' out of life of the priest. Torn between his love for his God (called devotion), and his love for a courtesan (called sacrilege), between his duty to the king and his duty to his wife, and the need to prove himself, the priest tells the story of his life, in a monologue, of what happens when all the loves and duties collide on a single night.

The beginning introduces us to the priest and to his 'private universe'. He knows this 'universe' so thoroughly that he says:

> ...even with my back to the temple, I could tell you what star is perched on the brass tip of its pinnacle. For I know every nook and cranny in these grounds. (243)

The priest who lived with his wife, children and parents, was treasured by the village people for his devotion to the god of the temple. He served at the Shiva temple and decorated the lingam with flowers. He was well appreciated for his unique decoration of the lingam. His skill was so well known that the chieftain of the land visited the temple every evening for evening prayers, accepted a *prasad* and also made it a point to commend the priest and his wife on the floral motif. The ritual, both of the pooja and that of the flower arrangement, was most sacred and engaging for the priest. He says, "Everything else then recedes into hazy, scarcely-felt distance and for an hour there is only the lingam and me" (244). He devised novel ways of adorning the phallic structure with flowers. The priest was obsessed with the lingam to the extent of talking to it, singing to it and even discussing political matters with it. His wife's complaint that the lingam was the priest's 'step wife' involved a certain pride, for it also brought him recognition. The isolation that the priest preferred, discouraging all friendly attention of the outside world, broke down when he met Ranganayaki, the courtesan, and began yearning for her.

As the protagonist continues, certain structural relations begin to emerge which tie the various particulars together and gives them significance. By the time the priest finishes his narration the structural relations are so firmly established that the incoherence in the plot, if any, and its contradictions acquire a new significance.

When the priest reports of his infatuation with Ranganayaki there is no pretence in him: "I wanted her" (245), and since he had never hungered for any woman before, he says that he felt powerless by the sudden budding of this particular weakness. But since he was a priest he could not afford a direct look at her and adore her features:

> ...each day as she received the *prasada, I* noticed the mole and as she looked up, hurriedly made a note of a fresh aspect of her face –the brilliant eyes which she quickly averted, the straight nose ending in a slight upward tilt, the lips which like thick petals rimmed her smile with dark sensuousness. Then at night I put them together as in a jig-saw puzzle. (246)

His relation with Ranganayaki makes him explore beyond the self-imposed seclusion and prescribed social norms, the passionate man within him, the lover and the artist.

> My wife had caught on the new element in my daily pooja. I looked for wider variety of flowers now, chose them with greater care and experimented with floral motifs on the linga which would be distinct from those I would devise later on Ranga.(251)

His relation with Ranganayaki gives rise to the obvious social disagreement; "I knew the main reaction would be of amazement that a beautiful and obviously wealthy courtesan should take up with such an unprepossessing lover. Eyebrows would be raised at my good fortune or virility" (251). At the same time this understandable fact is to be kept clandestine.

The moment it is revealed, or to say, becomes perceptible as thinly as a thin, long hair, problem arises.

Ranganayaki was highly appreciative of the dexterity of the priest and of the beauty of his floral motifs. She wanted the priest to decorate her body in a similar manner every night. She wanted the priest, who exhibited great mastery in art while bedecking the lingam, to apply the same mastery in decorating her body with flowers every night. The priest who was enthralled by Ranganayaki's ravishing looks observed it as a ritual. He made it a practice to visit her place every day after the chieftain's visit to the temple and the completion of his pooja. The ritual of decorating the female body with the same flowers used on the phallic symbol magnifies the monotony of the lingam that exists with no curves or/and shapely folds.

> And even as a whole new world of patterns was opening up to me, thoughts of the linga kept passing through my mind. I pitied it, felt exasperated at its unimaginative contours. Why did its shape have to be so bland and unindented that one had to balance garlands precariously on it and improvise superfluous knots to hide some ungainly strings? Why didn't Lord offer a form which inflamed invention like Ranga did? (250)

The act of worship at the temple is an elaborate ritual and is performed in details. "The beauty of a design lies in the detail, the priest later tells Ranganayaki" (250). He sits in a wet dhoti surrounded by baskets of flowers and the whole provisions of incense sticks, camphor and oblations. The everyday act of devotion is both a ritual as well as a ceremony. It is a ceremony because of its speciality and its ritual significance. It is also a ritual by its meticulous recurrence. His communion with Ranganayaki's body similarly becomes a ritual, by meticulous recurrence, similarly public with the presence of the woman, and a ceremony by being a special occasion always. When love is linked with truth (shiva) it is devotion, when love is linked with beauty (courtesan) it is 'sacrilege'. The priest feels it too, and so to purify himself takes a dip in the water before returning home.

He never ate in her place. But beauty is supposed to be truth and truth is ultimately beauty. The priest's passionate worship of the stone 'lingam' and the living female underlies a oneness.

Beyond the preferred isolation of the temple, the two spatial units that enclose the priest's physical being are his home, and the house of the courtesan. Home is where he lives with his parents, wife and children, which offers him shelter and food but denies him privacy, where he is accepted in a specific role, for, a little deviation from it leads to a disruption in conversation and ease. Home is a place that offers him food but where his desire is to be secretly expressed and stealthily indulged in. The other space, the courtesan's house, is where desire can be openly expressed and evoked but it offers him no shelter or food. "Ranganayaki had given up teasing me about consuming her body but not the food in her house" (251). It is a place he has to visit secretly and stealthily. At home love making is a "furtive scuffle in bed which demanded the minimum of uncovering", and at Ranganayaki's house it is a semi-public performance and a repetition of the ritual in the temple with the flowers now forming a pattern on the human body instead of on the stone image. While he decorates her body Ranganayaki sits so "calm and immobile that any amorous advances were out of question." (249)

The play also shows how power dominates the basics of human relationship: the fear of the divine power, Lord Shiva, and that of the worldly power, the chieftain. The pooja has to wait on that particular evening because the chieftain does not arrive on time and after a long wait, when it is nearly midnight, he decides to perform the pooja for he feels that they cannot leave the Lord waiting for ever (253). He reveals himself as unmindful and worried because the chieftain has not arrived on time. He can finally only hope that the god does not mind: "After all, the linga was Shiva and He was used to austerities" (253). It is vital for the priest that the chieftain visit the temple. The one hour he gets after the cannon goes off on the ramparts and the chieftain reaches the temple, the priest puts to good use. He decorates the lingam with his wife attending to the basic requirements of the ritual. By the time the chieftain arrives, the priest is perfectly ready for the pooja. The time of the pooja is thus set in accordance with the convenience of the chieftain. The chieftain's appreciation is also central to his own appraisal of himself, while he views the appreciation of others with scorn, only as a means to please the chieftain: "... he turns to his retinue which, needless to add, obediently spouts various standard phrases in agreement." (244)

When, on the particular night that alters his life, the priest returns to the temple at the sound of the cannon, which is a sure mark of the chieftain's visit, he returns with the 'used' flowers, that is, the flowers that he has used on Ranganayaki's body. This act merges his two separate worlds, the world of love and the world of devotion, also that of display and recognition. The flowers now, instead of journeying from the divine to the human, as it did with the chieftain's pressing one to his eye and sticking it behind his right ear and with the decoration of Ranganayaki's body, now comes from the human to the divine. It is a sacrilegious act violating all socio-religious codes. Such codes are parts of a culture which is made up of many such half-uttered or unutterable expressions of social value. They are hinted by small actions, sometimes by tone or simply a gesture. The priest's act eliminates the division between what is considered to be religious and the sacrilege, between the public and the private. But the narrator is no more an orthodox; he is rather heretical, divided and assembled by passion, a lover and an artist. The priest has broken out of his sole role performance by his relationship with the courtesan, and acquired a subjectivity. He becomes a lover, not merely a devotee but one who is also desirous. The chieftain does not fail to notice a long hair noticeably sticking out from the flowers that the priest holds up for him in a plate. The clandestine is subtly revealed by the ingenious comment of the chieftain: "Does God have long hair?" The priest's need to prove that God has long hair is an effort to restore himself in the eyes of the chieftain and in the eyes of the people.

It is noteworthy that the mind of the priest keeps turning to God when he is with the courtesan demanding the flowers to articulate something singular to God and then something completely unlike to Ranganayaki. Ranganayaki even rebukes him: "Why can't you concentrate on me? I am too gross for you, aren't I? I am not stupid you know. I can see your mind is somewhere else" (252). It is also noteworthy that the complete absorption of the mind is possible for the priest not in Ranganayaki but in the god with whom his association is the closest and longest, only when he can surrender completely to the god he has served. After the chieftain leaves dissatisfied and the priest sends his wife home forbidding her to disturb him and from stepping into the temple precincts and he sits in front of the linga cross-legged, only then does he surrender himself completely to a stupor. "I don't know whether prayer is the right word," he realizes, perhaps it is better expreesed in the words that follow later: "I pleaded with it to save my face. Just that."(258)

For twelve days, the priest reports, he cleanses his existence of everything, every name or person, except the linga. Cleaning oneself is known as Atma shuddhi. The idea of having a clean bath before pooja so that one feels light and uncontaminated in all the sensory organs along with the mind has been recommended. The priest dips in the water numerous times for his cleanliness but attains true cleansing only when he surrenders himself to his lord and shuts himself off from the world. The purification of body and mind is mandatory before special poojas.

The private and the public are merged again at the display of God's hair on the lingam, when a display of "waves and waves of jet black hair came billowing out, their tips gently eddying and swirling in the evening breeze" (258). The miracle saves the priest from public humiliation. The chieftain falls at his feet, crowds rush forward to take his blessings. The status of the priest rises. The priest who was humiliated by the public display of one long hair, from the head of a courtesan that is meant to be displayed, is restored by the public display of the hair on the phallic structure that is not meant to be displayed.

This miracle, while it saves the man from public humiliation and raises his status, deprives his wife of wifehood and claims the priest's single-minded devotion, denying him all enjoyment. The loss of gratification is rewarded by the new 'sainthood' that is bestowed upon on him. The monologue thus opens out several other layers of meanings and raises questions on the very idea of sainthood. In one sense sainthood is martyrdom, it is denunciation of human life. Such as faith itself is a constraint upon freedom. The theme of the play has two aspects. A socio-cultural aspect and a metaphysical aspect. It raises a question similar to that of *Hayavadana* that had questioned the very attainment of perfection. Does perfection mean the fusion of two extreme polarities that is symbolically achieved in *Hayavadana* by the transposition of heads? Does the monologue attempt this fusion within one human body?

The priest's articulation reveals that sainthood is martyrdom not only for the preferred person but also for those who are close to him. The priest's wife shows enough wisdom not to quarrel with the priest over the courtesan. She notes the priest's experimentation with a wider variety of flowers when he strikes a relationship with Ranganayaki. When the priest hears the cannon from Ranganayaki's house what he requires is the support of his wife to set things right before the arrival of the chieftain: "...hoped my wife had not slept through the canon shot" (256). She rebukes him only silently when he decorates the lingam with the flowers used on Ranganayaki's body. When he needs to prove himself he prohibits his wife from entering the precincts of the temple. Yet it is she who takes charge when the miracle happens and the crowd rushes towards him. She pushes the crowd and takes him home. It is she who informs the priest of Ranganayaki's departure. From her perspective the departure of the courtesan that leads to a sudden break in her husband's extra-marital affair and his rise to sainthood does not make a difference. She had served the priest when he was fulfilling his gratification, she would continue to do so through the change in situation:

> But it was clear that Ranganayaki's disappearance would make no difference to my wife. The courtesan had gone and had been replaced by Lord Shiva. I was among the chosen of the Lord and she could not possibly think of

> herself as a wife now, only as a slave and guardian, all shades of the marital bond expunged in favour of her devotion to me, her good fortune in having me for her husband.(259)

The priest who is raised to a status had only longed to save himself form embarrassment and humiliation. The ending of the play where the priest repeats what he had said in the beginning with a new revelation that he had decided to commit suicide, throws a new light on his entire monologue which now seem to be a deep rumination coming from the despair of someone about to die.

> And I have a quarrel to pick with God...Why am I worthy of this burden He has placed on my shoulders? I refuse to bear it. God must understand I simply cannot live on His terms....As a boy I used to shove my head into the hollow to test how long I could hold my breath. I shall do so again now, but not to test my lungs. I shall seek the narrow confines of that hollow the answers that God has denied me. (259-60)

The incident, more importantly the way it is reported, questions whether the act of the Lord was an act of mercy or was it a mockery, a cruel punishment from which the only release can be death.

Girish Karnad borrows themes from Indian history, myth and folktales and assesses them in new light. Like the Greek dramatists, he does not typically devise plots, but rather shows mastery in weaving complex dimensions into the pre-existing narrative. He makes use of the strategies of cultural and religious codes to expose its retrogressive values. He shares the disillusionment of modern Indian intelligentsia and is not fascinated by the make-believe solutions that the body of Indian myth and folktales customarily offer. Karnad's plays typically question the politics of power at play and attempt a redefinition and a restructuring of an existing narrative by ingeniously shifting the thematic emphasis. His *Yayati* redefines the old story of the king who, in his blind hunger for undying youth, seizes the youth and vitality of his son. *Hayavadana* is an embellishment of a tale found in *Kathasaritasagara* that deals with the crisis of incompatible incongruity between the opposites in human life. *Naga-Mandala* is a dramatization of two folk tales of Kannada. *Flowers* is based on a folktale dealing with the problems of self alienation and role play while it questions the very idea of sainthood.

Theatre is an institution that demands a different kind of writing. Even an unconventional arena or form outside the design of conventional theatre establishes specific actor–audience relationship as that can involuntarily come to be interpreted in predictable terms by the kind of spectators present. The playwright does not directly communicate with his readers but is literally interpreted by the agency of actors. At the same time the theatre's fundamental connection to physical reality and existing collective existence make it an important medium or transaction of ideas.

Works Cited

For all textual citations I have followed are from Girish Karnad's *Collected Plays*, New Delhi: OUP, 2005

Dodiya, Jaydipsingh (ed): *The Plays of Girish Karnard Critical Perspectives* Prestige Books, New Delhi, 2009.

Mukherjee, Tutun: *Performance and Critical Perspectives,* Pencraft, New Delhi, 2006.

Karnad, Girish: *Collected Plays*, New Delhi: OUP, 2005.

20

Encounter in Umbugland and *Ghashiram Kotwal*: Tendulkar's Comment on Power Politics

—Shailaja B. Wadikar

Tendulkar's plays can be categorized as social plays, historical plays and political plays. The play *Ghashiram Kotwal,* and *Encounter in Umbugland* reflect political reality and exhibit how political leaders render people mindless and thoughtless. Despite the fact that both the plays unveil the nature of the game of power politics, and reflect the political reality of India of a specific period, they differ completely from each other in terms of subject-matters and thematic concerns. The play *Encounter in Umbugland* is a political allegory as the characters represent historical personages and the story represents the political situation of India in the late sixties and the early seventies. It also refers to the emergence of a "New Woman" and comprises, in a small way, and quite obliquely, a critique on journalism. The play *Ghashiram Kotwal* is based on a particular incident in the eighteenth century Peshwa regime. However, the context is universal, for the characters such as Ghashiram, Nana and Gauri are symbolic and, hence, belong to all ages and societies.

Encounter in Umbugland: Allogorical Nature of the Play

The play *Encounter in Umbugland* is highly allegorical in nature. Even the title suggests something strange and symbolic about it. According to Manchi Sarat Babu, "Umbugland" intensifies the idea of hypocrisy. "Princess Vijaya stands for the

Prime Minister of India, Indira Gandhi.... The play draws parallels between the rule of Vijaya and that of Indira."[1]

The play begins with the announcement of King Vichitravirya's sixtieth coronation anniversary. However, he lies dead when he takes a posture for the painter to paint his portrait. The sudden death of the king rouses the question: "After Vichitravirya, who?" (284) Actually, the play reflects the political scene of India in the late sixties and early seventies. The question "After Nehru, who?" finds an echo in the play "After Vichitravirya, who?" (284)

After Vichitravirya's death, each minister tries to occupy the throne. But all their intriguing efforts are proved in vain for the lack of unity. At last, they unanimously decide to make Vijaya the queen so that they may rule the country in her name. Actually, they hand the authority over to her as part of their game. Vijaya, at first, rejects the responsibility, as she wants to have her freedom. However, Prannarayan helps her accept the responsibility and guides her in her journey from a Princess to a ruler. In the course of time, she learns to enjoy power by suppressing her humanity. Ultimately, the ministers' plans, once again, come to nothing as Vijaya refuses to be their pawn. Instead, she reverses the situation on her advisers. That is why she remains victorious over her rivals and becomes successful in her plan for the rehabilitation of Kadamba tribe.

Satire on Power Politics

The play appears to be Tendulkar's comment on power politics despite its topical nature. It throws light on the fact that in the political field, power is more important than duty. So, selfish designs of the power-mongers have replaced selfless service. All the ideals behind the establishment of democracy—"a state created by people for the welfare of people"[1]—get mingled with the dust. As soon as the power changes, those at the top try to make the ruler collapse or reduce him/ her to the stature of a pawn.

It is through the character of Prannarayan and through the device of the masked men that Tendulkar throws light on the ugliness and futility of power game. And it is through his objective observation that the playwright brings forth the central concern of the play: "Power corrupts itself; absolute power corrupts absolutely."

From Prannarayan's guidance to Princess Vijaya, the audience becomes aware of the fact that conspiracy and treachery are the characteristic features of the present-day politics. In the field of power-politics, nothing is real: appearances are deceptive; success and treachery go hand in hand. Deceitfulness is the way of life in it. Victory is impossible without resorting to treacherous ways and means. "One should take stock of the situation—give some advantages, and get some. Politics means sweet smiling enmity and the experience of sacrifice. A show of sacrifice is always profitable in politics" (306). A ruler should always remind himself that each of the persons is more important than the next"(299). The self-importance of the subjects should not be allowed to suffer at any cost. One should not be true to oneself and play false to others in politics. To accept and to digest these unpalatable things is difficult for a common and truthful person. So, the ruler does not need to be human, he should be either superhuman or even divine. Princess Vijaya's development from a headstrong, inexperienced princess to a prudent, intelligent ruler provides a proof of the fact that a ruler learns all these tricks of the trade gradually in the course of time.

The play projects how falsehood has become an inevitable part of the politician's life, the ultimate result of which is hypocritical behaviour. In order to enjoy power, the politicians "allow themselves to be dehumanized."[2] The play consists of a critique not only on the rulers but on the ruled also. Both of them are mentally deformed. The rulers go on deceiving their subjects and the subjects blindly trust their leaders. The play ends with Prannarayan criticizing people in the words: "I see you upside down, a formless, characterless, lifeless, existenceless gathering. The blind, deaf, and dumb spectators of the whole encounter—who allow men to become politicians, politicians to become statesmen, statesmen to become cunning men, and cunning men to become robots, mechanical men." (356)

The encounter that the play depicts is of dual nature: (i) the one between the ministers and the Kadamba tribe and (ii) the other between Vijaya and her ministers (i.e. an individual against the group). Under the guidance of Prannarayan, Vijaya succeeds in suppressing her humanity. Gradually, she learns and absorbs all the rules of the game of politics. In her transformation from a Princess to a ruler, she learns that hypocrisy leads a politician to words great success and achievement.

Topicality of the Play

Thus, it is observed, the play allegorically reflects the political encounter of the Sindicate group of the Indian National Congress with Indira Gandhi in 1971. It also illustrates the rules of the game of politics, which are difficult for simple, straightforward people to accept. The play exposes the evils in the political field. It shows how politicians make the people mindless by suppressing their capacity to think and by arousing their emotions.

The incident of the encounter in the play is reminiscent of the one in Indira Gandhi's regime in 1971 and the characters resemble those who have been the ministers in Indira Gandhi's cabinet. In the royalist regime of Umbugland, one can easily find the revolt resembling the one by the faction of the Indian National Congress called the Syndicate group represented by such ministers as Kamraj Nadar, S.K. Patil, Morarji Desai, Brahamanand Reddi, Y.B. Chavan, Nijalingappa, etc., to propose the candidature of Neelam Sanjeev Reddi for the post of the President of India in the teeth of their PM's opposition.

The story, thus, represents the political situation of India and the characters represent the historical personages. No doubt, the playwright successfully tries to keep a distance, but one can easily identify the characters with the political figures of the day who held ministerial positions in those years. Vijaya's victory, here, symbolically represents Indira's victory in the political crisis to see V.V. Giri elected as the President of India. Arundhati Banerjee rightly observes:

> Despite the distancing achieved through the creation of the fictitious milieu, it is easy to identify the characters with political figures who held ministerial positions in those years – the principled politician who spouts moral platitudes; his antitype, a bluntly immoral character; the statesman whose face is stretched in a constant smile and who gesticulates wildly but at the same time taciturn to a fault; the floor-crosser who pretends to be ill and sits on the fence till the eleventh hour. And, of course, there is the indomitable Princess Vijaya herself, the daughter of the autocratic king... who devises her own (successful) methods of vanquishing her enemies.[3]

Projection of New Woman

The most important character in the play is that of Vijaya. Her character is portrayed with utmost care. The playwright very minutely depicts the changes in her character and exhibits her development from a headstrong, self-willed and politically inexperienced Princess into an intelligent, witty, victorious ruler. She symbolizes the image of a new woman who is morally well-built, emotionally well-controlled, clear-headed, and clever. She rejects the treacherous plans of her advisers and turns the table on them at last. She is one of those rebellious and assertive women, who is capable of controlling not only her individual fate but the nation's destiny also.

In the political crisis, Vijay succeeds against her rivals as she takes the situation under her control, brings the crisis to an end, and imposes her own will on her subjects instead of allowing herself to be dictated by others. She is rational—guided by reason. She has the capacity to transform her dreams or plans into reality. She is the representative of the iron-willed personalities, who believe in the dictum: "My mind is my master and my thoughts are my power." So, in the royalist regime of Umbugland, the individual succeeds against the group. Likewise, her refusal to accept the authority of the ruler in the beginning and her relationship with Prannarayan reveal the human aspect in her character. It is seen that the character of Vijaya is delineated as exceptionally strong and is in contrast with the other suffering women in Tendulkar's plays.

Ghashiram Kotwal: Ahistorical Nature of the Play

The play *Ghashiram Kotwal* makes a room for Tendulkar in the international galaxy of the playwrights. Although the play is based on one of the incidents in the eighteenth century Peshwa regime, it is not a historical play. Using the historical incident, Tendulkar criticizes society that is responsible for the creation of such people as Nana and Ghashiram.

The new critics are always in favour of an ahistorical approach. The play *Ghashiram Kotwal* is considerably branched off to history and sociology. It is not difficult to find out in the play the reflections of the political situation of India in the eighteenth century Peshwa regime. However, the play has an autonomous existence. For the interpretation of the play, it is not necessary to take into account the historical background of the work or that of the author; just one close reading of the text creates a vivid picture of the political situation of the time and the people at the helm of power. The play belongs to all societies and all times.

The setting of the play *Ghashiram Kotwal* takes us back to the period of the eighteenth century Indian history, that of the Peshwa regime in Maharashtra. However, it may be seen as Tendulkar's dramatic comment on the power politics in society. The ideas put forward here are common to all ages and societies. An unknown Marathi critic writing in a very reputed literary journal discusses the play thus:

> The myth in the play gives the evidence of Tendulkar's extraordinary imagination. Using the classical and the folk forms such as Dashavatara, Gaulan, Tamasha, etc. he creates a suitable form according to the demands of the situation.[4]

But there are two very serious charges against the play and the playwright: (i) The play has been highly criticized as being anti-Brahmin, and (ii) Tendulkar is accused of distorting history. Tendulkar's reply to this criticism is as stated below:

> This is not a historical play. Although based on historical legend, I have no intention of commenting on the morals, lack of them, of the Peshwa, of Nana Phadnavis or

> Ghashiram. The moral of the story, if there is any, may be looked for elsewhere.[5]

According to Girish Karnad, in *Ghashiram Kotwal,* Tendulkar deals with the theme of "emergence of demons in public," created by political leaders for the fulfilment of their aims.[6]

No doubt, the play is based on the incident of the Peshwa regime but history has been transformed into a lively situation full of theatrical potential, supported by his worldview. This is exactly what Shakespeare did. He made use of history from Plutarch's lives and transformed the historical facts creatively into great drama that has withstood the test of time. So, Tendulkar appropriates history to create a powerful play that raises questions of the politics of power that have such a great relevance to Indian society even today. The success of the play lies in its contemporaneity: in the fact that it challenges contemporary values by exposing them.

The Theme of the Play

According to Girish Karnad, in *Ghashiram Kotwal,* Tendulkar deals with the theme of "emergence of demons in public," [7] who are created by the political leaders for the fulfilment of their dreams.

It is noticed that in this play, Tendulkar has used the three-fold tradition of the Indian theatre (i) the classical, (ii) the folk, and (iii) the modern. No other major Marathi playwright before Tendulkar has made such extensive and innovative use of the Indian folk theatre. Jabbar Patel's effective direction contributed a lot to the success and popularity of the play. He made use of humming in addition to the songs and music so that the audience witness and experience what Vasantrao Deshpande, a noted classical singer and composer himself, calls "the first sangeet natak (a musical play like opera) in the real sense of the term." [8] The music in the play seems to serve the following purposes:

1. The traditional songs and dances effectively create the scene of the decadence of the Peshwa regime and the city of Poona in the eighteenth century.

2. They provide entertainment and dramatic relief.
3. Sometimes they increase the intensity of the tense atmosphere. Satish Alekar, the play's assistant director opines: "After the ordeal by the fire, the tempo tended to slow down a little. But with the introduction of the '*Malhari*' song, the tense atmosphere, created by the sequence was reinforced." [9]
4. The use of 'lavni' (a folk song) brings into focus the sensuous and passionate elements in the situation. Similarly, it throws light on the contradiction in social values and norms.
5. The musical form helps to 'deglamourise' history by demythifying it through satire.

Briefly, the story of the play is about Ghasiram, a poor Brahmin from Kanauj who goes to the city of Poona in the search of livelihood. But he is tortured and humiliated on the false charge of theft. The inhuman treatment transforms an innocent new comer into an ambitious, sadistic perpetrator of injustice. He leaves the city with a vow that he will return and turn this city of Brahmins into a city of pigs. For the fulfilment of his ambition, he does not hesitate to bargain his daughter's chastity to Nana for a pecuniary gain of being the Kotwal of the city of Poona. He sends Gauri to Nana and in return, achieves the position of the Kotwal of the city.

The city of Poona starts trembling at the mention of his name due to his tyrannical rule, restrictions and punishments. To put out nails and to wash such fingers with lemon juice and soap, to seal the hands in a bag, to place red-hot iron ball on the hands, to cut off hands, etc. are the punishments he has meted out to the people who are caught under mere suspicion. However, Gauri becomes a scapegoat in the power game of Nana and Ghashiram. Nana is seen actually exercising his power through Ghashiram, the Kotwal. However, Ghashiram is too full of revenge against the Brahmins of Poona. For the time being, he is not aware of the treacherous ways of Nana. Gauri's death at the hands of a midwife during abortion of the babe she has conceived by Nana makes him more ruthless and sadistic. The death of Gauri makes Ghashiram a blood-thirsty and ferocious animal.

Nana foresees that Ghashiram may prove harmful to him also. He uses the policy of using a thorn to remove the thorn. Twenty-one people who are caught red-handed in the act of stealing fruits from Ghashiram's garden die of suffocation in the unventilated cellar. This genocide becomes the cause of Ghashiram's downfall. Nana does not shield him. He hands him over to the mad, revengeful crowd who stone him to death. Ghashiram dies a dog's death. Thus, Ghashiram has been treated like a toilet paper, a use-and-throw object, by the successful but wily, treacherous politician Nana Phadnavis. Thus, Ghashiram's role constantly changes from Victim to Rescuer (because he provides a kind of relief to Nana by sending his daughter to him), from rescuer to persecutor, and finally from persecutor to Victim. Such a kind of transformation, which may be seen also as role shifting, is noticeable in the roles played by the Brahmins of Poona and Nana, too.

The Brahmins, who torture Ghashiram at the beginning, perform the role of Persecutor. They become the victims of Ghashiram's anger and frustration, after he becomes the Kotwal of the city. Towards the end of the play, they are shown returning to their previous role of persecutors, when they punish Ghashiram for his indiscriminate, heartless cruelty.

Another role that is observed in the play is that of a Stage-Manager. It is performed by Nana. Ghashiram's ambition gives him a chance to work out his desire successfully. He seeks erotic pleasure with Gauri and exercies his power through Ghashiram. Gauri's ignominious death makes him conscious of the fact that Ghashiram may prove harmful to him also. So, he offers him to the bloodthirsty mob, that can avenge the wrongs done to them by Ghashiram.

Thus, from the beginning of the play to its end, Nana manages and at times manipulates to bring about changes in the role of Ghashiram and in that of the Brahmins according to the necessity of circumstance. He performs the role of Rescuer twice; for Ghashiram, when he appoints him as the

Kotwal, and the other time for the people, when he hands Ghashiram over to the frenzied mob.

Using the historical incident, Tendulkar criticizes society that is responsible for the creation of such people as Nana and Ghashiram. The playwright himself says:

> Though Ghashiram was a product of my reflections on the rise of the Shiv Sena, I was ultimately interested in examining the situations which led to the creation of Ghashiram-like forces in society. The Ghashirams of the world die, but the situations which give birth to such forces recur and are personified in the character of Nana Phadnavis. Beneath the superficial changes in history, the larger dynamics of power are cyclical.[10]

The characters here are types rather than individuals. Ghashiram is the representative of those people in society who pursue their goal unquestionably. Nana is the representative of those people in politics who use the needy people as their pawns and destroy them when they are no longer useful for them.

At the surface level, the personality clash between Nana and Ghashiram appears to be the theme of the play. However, the main objective of the playwright is to examine the use made of violence and sexuality in power politics. According to Samik Bandyopadhyay, "In Ghashiram, power is defined 'horizontally' in terms of individuals against individuals; from humiliation to revenge in assertion to eventual victimization...."[11]

Gauri's sacrifice of virtue brings rich dividends to Nana rather than to Ghashiram. Obviously, it gives Nana an opportunity to satisfy his physical lust; obliquely, he seeks to establish the reign of terror. It can be ascertained from his soliloquy: "What'll happen is that our misdeeds will be credited to your account. We do, our Kotwal pays. The opportunity comes in the shape of Ghashiram" (24-25). Doing nothing outwardly, he remains victorious and continues to thrive. It gives Ghashiram an opportunity to fulfil his inordinate ambition. The sadistic objective in his mind renders him blind and fails him as a father, as a Kotwal, and, finally, as a human being also. In his role as the Kotwal of the city, he creates a hell not only for the Brahmins but for himself and for his daughter also. He fails to realise the treacherous ways of the culprit Nana and is reduced to a stooge in Nana's power game. In this play, society is shown as succeeding against the individual, as opposed to what happens in the play *Encounter in Umbugland,* where the individual is shown prevailing upon the group in power politics.

Gulabi's dances, Nana's lustful pursuit of Gauri, the secret meetings of the Brahmin wives with their respective Maratha lovers—all these incidents bring out the underlying strain of eroticism present in the play, besides revealing the relationship between sex and power.

An effective use of pantomime, or to use the more recent term, "body language", is made very successfully to exhibit the punishments given to the Brahamins of Puna. The "gestures" and "silences" sometimes speak more than words.

The Relevance of the Play

The success of the play lies in the issues raised by the playwright. The play projects violence in its twofold aspects: (i) that of the state against the people and (ii) that of the people against the public authority. It also explores into the varied aspects of the sexual exploitation of women in power politics. The questions raised are not concerned just with the eighteenth century city life of the people in Poona. It means that the play is not topical; it relates to all societies and all ages. In a sense, it is universal. In the authorial note to the play's Hindi version by Vasant Deo, Tendulkar opines:

> In my view, *Ghashiram Kotwal* indicates a particular social situation which is neither old nor new. It is beyond time and space. Therefore, 'Ghashiram' and 'Nana' are also beyond space and time.[12]

The play is not so much about the historical personages like Ghashiram and Nana but about the way in which the power operates through social institutions like caste and religion to create and destroy the ghastly people like Ghashiram. It exposes the ugly nature of the power game, where people are used as pawns. It is for this reason that the play has been so relevant to our contemporary social situation. It is a satire on a society which shields the powerful and the corrupt and punishes the helpless and the innocent. Justice is exhibited to be done, and equilibrium of society appears to be restored. The play ends raising such questions as "Is it really justice? Is justice possible at all in a corrupt social system?"[13] From this perspectives, the play seems to analyse what is going on everywhere in the world:

> ...the rabble with their well-worn creeds, Their large profusions and their little deeds, Mingle in selfish strife, lo, freedom weeps, Wrong rules the land, and waiting justice sleeps.[14]

The play *Ghashiram Kotwal* is a classic, as it dissolves the boundaries between the temporality and eternity. It is sublime and universal since the situation depicted and the characters portrayed in it go beyond time and place. The issues raised in the play belong to all times and climes. Thus, the play is *par excellence* and has set a high watermark of dramatics and dramaturgy. It is, in short, Tendulkar's magnum opus.

Works Cited

1. Manchi Sarat Babu, *Indian Drama Today,* Prestige Books, New Delhi, 1997, p.109.
2. Ibid., p.115.
3. Arundhati Banerjee, Introduction, *Five Plays of Vijay Tendulkar,* OUP, Bombay, 1992, p. xi.
4. *Alochana.* May 1973, 24. The extract is translated into English by the research worker herself.
5. Quoted by Bandyopadhyay, Samik. Introduction. Vijay Tendulkar. *Ghashiram Kotwal.* (trans.) Jayant Karve and Eleanor Zelliot. Calcutta: Seagull, 1989, 2.
6. Manchi Sarat Babu, *Indian Drama Today,* Prestige Books, New Delhi, 1997, p.72.
7. Ibid.
8. Bhave, Pushpa. *Contemporary Indian Theatre: Interviews with Playwrights and Directors.* New Delhi: Sangeet Natak Akademi, 1989, 47.

9. *Ghashiram Kotwal: A Production Casebook. Ghashiram Kotwal*. xiv, xv.
10. An Internet Entry.
11. Samik Bandyopadhyay, Introduction, Vijay Tendulkar, *Ghashiram Kotwal*, translated by Jayant Karve and Eleanor Zelliot, Seagull, Calcutta, 1984, p.3.
12. Kanwar, Asha S. *Ghashiram Kotwal: A Study Guide*. New Delhi: IGNOU, 1993, 18.
13. Ibid., 20.
14. Holland J.G. "True Men". *English Reader: Kumar Bharati*. Standard IX. Pune: Maharashtra State Board of Secondary Education, 1994,174.

21

Communication in Drama: Exploration towards a New Analytical Model

—Umesh S. Jagadale

Communication in Drama

The communication in drama passes through various channels from the playwright to the audience, depending on the various mediums of performances like the literary medium, the theatrical medium, the radio medium and so on. Each of these mediums has its own medium-specific performance of the communicational acts. Yet, the medium-specific dimensions of one medium are found operating in the other mediums also, e.g. the literary dimension operates in the theatrical medium and vice-versa. Hence, in order to encompass the various medium-specific communicational dimensions, operating in each medium, the present article adopts a holistic pragmatic perspective.

The article views drama, or more precisely, communication in drama as one cf the 'culturally specific genres of transmission' (Posner, 1985: 255), and attempts to evolve a model of analysis. According to Posner:

> When we characterize the various media there are a number of different considerations we can take into account. The transmission of information brings into a play a particular biological sense, so that we talk about visual media, auditory media, etc. A particular physical channel is used, so that there are optical media, acoustic media, etc. the information may be distributed by a technical apparatus; for instance, there are print media

> and electronic media. There are sociological institutions for the organization of the transfer process, e.g. publishing houses, theatres, museums, film companies. There are culturally specific genres (emphasis mine) of transmission, e.g. drama, news, talk shows, action film, classical music, pop art. And the message has a code, verbal or nonverbal. (Posner, 1985: 255)

Posner's comment throws light on some key factors e.g. the biological sense, the physical channel, the technical apparatus, the sociological institutions, and the culturally specific genres of transmission, which influence the communication in the various media and so do they influence the communication process in drama or more precisely the use of English in drama. The said key factors obviously bring in some communicational complexities that are challenging yet interesting to make an assessment.

The Argument

Following the line of Posner's, it is the researcher's argument that the process of communication in drama or more precisely the use of language in the speech situations of drama is influenced by certain literary, theatrical and socio-cultural elements, for the assessment of which some new analytical model is essential.

The need for the new analytical model is supported even by the following comment of W.B. Hess-Luttich:

> The structure of audio-visual texts like theatre performances requires a somewhat more elaborative inventory of analytical instruments than linguists usually provide. In particular, the old sender-receiver model of communication is too simple to explain the communicative relationship between the participants of dialogues presented to audiences in theatre plays. (Hess-Luttich: 1991: 232)

Considering the need for some new analytical model, on the basis of some preliminary observations found in the speech situations in drama, the research comes out with a hypothetical model of speech situations in drama, which at a later stage needs be assessed against G.N. Leech's model of speech situations (Leech: 1983) and the model of playwright's communication with his audience by Hess-Luttich (Hess-Luttich: 1991). The hypothetical model basically considers certain socio-cultural, literary, and theatrical elements that influence the speech situations in drama, e.g. the socio-cultural context of situations, the literary feature of the use of the stage directions in drama, and the use of the theatrical means like the light effects, the musical punches, the stage property, etc. The speech situations in drama become very distinctive as they are processed in the context of these elements.

The model displays the pragmatic interactions like the operation of speech acts, and the 'ideational' (Halliday M.A.K., 1973 in Leech, 1983: 56) as well as the interpersonal verbal and nonverbal communication in drama. More importantly, it also displays the play of the socio-cultural, the literary, and the theatrical contexts in which the entire speech situation is processed.

Socio-cultural Dimension

The socio-cultural dimension operates as the beliefs, traditions, customs and the like of social practices, e.g. the beliefs like life after death, the existence of soul etc. In *The Dread Departure* by Satish Alekar (Alekar, 1989: 18-19) the rituals after death in Hindu religion like the funeral and the cremation operate as the context, wherein Bhaurao's death and his appearance as a soul become meaningful and acceptable throughout the play and more particularly in this speech situation.

A sample from the play *The Fire and the Rain* by Girish Karnad (1998) can also be cited here. The utterance *Fire* used in the very title of the play needs be processed in the socio-cultural context, or there are chances of but a partial perception of it. Unless the utterance is processed in the context of the Indian religious concept of *Yadnya,* the sacred fire and the *Homa-havana,* the custom of offering the sacred sacrifices to gods, the addressees of this utterance would not have the right perception of it.

Literary Dimension

The literary dimension of the context operates through various devices like certain techniques in the plot construction. The same is well observed in *The Dread Departure* by Satish Alekar, e.g. the interweaving of the game of 'Last letter starts the rhyme' (Alekar, 1989: 18-19) i.e. chaining up the rhymes by the *'Last letter'* and the game of the Prisoner's Base (chaining up the turns in the game by 'tagging') and the funeral process (chaining up the earthly existence with the Heavenly existence by the cremation of Bhaurao's dead body) in this situation.

So far as the literary context is concerned, some previous knowledge of the literary devices like personification, e.g. the personification of the Flames as seen in *Naga-Mandala* (Karnad, 1990) and the previous knowledge of the literary techniques like the use of stage directions—where the use of the characters' nonverbal communication, and the technicians' use of the theatrical devices are informed—in drama, operate as the literary context.

Theatrical Dimension

The operation of the theatrical context needs also be discussed thoroughly. To mention it briefly, the use of English utterances get some theatre-specific meanings in the context of the theatrical setup. All the utterances and the entire situation are processed in the context created by the use of music, light effects, stage property etc.

The use of music is a significant device to be discussed here. In *The Dread Departure by* Alekar the use of the drum beats and the jazzy beats in the singing and dancing at the 'Last letter starts the rhyme' (p.18-19); also the use of the chorus and the rhythm to make the utterance 'Hallelujah *!'* (ibid.) produce certain rhythmic effect. The musical effect of the 'shrill whistle' (ibid.) also remarkably causes the 'total silence' (ibid.).

The use of body language is a highly significant device in this context. For instance, this device operates effectively in the 'Last letter starts the rhyme' (ibid.) while playing the Prisoner's Base. A similar effect can be observed in Nana's confused state of mind and in his silent behavioural communication, where Neighbours talk to Nana but he remains silent and lastly exits.

The use of stage property is yet another important theatrical device. For instance, the bier and the ladder (ibid.) mentioned in *The Dread Departure* remain throughout there in the performance of that situation. All the communication in this situation becomes meaningful in the context of Bhaurao's death, what is visually realized by the bier. The very presence of the bier is suggestive of the omnipresence of Bhaurao's soul that remarkably influences the communication throughout this play. The use of the ladder and also of the binoculars helps establishing the space and the distance of the place of action, from the road Nana is supposed to arrive by.

Thus, the above discussed samples bring out the significance of the literary, socio-cultural and the theatrical devices in the process of communication in drama.

In the course of the exploration of the model, so as to authenticate the pragmatic approach adopted for the study, the hypothetical model needs be assessed against G.N. Leech's model of speech situations (Leech, 1983: 13-15) and also against Hess-Luttich's model of playwright's communication with his audience (Hess-Luttich, 1991: 232).

Leech's Model of Speech Situations

Leech, while working on the principles of pragmatics, derives various aspects of speech situations. So it is but obvious that his model has no direct concern as such with drama. As far as drama is concerned, the communication in general and the speech situations in particular operate very distinctively in drama than the same operate in the social scenario. Obviously the notion of pragmatics of communication in drama is bound to be equally distinctive. Hence, considering the distinguished notion of the pragmatics of communication in drama, though Leech's model of speech situations lays some authentic grounding for the proposed analysis, an exploration for a more suitable model is essential. Prior to the further exploration, Leech's model needs be discussed. According to Leech, there are mainly following aspects of speech situations.

1. Addressers or addressees
2. The context of an utterance
3. The goal(s) of an utterance
4. The utterance as a form of act or activity : a speech act
5. The utterance as a product of a verbal act

In addition to the above-mentioned aspects, Leech inclines to accommodate some more aspects like the time and the place of the utterance in his concept. In this connection Leech mentions:

> From the above-mentioned elements of (i) addresser and addressee, (ii) context, (iii) goals, (iv) illocutionary act, and (v) utterance, we can compose a notion of a SPEECH SITUATION, comprising all these elements, and perhaps other elements as well, such as the time and the place of the utterance. (Leech, 1983: 15)

Thus the components like the *time* and the *place* of the utterance also can be some more aspects of the speech situations. In this sense, Leech keeps his model open-ended.

About Hess-Luttich's Model

The model of playwright's communication with his audience produced by Hess-Luttich appears in a diagrammatic form. It is truly a polyperspectivistic model. Its polyperspectivity opens up from the following comment.

According to Hess-Luttich:

> The pragmatic model of an embedding hierarchy of communicative circles presented in dramatic texts and theatrical texts cannot show the whole complexity of their relationship. But it does attempt to co-ordinate the various problem-systems involved in the empirical analysis of a play. It helps to open up the semiotics, hermeneutics, and aesthetics of the meaning of drama and theatre as functioning in socio-cultural contexts—which is how the dramatist communicates with his audience. (Hess-Luttich, 1991: 239)

Limitations of the Models by Leech and Hess-Luttich

Leech's model of 'speech situations' (Leech, 1983: 13-15); and Hess-Luttich's model (Hess-Luttich, 1991: 232) have certain limitations for the present study. However, both the models are partially applicable to the study of communication in drama. Leech's model is partially inapplicable, for it speaks about the speech situations in the day today communication—where natural language is used—and not exclusively about the speech situations in drama. Hess-Luttich's model is partially inapplicable, for it discusses the entire process of communication in drama. So it is too wide to delimit it to a small implicit area of the speech situations.

However, so far as the partial inapplicability of both the models is concerned, it should be mentioned here that neither these linguists wish to claim a full and universal applicability of their models, nor does the researcher wish to blame them for the same.

The New Analytical Model

As a result of the assessment of the models by Leech and Hess-Luttich, a new the hypothetical model of analysis is evolved here to assess the speech situations in drama. The major aspects of the analytical model are discussed below.

The analysis of speech situations in a literary text of drama has its own scope and limitations. In the literary texts, the data of analysis appears in the form of three areas of communication: conversation, narration, and *co-text* (Crystal, 2003: 114) through which all the components of speech situations operate. These three areas together form message. Thus, in the literary texts of drama, as all the components of speech situations appear operating through conversation, narration, and co-text, and as these three areas form the message, the component message emerges as the central component of analysis, whereby all the other components too can be analyzed. As a result, the scope of analysis is focused on the central component message.

Precisely, to analyze a speech situation, here, is to analyze the central component message, what makes it possible also to collectively analyze the remaining components of the speech situations. The area of analysis that the model encompasses is specified below.

The Area of Analysis

The model specifying the scope and limitations of analysis is produced here for the scholars' critical inspection.

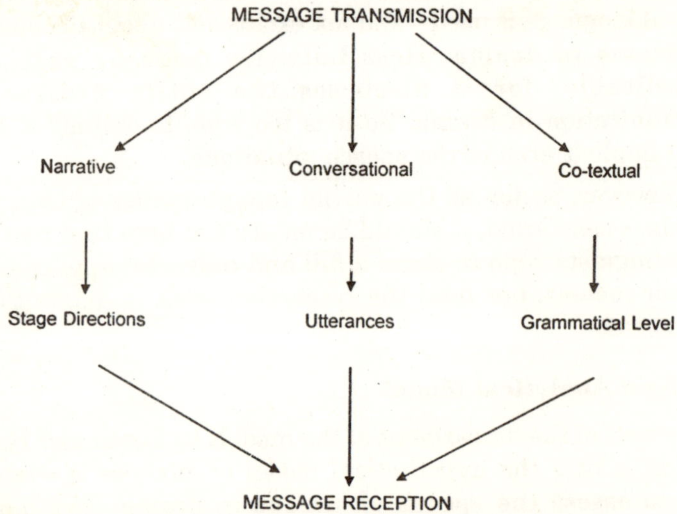

Considering the vastness of the communicational area in drama, the model delimits its scope to the speech situations in the print form of drama. However, besides and beyond the present delimitation, it is observed that the different communicational mediums overlap each other in the overall process of communication in drama, and the same way the overlapping is manifested, also in the print form of the speech situations in drama.

Conclusion

Precisely, the communication in drama is never a linear kind of verbal communication only, as produced in Saussure's 'speech circuit' (Saussure: 1974, in Chandler: 2002: 176), which is called 'a two-track linear model' (Chandler: 2002: 176). Moreover, the communication in drama is influenced by the various communicational components like the context, the non-verbal means of communication like the actors' body language, the theatrical and the technological setup, what make the communication in drama multi-dimensional.

In a sequel to the present article, the researcher proposes to apply the model produced above to analyze the communication in drama with reference to the study of speech situations in select plays.

Works Cited

Alekar, S. 1989. *The Dread Departure*. Trans. Deshpande Gauri. Calcutta: Seagull Books.

Chandler, D. 2002. *Semiotics: The Basics*. London: Routledge.

Crystal, David (2003) *A Dictionary of Linguistics and Phonetics*. Blackwell Publishing Ltd.

Halliday, M.A.K. (1973), *Explorations in the Functions of Language*, London: Edward Arnold.

Hess-Luttich (1991) in *Literary Pragmatics* ed. Roger D. Sell Routledge, London and New York.

Karnad, Girish (1990) *Naga-Mandala*. Oxford University Press, New Delhi, India 110001.

_____. (1998) *The Fire and the Rain*. Oxford University Press, New Delhi, India 110001.

Kramsch Claire (1998) *Language and Culture*. Oxford University Press, New York.

Leech, *Principles of Pragmatics*, 1983, Lancaster

Posner, R. (1985) in *Literary Pragmatics* (1991) ed. Roger D. Sell Routledge, London and New York.

Saussure, F. 1916/1974. *Course in General Linguistics*. Trans. Baskin W. London: Fontana / Collins.

Index

A Backward Place 39, 54
A Fine Balance 57
A Handful of Rice 93
A Man and A Woman 88
A Married Woman 117
A New Dominion 39
A River with Three Banks 100
A Silence of Desire 93
Abhedananda, Swami 12
Abrams, M.H. 1
Acharya, Shanta 200
Across the Black Waters 25
Actor–audience relationship 221
Adiga, Aravind 104
Age-old value systems 175
Aggressive novel 104
Agrarian revolution 92
All-India Home Rule League 22
Amriika 117
Analysis, hypothetical model of 243
Anand, Mulk Raj 21
Animal husbandry 92
Ardhangini 91
Ashok, A.V. 70
Ayala 119

Baldwin, James 105
Bandyopadhyay, Tarashankar 14
Banerjee, Lakshisree 197
Basu, Kunal 150
Besant, Anne 22
Best Loved Indian Stories of the Century 164
BhagavadGita 175
Bhalla, Allok 161
Bhatt, Sujata 199
Bombay Tiger 94
Booker Prize 37, 99
British Empire 117
British imperialism 116
British rule 116
Bronte, Emily 2
Brunizem 200
Buddha, Gautama 79

Charter of Human Rights 59
City centrism 99
Civilizational imperialism 117
Collected Plays 212
Colonial times 117
Commonwealth Poetry prize 200
Comrade Kirillov 31
Conrad, Joseph 2
Constitution of India 57
Contemporary fictional narratives 116
Contemporary Indian Short Stories 157
Coolie 24

Naga-Mandala 205
Naidu, Sarojini 192
Naik, M.K. 7, 160
Naipaul, V.S. 116
Nair, Anita 134
Namaste Book of Indian Short Stories 160
Narayan, R.K. 7
Narcissism 96
Nectar in a Sieve 93
New analytical model 241
Nietzsche 2
Nirmala 169
Noble savage 1
Non-Cooperation Movement 169
Nostalgia 137
Not This, Not That 200
Numbering Our Days' Illusions 200

Obscurantism 24
Only the Soul Knows How to Sing 193
Oscar Award 110

Parsi culture 58
Passage to India 25
Pati parameshwar 91
Patriarchal society 40, 205
Personal liberty 59
Philosophical wisdom 16
Pleasure City 94
Poetic ancestors 177
Political decolonization 117
Political evangelism 24
Political plays 222
Polyperspectivistic model 243
Portillo, Michael 104
Possession 93
Post-colonial novel 103
Post-Emergency era 99
Post-Independence period 175
Post-modern novel 100
Post-modern period 100
Post-modernism 99
Pragmatics, principles of 243
Prema 169
Premchand 169
Primitivism 1
Progressive Writers Conference 169
Puranas 175
Purdah 38

Quit India movement 23

Racist 150
Ramakrishna, Sri 12
Ramanujan, A.K. 184
Ramayana 175
Ranga Shankara Theatre Festival 212
Rangabhumi 169
Rao, Raja 21
Religious taboos 59
Right to Life 59
Riot 117
Robinson Crusoe 26
Rousseau 1
Roy, Arundati 100
Rushdie, Salman 104

Sabarmati Ashram 23
Sahani, Archana 197
Sahitya Akademi award 73
Sanskrit eroticists 177
Satyagraha 22
Sawhney, Kusum 119
Saxena, Manmohan 157
Sea of Poppies 104
Second Thoughts 123
Self fulfilment 93
Self-identity 88
Sexual assault 70
Sexual orientation 114
Shakti 92
Shakuntala 135

Shringara 200
Sidhwa, Bapsi 118
Singh, Gurupdesh 115
Singh, K. Natwar 158
Singh, Khushwant 118
Slumdog Millionaire 110
Smith, Zadic 137
Social commitment, sense of 73
Social criticism 193
Social plays 222
Social realism 169
Socio-cultural dimension 242
Some Inner Fury 93
Something Barely Remembered 144
Speech situations, model of 243
Spiritual enlightenment 18
Spiritual pre-eminence 92
Spiritualism 49, 115
Stories from India 158, 160
Strange Obsession 119
Such A Long Journey 118
Summer in Calcutta 193
Supernaturalism 10
Swami and Friends 21
Symbolism, device of 38

Technological age 136
Technology-oriented jobs 120
Tejpal, Tarun 119
Tendulkar, Vijay 222
Tennyson, Alfred Lord 91
Tharoor, Shashi 117
The Alchemy of Desire 119
The Assassin's Song 118
The Awakening 87
The Big Heart 25
The Burial at Sea 118
The Cat and Shakespeare 31
The City and the River 2
The Coffer Dams 93
The Company of Women 123
The Crow of the Barricades 31
The Dark Holds No Terrors 72
The Descendants 193
The Dread Departure 243
The English Teacher 7
The Fire and the Rain 243
The Glass Palace 104
The God of Small Things 99
The Golden Honeycomb 94
The Gunny Sack 117
The Hindu 137
The Householder 39
The Hungry Tide 129
The Impressionist 117, 119
The In-between World of Vikram Lall 117
The Inner Rooms 83
The Middleman and other Stories 146
The Miniaturist 150
The Nature of Passion 38, 39
The Nowhere Man 93
The Old Playhouse and Other Poems 193
The Opium Clerk 150
The Plumed Serpent 2
The Private Life of an Indian Prince 25
The Rime of the Ancient Mariner 42
The Serpent and the Rope 31
The Stinkin Roe 200
The Sword and the Sickle 25
The Village 25
The Vintage Book of Indian Writing: 1947-1997 158
The White Tiger 104
The Woman Who Rode Away 2
Theatrical dimension 243
Thematic anthology 161
Three Continents 43
To Whom She Will 55
Touch 202
Tradition-bound society 79

Traditional image 91
Transmission 127
Truth Tales 159
Two Leaves and a Bud 24
Two Monologues. Flowers 212
Two Virgins 93

Unaccustomed Earth 140
United Nations 59
Universal civilization 116
Untouchable 21
Upanishads 33, 51
Upanishads 175
Urbanization 114
Utilitarianism 184

Values, crisis of 175
Vardaan 169
Vassanji, M.G. 116
Vasudhaiva kutumbakam 175
Vedas 175
Village centrism 99
Visvanathan, Susan 144

West, Elizabeth 158
Womanhood 79
Woolf, Virginia 103
Wordsworth 2
World War II 23
Wright, Richard 105
Writers Workshop Anthology 159
Writings of India's Partition 161

Yadnya 243
Yajnas 2
Yayati 220